M000240272

THE WEAVE OF MY LIFE

Urmila Pawar

The Weave of My Life

A DALIT WOMAN'S MEMOIRS

URMILA PAWAR

TRANSLATED BY MAYA PANDIT

COLUMBIA UNIVERSITY PRESS   NEW YORK

COLUMBIA UNIVERSITY PRESS
Publishers Since 1893
New York   Chichester, West Sussex

Aaydan copyright © 2003 Urmila Pawar; English translation copyright © 2008 Stree.
Copyright © 2009 Columbia University Press
The Weave of My Life: A Dalit Woman's Memoir was first published by Stree, an imprint of
    Bhatkal and Sen, 16 Southern Avenue, Kolkata 700 026, India, in 2008.
This edition for sale in North America only

All rights reserved

Library of Congress Cataloging-in-Publication Data
Pavara, Urmila.
    [Ayadana. English]
    The weave of my life: a Dalit woman's memoirs / Urmila Pawar; translated by
Maya Pundit.
        p.   cm.
    Includes bibliographical references.
    ISBN 978-0-231-14900-6 (cloth: alk. paper)
    1. Pavara, Urmila. 2. Authors, Marathi—20th century—Biography. 3. Dalits—India—
Maharashtra—Biography. 4. Women—India—Maharashtra—Biography. 5. Political
activists—India—Biography. 6. Feminists—India—Biography. 7. Maharashtra (India)—
Biography. I. Title.

    PK2418.P344Z463813   2009
    891.4'687109—dc22
    [B]   2008052564

Casebound editions of Columbia University Press books are printed on permanent
    and durable acid-free paper.

Printed in the United States of America
c 10 9 8 7 6 5 4 3 2 1

References to Internet Web Sites (URLs) were accurate at the time of writing.
    Neither the author nor Columbia University Press is responsible for Web sites
    that may have expired or changed since the book was prepared.

To the memory of my mother, Laxmibai

Contents

Illustrations follow page 170.

Preface

Aaydan! What does it mean?

Before plastic began to be utilized for making different objects of everyday use, bamboo was the most common material used to make baskets, containers, and other things of general utility in households. *Aaydan* is the generic term that refers to all things made from bamboo; *awata* is another word. Outside the Konkan, the job of weaving bamboo baskets was traditionally assigned to nomadic tribes like the Burud. In the Konkan region, however, it was the Mahar caste that undertook this task. Nobody knows why. Even today, the practice, though considerably weaker, is still prevalent.

The other meanings of *aaydan* are "utensil" and "weapon."

My mother used to weave *aaydans*. I find that her act of weaving and my act of writing are organically linked. The weave is similar. It is the weave of pain, suffering, and agony that links us.

When I look back upon my life, I see the period of conversion from Hinduism to Buddhism as its most significant. Neither the children nor the elders had any idea what religion or conversion meant, of its significance, and about who could act as our guide as far as conversion was concerned. Yet we did convert. The meaning of the transformation began to become clearer to us gradually through the changing rituals and traditions and through the guidance of our political leaders.

Dalit houses in the Konkan region were usually not located on the margins of the village but found at its center, probably as a matter of convenience for the upper castes, who could summon us at any time and wanted us at their beck and call. The community was haunted by a sense of perpetual insecurity, fearing that it could be attacked from all four sides in times of conflict. That is why there was always a tendency in our people to shrink within ourselves like a tortoise and proceed at a snail's pace. This slow pace picked up radically after the conversion to Buddhism. To begin with, there was a tremendous interest in the new religion and in the images of the Buddha and Dr. Ambedkar. Initially it was difficult to replace the images of Gods with those of the Buddha and Ambedkar. The age-old habits of praying to the Gods, worshipping them for some boon or praying for help in difficult times, were too strong to be given up. Then we came to know from our leaders that one was not supposed to pray to these images for selfish motives, individual benefits, or getting some personal wish gratified. The new way of looking at religion had already given us what we needed; we learned that we folded our hands to the Buddha not as a *dharma* but a *dhamma*—a way of life, with tremendous social strength. At that time, of course, all this was new and way beyond our understanding!

The other interesting thing was the white clothes that we were asked to wear. In fact, we had not had sufficient clothes to cover our bodies till then and were therefore thrilled with the white clothes. We also came to know that a new rule had come into existence: one had to wear only white clothes on occasions such as the naming ceremony, marriages, and the last rites. Why white clothes? Our leaders convinced us that white is a color of purity. Just as white clothes display any stain prominently; we had to be careful about our conduct being flawless; so that our characters appeared without any stain. This made the question the non-Dalits asked us, "Why give the married woman a widow's garb?" completely irrelevant and superfluous. Even young children like us learned to answer such questions well. But the principle of *ahimsa* was a bit difficult to understand. We were used to eating meat. Even the Tathagata had accepted that creatures survived on other creatures' lives.[1] But for him the human mind was more important. What he meant was that we should not commit violence for the sake of violence. If you strike someone with a sword, you will receive a similar blow in answer. You cannot conquer people with violence, but with love. Our leaders simplified the Buddha's philosophy for us.

Later on we became acquainted with Dalit literature and participated in the Dalit movement. The word *dalit* achieved a prominence. Some Dalits themselves opposed this word. "Now we have become Buddhists, so why call us Dalits?" they asked. Dalit writers defined the word *dalit* in a new way. *Dalit* means people who have been oppressed by a repressive social system and challenge the oppression from a scientific, rational, and humanitarian perspective. Now this meaning of the term *Dalit* is acceptable all over the world. But far more important than mere words such as *savarna, avarna, Dalit, Buddhist,* or *woman* is the awareness of each and every individual about who he or she is.[2] The Dalit communities got this self-awareness from Ambedkarite philosophy.[3]

Today, because of education and job opportunities, many Dalits have made a transition from being below the poverty line to the middle class. A Dalit looks no different from any other person in society. This has blunted the edge of casteism or discrimination. Like wild animals fast disappearing from the woods, caste seems to have "disappeared." Yet, like a wild animal hiding behind a bush, it remains hidden, poised for attack. People traveling in fast vehicles may not notice the wild eyes looking at them, but those who walk do and are struck with terror.

Women are in a similar position. Today women are aware that they hold up half the sky; are educated and work on an equal footing with men in all walks of life. In that case, I ask myself, where is the Dalit woman in all this? I see two streams of her existence: one, below the poverty line, which is worrisome. This woman lives in slums, beside gutters and dung heaps, on railway stations. With her children in her arms; she ekes out an existence by begging or collecting and selling stuff picked up from the garbage heaps. This woman works herself to death as a maid, doing odd jobs, and tries to send her children to school—sometimes even to English-medium schools.[4]

The woman in the other stream is educated and most probably has a job. As both husband and wife work, their economic status is a little better. The distance between the Dalit and non-Dalit communities fifty years ago is reduced by half today. Now we are confronted by the phenomenon of globalization, privatization, and politicization of religions, which has led to unprecedented competition and tensions. This is going to have an adverse impact on the future of succeeding generations and society in general. Yet the fact that the human being has tremendous resilience and capacity to survive is a ray of hope. I am sure people will be able to explore new paths and protect their humanity against all odds.

Mumbai, January 2008

Acknowledgments

I must first mention a longstanding debt that I owe. The toiling women of my village climbed up and down the hills with terribly heavy loads on their heads in order to make ends meet. They carried me in their arms during this arduous journey. They indulged me so much when I was a child. I wanted to repay this debt, however inadequately. That is why I began to write about my childhood which was published for the first time in the Diwali issue of *Ababa Hatti*, a children's magazine in Marathi, in 1989, and continued to be published for the next three or four years.

I realized that I could also write about my life for the grown-ups. Some of these attempts were published in magazines like *Akshar, Charvak,* and *Prerak Lalakari. Milun Saryajani* published my outspoken account of the "first night," which created curiosity about my autobiographical writing. I could perceive that readers appreciated what I had written. Because of my many commitments and busy schedule, it was very difficult to find any time to write about myself. Usha Mehta noticed this and reminded me time and again. It was because of her relentless prodding that I completed this task, the "weave" that I have inherited from my mother.

Pramila Shantaram Pawar, my *vahini* Nirmala Krishna Pawar, my *akka* Shantabai Dharmaji Jadhav, and brother Shahu Arjun Pawar brought out the memories of the past. Cecilia Carvalho and Kunda P.M. and Bhagoji Laxman Jadhav pointed out the shortcomings. Dinkar Gangal took pains to give a felicitous shape to the *Aaydan* I had woven. So many people have helped me to have *The Weave of My Life* reach many more people: C.S. Lakshmi, the writer, filmmaker, and activist who heads the organization Sparrow; Maya Pandit, who translated the Marathi text to English, thus starting the ball rolling; Ramdas Bhatkal, of Popular Prakashan, who read the translated text and the proof for me, and his colleague, Asmita Mohite, who provided such unstinting support to my publisher Stree; Sharmila Rege, who was instrumental in persuading Maya Pandit to undertake the work; Aruna Burte; my son-in-law Ravi Ahalawat, my daughters Malavika and Manini; everyone at Stree; I am indebted to them.

Introduction

Wandana Sonalkar

The original title of Urmila Pawar's memoir is *Aaydan*, a word from the local dialect spoken in the villages that form the background of her life. *Aaydan* is the name for the cane baskets that her mother wove to sell for additional income for the family. Translated into English as *The Weave of My Life: A Dalit Woman's Memoirs*, it takes us from her childhood memories of life in the village, and her mother's constant struggle to make ends meet, through her school and college days in the town of Ratnagiri, to her life after her marriage, in Mumbai, where she enounters a feminist group and later becomes a writer and organizer of Dalit women. The time span it covers is from just after India's independence in 1947 to the end of the century.

But this trajectory is not the essential narrative line in a book whose title is a better metaphor for the writing technique that Urmila Pawar adopts. The lives of different members of her family, her husband's family, her neighbors and classmates, are woven together in a narrative that gradually reveals different aspects of the everyday life of Dalits,[1] the manifold ways in which caste asserts itself and grinds them down. The author's point of view is also woven from two strands: that of the young girl uncomprehendingly witnessing instances of caste injustice, patriarchal domination, and the daily compulsions of poverty, and of the mature woman looking back on these with the insights she has gained later on in her life. And yet the narrator's position is neither central nor distanced: it is constantly engaged.

We can make a comparison here with what M. S. S. Pandian[2] says about two recent Dalit autobiographical texts, *Karukku* and *Vadu*, originally written in Tamil. "The everyday, the ordinary, a temporality that is not teleological, and a language of affect and incomprehension invest caste with certain presentness and immediacy and opens up a space for moral and political appeal to the upper castes. The burden of caste is thus returned to the upper castes."

In Urmila Pawar's writing there is plenty of the ordinary and everyday, and a temporality that goes back and forth, from her own childhood to episodes in the life of her mother and her elder brothers and sisters and back. Much has been written of how Dalit autobiographies play down the role of the narrator subject; Pandian also refers to this. The sufferings of the Dalit are, like those of the black slave in America, the sufferings of her community. Not only this, because the path to emancipation is also a social project rather than an individual one, the Dalit autobiography combines witnessing and experiencing in an act of sharing that gives it a political force. The first Dalit autobiographies written in the Marathi language appeared in the 1970s, and women writers soon followed the men. Sharmila Rege's recent book on what she calls the *testimonio* of the Dalit woman brings out its unique role in exposing the reality of both caste and gender domination in Indian society.[3]

Urmila Pawar's memoir follows in this genre; what is different is that, unlike her predecessors, she approaches her subject both as a writer with some literary achievement already under her belt and as an activist who has tried to organize Dalit women and has a specific stance on Dalit feminism. It seems that her objective is to document both caste and patriarchy in the lives that enter into the weave of her memoir. "The language of affect and of incomprehension" that Pandian writes of are somewhat toned down as compared to some of the earlier Dalit autobiographies.

I will try, in this introduction for readers unfamiliar with the Marathi language and with the history and contemporary context of caste, to fill in some of the background and underline some of Pawar's insights.

The Weave of My Life begins with a detailed description of the harsh landscape of the Konkan region on the west coast of India and the relation these Dalit women—their own lives harsh and full of toil—have with this landscape. The range of the Sahyadris runs along the coastline, and there is a sheer drop down to the sea. The main crop is rice; the poor grow a form of red millet that thrives on the thin soil, but there are also fruits that are native to the region, like several choice species of mangoes, cashews, and the red *ratamba* fruit that is dried and used as a flavoring for curries. There are heavy rains during the monsoon, but the water runs down into the sea, and, paradoxically, it is hard to find enough water for drinking and washing during most of the year.

The first chapter begins with the village Dalit women's journey to sell their wares—rice bags, firewood, grass, in the town market. The women walk in a group, accompanied by their children, for how can they leave them behind and who will look after them back in the village? They talk, curse, and gossip among themselves as they climb the hills, along thorny paths, buffeted by strong winds. Their rambling progress, as they trace their zigzag route, is echoed in their talk and sets the tone for Urmila Pawar's writing in this memoir of a Dalit woman's life.

Urmila Pawar is now a well-known writer in Marathi; her work consists mainly of short stories and a history of the role of women in the movement for the emancipation of the Dalits, or untouchables, led by Bhimrao Ramji (affectionately and respectfully known as Babasaheb) Ambedkar in the early twentieth century, which she wrote in collaboration with Meenakshi Moon, published in 1989.[4] In chapter 8 of her autobiography, Pawar tells us about starting out as a writer. Earlier she had been an enthusiastic participant in school and village plays; this gave her confidence to speak on the stage, and while she was working in Mumbai she came in contact with organizers and political activists among different groups of Dalits. She is struck by situations involving caste and gender prejudice and begins to put down her thoughts in the form of short stories. After some of these are published, she meets other writers and becomes aware of matters of style and structure. Toward the end of the book she takes up her project of recording the histories of older Dalit women who took part in the Ambedkar movement.

The transition from an oral to a written form of self-expression in Urmila Pawar's own life echoes the story of emancipation of the Dalits. It is interesting that Pawar's first attempt to form an organization of Dalit women later in her life, in Mumbai, is by starting a literary group called

Samvadini, a coined name that adds a feminine ending to the word for conversation or dialogue. In Pawar and Moon's account of an earlier era of the struggle for Dalit liberation, we find repeated accounts of Dalit women in the 1930s and 1940s going up onstage in a public meeting, where even to read an announcement or to propose or second a motion is an extraordinary act of self-emancipation.

This is because untouchability, the most extreme manifestation of caste in Indian society, functions through a prohibition not only of touch, and of certain occupations, but also of the public use of speech; it is only the Brahmins who can enunciate sacred texts, but the untouchables are even further silenced by the authority of caste. So for these Dalit women, who were also silenced by the authority of patriarchy, to make a public use of speech was at the time truly revolutionary.

The political scientist Gopal Guru has underlined how Dalit women preserved the emancipatory character of the public use of language in the postindependence period, when, according to him, Dalit cultural politics was beginning to lose its edge.[5] During Ambedkar's lifetime, and also after his death in 1956, the tradition of Ambedkari *jalsas* did much to mobilize and politically awaken Dalits across Maharashtra. These troupes drew upon the musical traditions of the Mahars,[6] the largest Dalit caste in Maharashtra, and also on different forms of religious and folksinging, imbuing them with a message of Dalit liberation. However, Guru says, "Dalit women were invisible in the cultural landscape that was completely dominated by Dalit males." Further, traditionally Dalit women had performed in the erotic song and dance form of the *tamashas*, patronized by upper-caste men. Ambedkar urged Dalits to give up those occupations and traditions that were demeaning and humiliating, or in the women's case, sexually exploitative. And so, according to Guru, "the moral code imposed by Dalit patriarchy forced women into private spheres and denied them public visibility." However, he adds that in the post-Ambedkar era, women also developed their own cultural forms of protest. Urmila Pawar writes about how, after they became Buddhist, the women of her village at first found it hard that they could no longer sing the old religious songs, but later on they wove their own words into the old tunes, talking of their beloved leader affectionately as Baba or Bhim, of his first wife Ramabai (Rama-aai), and of his social message.

After Ambedkar's conversion in 1956, shortly before his death, Dalits all over the state followed him in giving up the worship of Hindu gods and goddesses and embraced the Buddhist faith.[7] Urmila Pawar was a young schoolgirl at the time. While thousands of Dalits became Buddhist on the occasion of Ambedkar's own conversion in Nagpur in eastern Maharashtra in October 1956, this wave of conversion reached her village in the Konkan only after Ambedkar's death on December 6. Pawar describes the grief expressed by all around her on that day, young and old, women and men "weeping uncontrollably," while she was only just beginning to understand what had happened. And, she tells us, "then the conversion happened quite suddenly.... Crowds of people from the surrounding villages marched to the grounds of Gogate College in Ratnagiri until it resembled a sea of humanity. We went there too, along with Govindadada and the other villagers. Several instructions were being issued from the loudspeakers hanging overhead. Then came the reverberating sound of *Buddham Saranam Gachchami,* and we too joined the chanting of the crowd.

After the ceremony, we went home. Govindadada and the villagers collected the idols and various pictures of the gods and goddesses adorning our walls, which Aaye used to worship every day, and threw them into a basket."

This was a historic moment in the lives of Dalits in Maharashtra. Throwing away the pictures and idols of Hindu gods and goddesses was significant in two major senses: it meant renouncing the lowly place that was accorded to Dalits in the Hindu caste hierarchy and it also entailed giving up superstition and ritual in favor of a more enlightened view of the world. Buddhism gave the Dalits a new vision of life, the possibility of living in a totally new way, free of bondage and subjugation.

Toward the end of *The Weave of My Life,* Urmila Pawar returns to her village after living in Mumbai for many years. She sees tarred roads in place of the stony, thorny pathways she used to walk to school on and tiled houses in place of huts. But when she looks into the interior, she is disturbed to find that the old gods and goddesses, and rustic talismans to ward off evil spirits, have returned to the homes of the neo-Buddhist villagers.

The Konkan region, with its rocky paths, its precipitous slopes, and the nearness of the sea, the always palpable presence of a wild and unruly nature, has traditionally been a breeding ground for all kinds of superstitions and belief in ghosts and the occult doings of neighbors. This is an integral part of the culture of the Konkan, and with the Dalits there is added the constant struggle for survival, in conditions of unremitting labor and extreme poverty. This region was also one of the areas that many of Ambedkar's followers originated from. Urmila Pawar tells us about the villagers' fight to emerge from these conditions to a better life through the eyes of the rebellious child that she then was, who sees her father merely as a hard and even cruel man. He is willing to thrash his children and his nephews and nieces to put them through school. Yet the narrator also makes us see that his harshness is necessary, for the Dalit child's road to education is full of obstacles. The children are made to sit apart, they are singled out to perform duties like sweeping the school, they are beaten without reason, for the Brahmin teacher still feels that untouchables have no right to an education. Pawar's father set up house in Ratnagiri so that his children and his nephews and nieces would have access to better schools. When Urmila's sister takes up a job and is about to give it up because of the hardships it entails, her father helps out: "That's when Baba decided to stay with her. He brought his luggage to her tiny room and helped her hold on to the job."

Pawar's father also serves as a village priest; he has inherited this mantle from an ancestor who directly challenged the authority of the Brahmin. For a Dalit to take on the duties of a village priest for his community was itself part of a tradition of resistance. The Brahmin, who usually had a monopoly on the priesthood, exacted tribute and profit from every occasion in the villagers' lives, from birth, marriage, and death to illness, infertility, or madness. The Dalit priest, on the other hand, is partly healer, partly teacher and counselor. His approach to religion is pragmatic; certain rites have to be carried out as a matter of custom. (Later, of course, there is a conscious rejection of these by the Dalits who have turned to Buddhism). He is not above using meaningless mantras to lend dignity to his ministrations, as long as this serves to comfort the supplicant who comes to him. The religious practice of the Dalits is thus shorn of the mystification that surrounds the figure of the Brahmin priest, his monopoly over the interpretation of the sacred law thinly disguising his economic greed. The Dalit priest's role is to dispense human wisdom in the context of the everyday.

After their father's death, Urmila's brother Shahu inherited the priesthood, though he was only twelve years old. People made concessions for the "small" priest and gave him only jobs he could handle.

Anecdotes like these in Urmila Pawar's memoir can be read for their deep insights into caste as it is lived by the Dalits, with its small cultures of resistance that help to make the ever-present pain of untouchability more bearable. Her own experiences of caste discrimination are narrated with an interweaving of humor or with wry asides of self-deprecation. At school, the Dalit children are saddled with bothersome tasks; on one occasion the master hits Urmila with the unjustified accusation that their family cow has made a mess in the verandah! She runs home crying and is cheered to find that her mother is willing to confront the teacher and demand justice. After her marriage, Pawar is subjected to discrimination when she and her husband look for rented accommodations in the town of Ratnagiri; they have to vacate two rooms after the landlady discovers their caste. In one place, her landlady's daughter strikes up a friendship and wants to borrow a sari. Urmila generously shows her all her wedding saris; but when the girl discovers Urmila's caste, "she suddenly lost her voice. Picking up my brocade sari, she walked off." Here is the paradox of untouchability, that it is fine to borrow a Dalit girl's sari (and to return it in a soiled and stained condition), but not to have social intercourse with her or drink tea in her house! But Urmila Pawar's tone in telling us this story is not the "incomprehension" of the suffering subject of the worst kinds of Dalit oppression and violence; rather it is ironic. After all, landladies in small towns are notorious for their caste sensitivities, and it would not be only Dalits who are likely to undergo this kind of discrimination.

One of the most moving anecdotes recounted in this memoir is of the village celebrations of the spring festival of Holi. Mahar youths are made to do the hard work of cutting down branches and trunks of trees and carrying them to the field where a fire will be lighted at dusk. But they are not allowed a place in the celebrations: it is the upper-caste men who carry the palanquin of the goddess, and the Mahars are forbidden to touch it. But the Mahar boys, who by this time have poured lots of drink down their throats, jump up and try to touch the palanquin. They have been affected by the mood of defiance that is peculiar to the Holi festival, when it is acceptable for men and women to howl and curse in public. These are age-old traditions that have been followed by all castes for centuries. On the day after the full moon, people throw dust and cow dung at each other; these days it is customary to spray one another with colored water. While praying for prosperity and the diversion of calamities from the village, the upper castes also ask that the calamities be visited on the Mahars! This is another role thrust on the untouchables, that of carriers of misfortune as well as pollution, protectors and sanitizers of the village who are reviled rather than revered. The defiant Mahar boys are soundly kicked and beaten for their transgression. The narrative here chillingly adopts the technique of "the ordinary": the youths return to their families, receive some comfort from their mothers and sisters, and run back into the fray, only to get beaten up again. Then the festival moves on to the next stage, and everyone enjoys the dramatic performances staged in the light of the full moon, petromax lamps, and the raging Holi fire.

One of the special features of Urmila Pawar's memoirs is her account of patriarchy among the Dalits. It begins in the second chapter with the description of the marriage ceremony of her eldest brother. This marrriage took place before the Mahars converted to Buddhism; but Urmila Pawar's family had already cut down on the number of rites to be performed. She gives details of the rituals of a Mahar wedding, which the reader of the Marathi original will easily recognize as being different from those of a traditional Hindu wedding. The all-important *saptaphera* or seven circlings of the sacred fire by the bride and groom, for instance, is replaced by arranging seven piles of rice on a wooden plank for the bride to step on. When the rituals are over, the traditional games begin. After her account of several games, Pawar remarks: "All these games were basically intended to control the bride and keep her in check. But when they were being played, everybody laughed and had a good time. These were happy occasions in their lives."

Later on in the book, Pawar gives us more serious examples of patriarchal oppression of women both within the Dalit community and along the lines of caste hierarchy, with upper-caste men enjoying a licence to exploit Dalit women sexually. The temple priest sexually abuses a young girl from the nomadic Komti community; the young Urmila sees her coming out of the inner sanctum in tears and does not understand. Her mother and her elder sister Bhikiakka are more victims of dire poverty than patriarchy, but in chapter 5 we have a detailed account of the ill-treatment of another sister, Manjula, at the hands of her in-laws, followed by several cases of similar treatment of daughters-in-law. On the other hand, Urmila Pawar also tells us of her own experience of affection and friendship from members of her husband's family.

There is a terrible story of a widow who becomes pregnant and is kicked in the stomach by women of the village till she aborts the fetus and later dies. Noting the self-righteousness of the village women who feel that they are upholding the "honor" of their community is the only comment Pawar offers us with regard to this incident. She does not mention whether the woman in question was a Dalit, though that seems unlikely. However, the Dalit women of the village certainly participated in the spirit if not the act of punitive violence.

On the whole, however, Dalit widows were not treated with the same degree of exclusion as in the Brahmin community. Although Pawar does not touch on the issue of widow remarriage, she gives us a small linguistic essay on the interesting term *randki sooj*, which translates as widow's swelling or widow swelling. Urmila has heard the phrase from her mother, who claims that, although she is a widow, she does not have the *randki sooj*. She asks her elder sister about it and gets the following reply: "'You know, for some women, when their husbands die, it is a release from oppression. Then they look a little better, fresh, so people say they have got the *randki sooj*.' Then she grew grave and said, 'But let me tell you, I have always been like this, somewhat plump, even before my husband died.'" This explanation is perhaps an adequate comment on the nature of Dalit patriarchy. The earthy phrase—more so because the word *raand* means both a widow and a prostitute in Marathi—tells us that many a woman is so badly treated by her husband that she blossoms out a little after his death. And yet, the freedom to joke about it, the common use of such a phrase, also signifies that widows are not completely suppressed.

Urmila Pawar's use of earthy language is no longer a new stylistic device. Both Dalit autobiographers and Dalit poets have used the vocabulary of the Mahars and the Mangs to delineate a world foreign to the experience of most readers of literature. Pawar is aware that there is not much shock value left in the use of this vocabulary. But she gives us a taste of the women's cursing, the words they use in quarrels, the open discussion of bodily functions, and of the "polluting" work that the untouchables are forced to do. The raunchy language, the openness, is also an integral part of Dalit culture. The women's songs, especially those composed after the conversion to Buddhism, carry the touch of the soil, the strength of bodies accustomed to hard labor. Her account of her romance with Harishchandra, the man she eventually marries, also does not shy away from discussing the physical aspects of their relationship.

Maya Pandit's translation succeeds to a great extent in conveying the flavor of this speech and the down-to-earth humor of Pawar's writing style. She retains the use of Marathi kinship terms that are so much a part of family relationships and gives us a glossary to their meaning. It is always challenging to translate a linguistically diverse text from one language to another, and here it has been done with considerable accuracy and ease.

Urmila Pawar devotes an entire chapter, the third, to a description of food and eating habits in her family and community. This helps her to accomplish a number of distinct objectives. First, the experience of extreme poverty, of living with a persistent lack of adequate nourishment, is most effectively conveyed through the child's viewpoint. The mother is described as stingy, fending off her children's demands, while we also see her efforts to make ends meet and to give them what taste and variety she can. Then there is the contrast with the food habits of young Urmila's upper-caste schoolmates. The children's negotiations with each other and the pain the girl feels tell us a great deal about one of the central aspects of caste hierarchy. And, finally, throughout the hierarchy, it is the women who nurture the culture of their caste, and there is an enjoyment and a pride in talking about the food characteristic to one's caste and the food prepared at festivals, however meager it may be. Women are the cultural carriers of caste, and it is through the patriarchal control of women that caste divisions are maintained.

In the later chapters of *The Weave of My Life*, Urmila Pawar moves with her husband to Mumbai and works at a job in a government office. Here the narrative picks up speed as she adjusts to life in a metropolitan city. The ubiquitous presence of caste cannot be entirely forgotten even here; there are daily pinpricks and occasionally bigger jolts of caste discrimination. But Pawar makes good use of the newfound freedom and attends meetings, meets women's groups, and, most important, begins to write. Here, too, her weaving technique is at play as she intersperses the narrative of her own achievements with her observations about the society around her. Her feminism becomes more pronounced. Her increasing activity and fame as a writer makes her husband uncomfortable. There is tragedy—she loses a college-going son—and there are problems to be resolved. She stands by both her daughters when they go against their father's wishes, marrying men of their choice.

Pawar's autobiography has been much acclaimed in Marathi literary circles.[8] It has won prizes and is currently in its third edition. But she says that the book has also received its share of flak, especially in the Dalit community. She has been criticized for her association with upper-caste women's groups, and her open exposition of Dalit patriarchy has not been welcomed.

The movement for the emancipation of the untouchables carried on for some time after Ambedkar's death, but the co-optation of many of its leaders by the ruling Congress Party eventually blunted its revolutionary edge. Ambedkar, for his part, like the nineteenth-century social reformer Jotiba Phule before him, was always very clear that a fight for the emancipation of Dalits would have to take up the cause of gender equality. Even today, cultural and political movement leaders organizing against caste invoke the names of Ambedkar and Phule. But—and Urmila Pawar talks about this several times in the later chapters of her book—today's Dalit leaders are not very open to women raising issues of gender. Some might say that patriarchal attitudes have hardened since the 1990s, when fundamentalist religious organizations began to dig in their heels on the Indian political scene. In fact, the radical face of the Dalit movement began eroding even earlier, with the rise of the Shiv Sena in Mumbai: a party that mobilized disaffected non-Brahmin youth of the city using a fascist rhetoric directed first against "southerners" in Mumbai and later against Muslims.

Similarly, though some dialogue between Dalit women's organizations and the "mainstream women's movement"—itself a problematic term today—have been initiated, there is still distrust and suspicion. The issues raised on each side do not translate well into the rhetoric of the other. There has not been enough genuine dialogue or attempts to forge a common program, though there is more talk of gender and caste today than at any time in the past.

In any case, Urmila Pawar is today quite deeply involved in a political attempt by Dalit women's organizations to bring together the movements against gender and caste inequality. Recently, she was one of the organizers of protests in Mumbai on the brutal murder of a Dalit woman, her daughter, and two sons in a village named Khairlanji in the Bhandara district at the eastern end of Maharashtra state. The story is depressingly familiar. An upwardly mobile Dalit family attracted the ire of the village non-Dalits, as they owned a bit of land, a daughter was studying in college, and her mother bought her a bicycle. Attempts to harass them by trying to encroach into their land were resisted. The retaliation of the upper castes was visited upon the two women, Surekha and Priyanka Bhotmange. Their bodies, stripped naked, were found dumped in a river. A recent court verdict has acquitted three of the accused and pronounced a death sentence on five others for murder.[9] However, the judgment denies any caste motivation for the crime and also refuses to take cognizance of the accusation of gang rape, since evidence of the latter has been systematically destroyed. Dalit women's organizations, in demanding justice for the victims of this crime, seek to underline how violence, especially sexual violence, is perpetrated on Dalit women whenever it is felt that the caste order has been transgressed. The involvement of the state and the media in suppressing these implications of the Khairlanji violence has, however, not been taken up either by Dalit political organizations or women's organizations as a major issue, though some protests have been organized by women'a organizations at the local and national levels.

If one wishes to understand the complex interweaving of caste and patriarchy and how it affects the lives not only of Dalit women but of men and women of all castes living in contemporary India, Urmila Pawar's book has much to offer. I am sure that non-Indian readers, too, will find articulations here that they can resonate with. A careful reader will learn much about how the politics of culture is played out in the lives of ordinary women and men in a situational context vastly different from her own. She may also understand something of the role that Dalit women can play in shaping the politics of the future.

A Note on Kinship Terms

In general, the translation uses English words as far as possible.

aai   mother in standard Marathi

aatoji   a more respectful way of addressing an older sister in Konkani

aaye   mother in a dialect version

akka   a respectful way of addressing the oldest sister; sometimes added as suffix

anna   (used by the author's children) father; or sometimes an older brother if he is like a guardian

attya   aunt

baba   father

bai   a suffix added to a woman's name

bay   a suffix added to a woman's name in a dialect version

bhau   brother; the author refers only to her eldest brother thus

chulti   paternal aunt; also father's brother's wife

dada	grandfather's brother or cousin; suffix added to the name of a much older man in general
kaka	uncle, father's younger brother
diu	husband's brother
jaau	husband's brother's wife
jawai	son-in-law
mama	mother's brother
mami	mother's brother's wife; village women in general
maushi	mother's sister
mehuna	wife's brother
mehuni	wife's sister
nanand	husband's sister
sasu	mother-in-law
sasra	father-in-law
suun	daughter-in-law
tai	a suffix added to an older sister's name as a sign of respect; also added to any woman's name
vahini	brother's wife; also term of respect for any married woman (*vayani* in Malavani)

THE WEAVE OF MY LIFE

One

Women from our village traveled to the market at Ratnagiri to sell various things. They trudged the whole distance with huge, heavy bundles on their heads, filled with firewood or grass, rice or semolina, long pieces of bamboo, baskets of ripe or raw mangoes. Their loads would be heavy enough to break their necks. They would start their journey to Ratnagiri early in the morning. Between our village and Ratnagiri the road was difficult to negotiate as it wound up and down the hills. It was quite an exhausting trip.

When they came to the first hill, the vexed women would utter the choicest abuses, cursing, the *mool purush* of our family, who, had he heard them, would have died again. The reason for the abuse was quite simple. It was he who had chosen this particular village, Phansawale, in the back of beyond, for his people to settle. It was an extremely difficult and inconvenient terrain, as it lay in an obscure ditch in a far-off corner of the hills. Two high hills stood between the village and the outside world. The steep climbs, with their narrow winding paths full of jutting sharp stones and pebbles, were extremely slippery. One wrong step and one would straightway roll down to one's death somewhere in the bottom of the deep valleys. Then there were two big rivers to cross. These rushed down the hills, looping through thick forests and valleys, their bellies carrying who knows what under the deep water. But that wasn't all! After crossing the hills and the rivers, the women had to walk quite a distance on a long, dusty, and dirty path till they reached the city. Every time a toe crushed against a jutting stone, a curse rang out, probably making the poor ancestor turn in his grave.

Occasionally, the women heard the bloodcurdling roars of a tiger even in broad daylight and, indeed, incidents of tigers attacking people on their way were not uncommon. Danger lurked everywhere. It crawled across one's path in the form of poisonous snakes such as *ghonus* and *phurse* who looked as if they wanted to inquire casually after the travelers. The barren open spaces were covered with shrubs as sharp as the teeth of those creatures and resembled some ancient armor. The howling wind, ferocious enough to topple one to one's death, blew continuously. Then there was a huge deep well on the way, without any protective walls around, shrouded in the mist of chilling stories of evil spirits lurking there. All of these would strike one's heart cold with terror. And as if all this were not enough, there would be freaks and perverts, hiding in shrubs and trees, who occasionally assaulted the helpless women. They would be tense not only because of the obvious threat these miscreants posed but also because of what it would do to their reputations.

During the rains, especially, life hung by a thin thread. Survival was as dicey as gambling. The rain pouring down in huge torrents, as if the sky itself was collapsing; lightning striking across the sky in deafening roars; streams fiercely gushing down the hills; rocks exposed under receding layers of soil, like teeth jutting out of monstrous mouths, ready to tear the traveler's feet to shreds; thick shrubs, huge trees with wild creepers weaving tangled webs, and dense, dark forests sprawling around; rivers swollen with floods, weathered wooden bridges over them, ready to collapse at any moment ... life indeed hung by a thin thread! Eternal hunger gnawing one's insides overpowered all fear. Women were compelled to make the journey to the market because they had to sell their wares in order to survive: bundles of firewood or rice bags or grass or whatever merchandise, covered with leaves or woollen blankets. With their emaciated bodies covered in rags, bony sticklike legs, bare feet, pale, lifeless faces dripping either with sweat or rain, sunken stomachs, palms thickened with work, and feet with huge crevices like a patch freshly tilled, they looked like cadavers floating in powerful streams, propelled by a force hurtling them along the strong currents, being dashed against rocks and thrust forward by powerful waves.

So the women heaped abuses on the head of their mool purush who they felt was responsible for the difficult lives they had to live. "Just give us one good reason why we shouldn't abuse him?" the irate women asked. The rhetorical question was followed by still more curses.

"May his dead body rot ... why did he have to come and stay here, in this godforsaken place?" "May his face burn in the stove." "Was that bastard blind or what? Couldn't he see this bloody land for himself?" "Didn't that motherfucker see these deadly hills, paths, forests? How I wish somebody had slapped him hard for making this decision!"

My mother also belonged to the group of the cursing women. We heard so many curses from her! My father, who was a teacher, had built a small little hutlike house on the road to the bazaar, in Ratnagiri proper, especially for his children's education. So we siblings lived in the town. But before we shifted to the town, my mother had lived in the village and suffered all the pain and travails of traveling through the wretched hills.

The village held a terrific attraction for us children. Whenever there was a holiday and no school, we rushed to our village, which was located in a far-flung corner among the hills. Swimming in the river, plucking raw mangoes and berries to eat, roaming the hills ... these attractions drew us like a magnet. My sister Akka's children accompanied us quite often. But we did not make the journey by ourselves. We always went with the women who returned home after conducting business in the market. And we always came back with them when they returned with their wares to sell. The women chatted with each other ceaselessly on their way. It was great fun listening to their gossip! They would talk freely, without any restraint, in a language, vivid and robust, full of various cadences, tones, and rhythms that evoked many colors and smells of things from different places.

Their voices would be fresh and strong early in the morning when they started from their village with bundles on their heads. Someone would complain to her friend, "Haven't you stuffed your firewood yet? You silly woman, why didn't you pack it up yesterday and keep it ready? Come on, hurry up, we're getting late!' Yet another would loudly tell the old woman in the house, "Grandma, keep an eye on the kids! They might go to the river!" And a third one would beg her neighbor, "Could you please look after my baby? He's got a high fever. You'll give him his medicine on time, won't you? And please don't forget the holy ash under his bed. Put a pinch on his forehead, will you? I will be back in no time at all." Although this promise was given most solemnly, both she and her neighbor knew that it did not mean much and that there was no chance of her returning before dusk.

Their children always insisted on being taken along. The women would dissuade the children with honeyed words and promise of gifts. "I'll get you sweets," "I'll bring you *chana*," "Would you like dry Bombil fish?" When the children persisted, the women chased them away with threats, even sticks or stones, "You dead one, get along, you! You want your nose pinched, want to get your leg broken?" In spite of these dire threats, however, some kids persisted, creating such a racket with their crying and howling that the entire village woke up with a start from sleep. Somehow the women managed to pacify their kids and took off. They inquired after each other, "Why, what's wrong with your son? How long has he been sick?" These exchanges helped them forget the long road and eased the strain of walking with heavy loads on their heads; they chatted away.

In the process, however, even something insignificant became a long-winded narrative of epic proportions. For instance, "You know, I got up bang at the first cock crow. Kicked my blanket away with my feet ... went to the stove ... picked up the clay pitcher in the corner and came out ... when I came out, it was still moonlight ... yet I went to the river ... filled up the pot with water ... by that time the cock crowed again ... I said now I need a live coal ... but who will give it to me? Then I saw the children's *chulti*, their aunt, get up as her nephews were returning to Ratnagiri ... so I took a small dung cake and went to her ... she gave me a small live coal which I placed on the dung cake ... I came back blowing on it."

This would be followed by a detailed account of how she had lit the stove by putting more dung cakes on the burning coal, blown on it, and then made *bhakris* and cooked a vegetable dish; how she had hidden the bhakris in the hanging pot to keep them safe from cats. By the time this slow motion account came to an end, they would be halfway through the steep climb. That particular climb was called the Climb of the Lame. Nobody knows why! Maybe because it was so steep that one wrong step and one would be maimed forever.

Every house had its own share of drunkards. There would be at least one woman among them badly bashed up by her husband. She would walk painfully, somehow managing to drag her aching body along the way. If someone asked her what was wrong, her anger gushed out, "Let his drinking mouth be burned off forever. Let his hands rot." This would be followed by a detailed account of the reasons for the beating. He demanded money for liquor, she was late in serving his meal; she asked for money for household expenses, for buying medicines for the sick child. The narrative would be followed by spirited discussions and curses, which propelled them forward on their way.

Daughters-in-law were always despised and bashed up. There was a common expression that mothers-in-law would use about their daughters-in-law. "Trust the bitch to oblige you with a few drops from her private hair!" I could not understand what the expression meant then. Today, of course, it simply makes me laugh! Similarly, the wives of people who had migrated to Mumbai for work also invited ridicule, "Do you think the bitch will move her thick neck? No way!"

Chatting away like this, women climbed the hill. The steep climb would cause cramps in our legs. Somehow we dragged our feet to the flat plateau with that frightful well and the flat terrain would ease out the strain the climb had induced. But a new fear would now grip us—that of the evil spirits called Asaras! Here the talk switched track. The women's voices and the subject of their conversation also changed. It would be extremely windy there. Strong winds tried to fling the loads off the heads of the women whose necks almost got twisted with the strenuous effort of holding onto them. Women would somehow manage to keep their wares on their heads against the force of the pushing winds. They would stumble forward, trying to keep their balance and maintain direction. All chatting would cease. It was believed that the Asaras did not like loud voices. So women walked on with folded hands and fervently whispered prayers in the direction of the well, "Please bless our children with your mercy." And then they would silently move on.

Once we had crossed the barren plain on the hilltop, we started descending on the other side of the hill. Then women would whisper their complaints to each other. The topics had an amazing range: about people sneaking in somewhere on the last moonless night, how they had covered themselves in black blankets and how they stole mangoes from someone's garden, who had chopped off whose tree for fuel or stolen whose paddy from the field, who had taken cows and buffaloes for grazing in whose fields, who had got into whose bed. The stories would be narrated in a competitive spirit of "mine is better than yours." The stories, of course, would have many embellishments.

If they suspected that we listened to their gossip most keenly, they would shout at us, "You dead ones, why do you get in our way? Go on, walk ahead; your mother is waiting for you. Come on, faster." But we could be sure that the molehills of their gossip would grow into mountains in a short while.

Once we had climbed down the hill, we would hear the splashing noise of the Mirjole River and our heavy feet moved a little faster.

Suddenly someone would remember people back home, especially children, whom they had left behind. "How's my baby, I'm so worried! Did they give him his medicine?" A young mother would find her breasts aching, heavy with milk. Often while crossing boulders it would drip out, wetting her blouse. The young mother would interpret this as a sign of her baby crying at home for milk and break down into uncontrollable sobs. The other women would console her.

"Why do you cry? Last time when Jani came to the market, you had fed her baby with your milk. Now won't she return your favor and feed your baby? And suppose she doesn't! Somebody is bound to do so in the village, willing to feed him with a little something. No, no, don't cry like that! Come on." In case it was a new, first-time mother, they would advise her, "Your milk is spilling out, isn't it? Don't let it spill on the ground; if ants taste it, you'll go dry. So collect it in a leaf. Here, take this leaf, gather your milk in this and then pour it in the tree trunk. See, your milk will increase."

"What a wretched life!" they would exclaim and then lower the heavy loads on the bank of the river, flowing with waist-high water. We would run along and cool our feet in the waters. Then we drank the cool water of a nearby stream. They told us that the stream water was cooler and cleaner than river water. Cupping their hands together, they drank water in great gulps as if they had been thirsty for ages. Then they washed their faces. Their sunburned cheeks glistened with the water, and their sparkling nose tips stood out on their dark wet faces. The wet *kumkum* on their foreheads slowly trickled down on their noses. They patted their hair in place and offered each other *paan,* betel nuts, and quicklime. Pushing the leaf into the mouth, they would twist the tender stem of the paan and throw it out. Then slowly gathering the paan in the mouth, pushing it behind their molars and happily chewing on it, they would turn toward us to admonish us. "Come on kids, we still have to climb one more hill. If you want to pass water and stuff, do it now. Otherwise you will do it in your knickers while climbing the hill."

Making fun of us, they would walk on. The hill of Mirjole was terrible; it was very steep and we used to get cramps climbing it. We could hear the dry leaves crunching under our feet and our panting breaths echoed in our ears. This was also the place for confrontation with gossipmongers. A woman, hurt by the whispers she had overheard a while ago, would decide to allow the others to go on. Then she would turn to the woman she'd heard bitching about her and confront her, "What were you telling them about me a while ago?"

"What? What did I say?" The woman being confronted would warily counter back, in an equally high-pitched voice. She would guess that now there was no easy escape.

"Didn't you say something about somebody getting into someone's bed? Now who's got in whose bed?"

"Who? Me? No! Why should I be saying a thing like that? Maybe it was Yesu … or someone else talking to somebody, I don't know … "

The speaker would just try to wriggle out of the mess by squarely pushing the blame onto a woman who hadn't even come with them. But from the hurt tones of the accusing woman, we could imagine the fireworks that would soon ensue in her house. We could smell many such future quarrels from the gossiping around us.

The women and their clothes would carry mixed smells of cashew nuts, mangoes, the medicinal nut *bibbe,* grass, wood, ash, cow dung, and earth. Even the memories and anecdotes they narrated to us carried the smells of various objects and things, living and otherwise. They evoked the fragrance of mango blossoms and flowering kuda trees, the soil soaked in the first rains, of mud, moss, gum, and other juices oozing from the trees … these smells anywhere evoke those memories in my mind! And sometimes they carried sounds such as the murmur of the flowing river, the splashing of streams, and the chirruping of birds that provided some sort of background music.

After climbing atop the hill of Mirjole, we would step onto the plateau, where there was a huge jamun tree, so tall that its top almost touched the sky. So we would tell each other that we were nearly there. The women would tell us, "Now come on, hurry up, we have crossed the whole elephant, only the tail remains ... Here, you can see Ratnagiri right in front! See ... here comes the broken man's bungalow." This broken man's bungalow was the Leper Hospital, which was located on the outskirts of the city. Lonely, isolated! The broad road coming from small places like Mazgaon, Sheel, Mirjole, Kelaye would reach up to the big jamun tree, and buses, trucks, cycles, bullock carts would zoom past, raising a thick dust cloud, driving the poor hawkers helter-skelter. The rich people in the villages, who traveled in a bullock cart, always took another road that was longer. But this was the main road. We somehow dragged our weary feet and finally reached home.

Our house was right on this road. Once it came into sight, we would run and reach the door. Aaye would be sitting in the courtyard, weaving cane baskets. The women, our chaperons, would shout from the road that they had safely brought us home, "Masterni, we got your kids back safe and sound.[1] They did not fall down or stub their toes. They are all in one piece, quite intact! Check them well. Otherwise later on you may blame us." Then they would rush off to the market.

The women had to trudge through various small lanes and nooks and corners of the town to sell the heavy loads on their heads. Once they had struck bargains, they walked all over the bazaar, looking for places where they could get cooking ingredients like molasses, oil, and red chilli powder at cheap rates. Then they threw the tiny packets in their baskets, bought some cheap, low-quality fish, tidbits for their kids waiting at home, and started on their way back ...

The walk back home would be quite different. Their baskets would be light. Some of the women, before they started their journey back, would first sit in our yard, draw water from the well, quench their thirst, roast cheap tiny fish on dry twigs and eat them with some dry bread. But some, who did not have any time even for this meager refreshment, would start walking the long way. They would just take some morsels of dry bread and fish in their hand and nibble on them while walking. Their talk would again be quite interesting and long-winded. Yet the chatting would be light, like the baskets on their heads. And the things that they talked about! Relatives they had met in the market, the sad and happy incidents in their lives, "seeing" prospective brides, a program carried out successfully in the market itself, marriages arranged and broken, divorces, and, of course, their experiences while selling the wares. But their voices lacked the morning's excitement and enthusiasm. Their talk now took on the colors and smells of slightly decomposing fish, of provisions they had bought in tiny packets, their sweat, and the setting sun.

While chewing on a betel nut, one would ask her friend, "Tell me, did that red sari near the Ithoba temple finally buy your bundle of firewood or not?"

"Ha, as if she was really going to, the bitch!" The woman would explode into fiery expletives, spitting the fiery red paan juice into the dust. "How many times did I tell her that the firewood was good and dry and wouldn't smoke! But would she buy? No way! The bitch that she is, she just lifted her leg over my bunch of sticks and left." Then the woman who had asked her would tell her own story. "You know, even I came across one of them bitches, up in the Tambat Lane. This one says to me, your sticks look so porous; they won't burn long … so I told her, look at it well, this is proper mango wood, not some useless twigs. And then you know how much she offers me? Five annas … I immediately said, to her face, go stuff your stove with this money and see if it burns well." This raised a collective burst of laughter from everyone!

The women, of course, had not said anything like this to their customers. Nonetheless, it would give vent to their pent-up anger. Somebody would burst out, "And there was this oldie asking for my bunch of sticks. Offered me seven and a half annas; I told him straightaway, try feeding that money to your bull and see if he can eat it." Yet another one exposed the ignorance of her customer, "See I took my bunch of sticks on the stand. Two guys came asking me about the price. Then they started chatting about something else. So I said, you are buying this, aren't you? This bunch is quite heavy on my head. So they said, all right, put it down. So I did. Then they tried to lift it and feel its weight. Then one says, Ha, this is so light; how can you say it's heavy? I told him straight to his face, it's heavy for us because we come crossing two-three hills with that on our heads! We are bound to find it heavy! You just lift it for a minute. Obviously it's light for you!" Then a fourth would comment, "Just let him try and lift our bundles; I bet his bums would tear apart!" This would provoke peels of laughter from the other women. But that laughter often camouflaged a deep anguish in their hearts at their wretched lives.

There would be some experiences, however, far beyond the grasp of children like us. "When I put down my bundle of grass on the stand, an old guy came, the bastard! Winking at me, he kept pressing the grass bundle. So I said, "Why are you pressing the grass; do you think I've hidden a grain bag inside? These are just paddy stems. Your cows and buffaloes will gobble it like candy. Buy if you want! The bastard just pushed his dhoti aside and showed me his "cobra." I was going to beat him to a pulp but he ran away fast."

Here all the women would heartily heap abuse, in chorus, on that man's head. Then they would become their former serious selves once again and start treading the path back home.

Someone munched on the slightly decomposed fish, babbling away, "Bah, this fish is bad; that Mussalman woman told me it was fresh; that's why I bought it! May her heart roast in the stove."

Then another would remember, "I asked for oil worth two annas; the bastard gave me only one anna's worth. Oh God! How was I deceived like this? I am so stupid!" She would keep blaming herself, muttering curses all through.

In the meantime someone coming from the back would shout at the woman in the front, "Hey, look, a crow is stealing your chana packet!" On hearing this, the woman being plundered thus would dance on the balls of her feet, protecting her basket and the precious packets in it. The crows would fly off with someone's fish and another's liver. Then a collective shout would go up, "Hey, the crow is flying off with your liver," to provoke peals of laughter.

Sometimes, a bunch of Kulwadi women coming from behind would cross them, taking care to avoid their touch. Someone would notice that and flare up, "Look at them! See how they kept far from us! As if they are wearing the holy cloth like the Brahmin women!" Then another would be sure to answer her, "Let me tell you, a Kulwadi woman I knew kept a dead snake in her sari for eight days—completely rotten! And see how they show off as if we pollute them!" Then there would be a discussion about how the show-offs were really filthy. There would be frequent references to a "decomposed snake"! This would excite laughter from all!

Their feet kept walking.

Then somebody would remember people at home. "My baby is sick at home! Will they have remembered to feed milk to my young one? Has that drunkard, that husband of mine, bashed up the kids?" These fears and doubts made their feet tread the rough-hewn path home faster.

On this same road, we heard hundreds of stories about the history of our family, across generations. Once we came to hear a very strange tale about our great-great-great grandfather, the same man who had founded our settlement and whom women abused while climbing up and down the hill. That original founder went on to have a huge family, which developed into several branches that had settled together in our wadi. There was a man called Hari in this family who went to Pune and joined the British army. During one of his visits to the village he did something completely unprecedented.

The story went thus. At that time Brahmin priests performed the rituals of marriage and ceremonial worship for the lower castes, like the Mahars and Chambhars. But the priest would never enter the Maharwada to perform these tasks. He would climb a tree on the outskirts of the neighborhood, muttering some chants. The holy moment for solemnizing the marriage would be either in the morning or evening, when the trees cast long shadows. So the bhatji would climb the tree because he did not want to be polluted with the shadows cast by the people of our Mahar neighborhood. When a marriage took place, the bride and groom would be standing in the *pandal* in the Maharwada with the *antarpat*—a piece of cloth that is held between the bride and groom at the time of marriage, barring them from looking at each other—and the Brahmin priest would climb a tree at a distance muttering mantras under his breath. Then he would shout the word *sawadhan* (a ritual chanting that literally means "attention") from the tree. At that instant the drummers started beating their drums and the marriage would take place. Then the priest would climb down, sprinkle holy water from his *panchapatra*—a vessel with five compartments—with a *pali*, a small ritual spoon, on the coins kept as his *dakshina* to wash away the pollution and make them clean, and push it into his waistband. He would also make it a point to take away all the offerings: rice, coconuts, and so on, as part of his dakshina. He never carried these himself, of course! He had his servant for that task.

If one wanted to consult the priest about choosing a proper name according to the almanac or collect some holy ash for a sick person, he had to wait endlessly outside the priest's house, that too beyond the courtyard.

Hari felt it was humiliating to have the rituals conducted from a distance. It must have been the influence of Mahatma Jotiba Phule's Satyashodhak movement in 1873.[2] So, during one of his visits to the village, Hari called a meeting of the villagers. They decided that in future they would perform all the rituals themselves.

Now the bhat found this terribly insulting. He told Hari, "You must know Sanskrit to conduct a marriage." Hari said, "Of course, I do know Sanskrit." He recited some *shlokas* and demonstrated his knowledge of Sanskrit. Then the bhat said, "If you want to counsel people about the past and future, you also must know *pranayam*." Hari said, "I know it; I can do it." The bhat did not believe this so he challenged Hari. "For eight days, we will sit in pits dug deep into our respective cremation and burial grounds. The pits will be covered with earth on top. If you win, I have no objection to you performing your own religious rituals."

All the wise people in the village held a meeting and endorsed this challenge. Accordingly, two deep pits were dug in the respective grounds. The two contestants were made to sit inside their own pits; the bhat in a pit in the upper-caste burning ground and Hari in the Mahars' burial ground. Wooden planks were used to cover the pit mouths, which were then sealed off with wet soil. Two tubes were inserted inside the pits, to feed milk to the contestants. This horrible ordeal was carried out under police protection too! People kept vigil day and night at both places. Both contestants were alive in their respective pits for five days. On the last day, the milk in the tube provided for the bhat came up unconsumed. The bhat was dead. Hari survived the ordeal and won.

From that day on, the responsibility of carrying out various rituals in nine surrounding villages, including our Phansawale, was given to Hari. He earned a second name, "The Buwa of the Burning Ground." It was this tradition that my family had inherited. All the men in our family, and even a woman, Phatiakka, Hari's daughter and my father's sister, would function as the "bhat" for the community. They read holy texts and performed religious rituals too. Hari had got Phatiakka married off to a man called Kavalekar, who served in the army. Hari brought him to live in our village, Phansawale. So Phatiakka performed as a priest even after her marriage.

We used to feel extremely proud of Hari, our great grandfather, for having achieved something so wonderful. We would circulate his story. But now ... now I feel sorry for the poor Brahmin who lost his life unnecessarily trying to protect a preposterous tradition. This particular memory has lost all the exuberance now; it has become painful and sad like a looking glass without mercury.

On the way between Ratnagiri and Phansawale, women villagers used to tell us many stories about our aaye and baba. They had a terrific talent for histrionics, and we loved their forceful narration. They would bring events from the past alive before our eyes. I often feel that a couple of them would certainly have emerged as quite powerful actors had they got a chance. But that godforsaken village of ours did not have even a proper school! Just one *pantoji* used to teach only Brahmin kids, on the verandah of a Brahmin house. My grandfather, Chimaji, had a great wish to educate his son, my father. His elder daughter was married to a man from a village near Ratnagiri, called Partavane. He was a havaldar who had given his house to Christian missionaries to set up a school. Since only the children of converted Mahar-Christians went to that school, it was called the "school of the polluted converts." My grandfather sent my father to this school. My father got married at a very young age. While at the school, he got a chance to go to England, but my grandfather refused permission. The story goes like this:

At that time, missionaries used to visit schools and went from door to door as part of their proselytizing campaign. They would give sermons on Christianity and encouraged people to convert. Some poor people did get converted. But because of the false caste pride (it was said that one should bear any calamity for the sake of maintaining one's caste), conversion was not a regular thing. Maybe because Baba was a good student, or maybe they wanted to prepare him for conversion, nobody knows why, but a woman missionary had made all the preparations to take Baba along with her to England. Grandfather was invited for a consultation, and his permission was sought. England was way beyond his imagination. Maybe he was afraid that once his son went beyond the seven seas, he would not be able see him alive again! So he refused to give his permission under the pretext that his son was married. And thus the possibility of change this trip would have brought about in my father's life, and ours too as his children, was nipped in the bud. When young we often regretted this; Father should not have done that! Even today, after having experienced the horrors of the caste system, the same feeling haunts me. Of course, it was also true that our mother was a native of this place.

Now my father's wife (not my mother, the previous one), who had provided my grandfather with a solid pretext for why his son could not go to England, was later taken seriously ill. What began as an ordinary fever turned into something serious. She gradually lost her appetite and zest and never recovered. Immediately afterward, my uncle also died. My grandfather died in shock. Now in those days it was believed that if people in the house died quickly in succession, someone must have been dabbling in black magic. Our family was no exception. My aaye and my chulti, Thoralibay, were convinced that somebody had indeed done black magic on our family. They suspected some people from our neighborhood and went on flinging curses at them for a long time. This drama of superstitions took on still more novel forms after my father's death.

My father completed his sixth standard and became a teacher in a school for untouchable children, opened on a hill called Sinal where many Mahar families used to live, with surnames like Tondekar, Kashelkar, Naneejkar, and so on. It was said that the hill was called Sinal because women living there were sinners. But the name Sinal was a distorted form of "signal" as the hill was used for giving signals to boats sailing in the Arabian Sea. The name Signal Hill changed to Sinal Hill. After conversion, when all the Mahars there converted to Buddhism, they renamed their neighborhood Ambedkar Wadi.

My father was a man with many qualities. While he was a student and even later on, when he became a teacher, he used to work for a couple of hours every day in the cloth shop of Shri Rangoba Lanjekar, near where the bullock carts stood, where the Savarkar statue stands today. He would do anything he was asked to do. Lanjekar was a big-time mango merchant who bought mango trees on contract immediately after they flowered. That is how he came to know Baba.

Baba had lost his wife and wanted to remarry. He had consented to marry my mother because she could weave cane baskets. But my other *aajoba,* my mother's father, rejected him because he was a *bijwar,* that is, getting married the second time. He was also dark and ugly compared to his daughter, who was fair and beautiful. He was also shorter than her. Even if these flaws could be overlooked, that he was educated in the school of converts and taught in one, that too on the Sinal Hill, couldn't be. Besides, my father's house was in a far-off, obscure village, far from the sea, whereas my mother came from a house that was right on the seashore. "My daughter eats fish fresh from the sea, every day, but this guy can get only dried fish! I won't give him my daughter!" my mother's father declared. He had many other reasons too, but finally my mother's elder brother Vithu, who was a soldier in the army, intervened, and at last the marriage did take place.

By the time Baba became a teacher, the Brahmin school was moved from the verandah to the courtyard of the house (it was held under the canopy of a creeper there). A few others, children from other castes like the Bhandaris and Kunbis, started attending school with the Brahmin boys. Some Mahar children also went to school, but they had to sit outside in the courtyard. The teachers taught them and examined their slates from a distance. They would hit the children with stones if they made any mistakes. Naturally, our cousins lost all interest in learning and bunked school. Baba would be teaching in some far-off school, as he was often transferred by the authorities from school to school. He would constantly tell everybody to go to school. When he came home and discovered that his nephews skipped school, he would go wild with anger and give them a good thrashing. He was quite a thrasher! He used to take the skin off our backs too.

Once he thrashed my cousin Babi so much that Babi's mother, my aunt Thoralibay, became furious. She broke a ripe ratamba fruit open, squeezed out its red juice, and rubbed it against the child's buttocks. Then she howled loudly, "Oh look, my poor child has been beaten up by his uncle so badly that he has shat blood." She began to cry, scream, and curse. The old men from the village got very angry and they too started abusing my father. Since that day my father never laid even a finger on his nephews. He would take them along to the school he was teaching in and made them attend classes. But neither of them was ever interested in attending school. My elder sister, Shantiakka, however, lived with my father and reached the fourth standard. My father taught at a place called Karbude for a long time. He would coach children free of cost and encouraged them to attend school. Our village had a school, but it was only till the fourth standard. Moreover, girls were not allowed to enroll. My father kept my sister at a friend's house at Partavane, though he could not afford it, and enrolled her in the fifth standard. This friend was Jadhav Guruji.

Jadhav Guruji had five or six children of his own with whom Shantiakka started attending a school opened by the school board. The Patit Pavan Temple, built by Bhagoji Keer, who was inspired by Savarkar, is on the way to this school. In this temple, Savarkar used to organize *sahabhojan* programs, in which untouchables and high castes ate together. The Mahars from Partavane attended these programs, but not Baba. Ambedkar had organized Satyagraha at Mahad (Chavdar Tale) in 1927, but Father probably ignored that as well. In the *sahabhojan* programs, sweet dishes, such as huge *bundi larus, jalebis,* and so on, were served, and Akka often ran away from school to eat these. Besides, rich girls from the Surve family in the Mandavi area were her friends. She would roam around with them in their two-horse carriage. As a result, she somehow managed to go up to the sixth standard. Then Baba decided to get her married.

Actually nobody was in favor of Akka's going to school and her staying so far away from home. All the women complained, "Bah! What do women have to do with education? Ultimately she would be blowing on the stove, wouldn't she?" or "Is she going to be a teacher, a Brahmin lady, that she goes to school?" When word spread that the teacher who lived in a house with a well-tiled roof, and who functioned like a bhat, wanted to fix the marriage of his daughter, many proposals came from various places. In those days people would consider a proposal from Mumbai as one from a foreign country.

Once a woman from Velund came with her nephew from Mumbai to see Akka. She was related to my chulti from her mother's side. The nephew had lost his first wife and now wanted another. He worked as a sweeper. A stout fellow with dark, red eyes, mouth stained red with betel nut juice, he had come neatly dressed in shirt and pajamas. He wore several gold rings on his fingers. He sat there, displaying them, patting his hair in place. It was his aunt who did the talking, praising his job in Mumbai, his fields in the village, and his house. Baba was a teacher in some far-off school then. My aunt was mighty impressed with his four or five gold rings, but my mother thought he was as dark as a burned griddle. So there was a big argument, which went on and on till my father arrived. Finally, my father put an end to the argument, saying, "I'll give away my daughter to a coolie rather than to a sweeper." But Govindadada was really angry that the boy from the village of his mother's family and related to Thoralibay was rejected.

Next Baba selected a boy from my mother's village, Mire, and even this caused a big fight between Aaye and Baba. He was the first boy among the Dalits of Mire to have passed the vernacular examination, that is, the seventh standard. He had a small family with two sisters and his parents. There was nothing to object to. But there was a terrible scarcity of water in this village. Their house was atop a hill and they had to carry water all the way up from a stream, which met the sea several feet below. The daughters-in-law of the village were worn out doing this essential task. Some even succumbed to tuberculosis.

Aaye was angry, however, for a completely different reason. She knew those people very well. It was a joint family where the boy, his parents, his four or five aunts, uncles, and their wives and daughters all lived together. They were terribly poor. They did not have any land. They carried out the traditional duties that had befallen them because of their caste for their village and also did sundry jobs such as breaking firewood and so on. They somehow managed to buy a little rice, which they would cook in a big mud pot and serve with some watery soup. This was served to the men first, in one big common dish. They sat on their haunches to dine, as if they had sat down to shit! It was true that Dalits had the custom of all people eating from one plate, but that was usually because there were few plates in the homes. But this eating was a shade different. When men sat down to eat, they would count how many bites each one had. Everybody would count how much everybody else had eaten. Then they would fight, "You had two bites, I had only one." Or, "Now wait, your turn is over." Or, "He had one bite just now, now it's my turn!" This "conversation" went on all the time. If someone took one morsel more, there would be bitter fights. That's why they were known as "bite-counters" and the house was known as the "bite-counters family."

The Mahars were generally known for talking loudly while eating. So whenever there was a cacophony, others would say, "Don't worry; it's the Mahars eating!"

Anyway, when Baba fixed his daughter's marriage with a boy of this family, Aaye exploded. "No, I'll never allow my daughter to be given to that family." Baba coolly replied, "Remember, no one lives in the same situation all the time. An insect may be born in dung; that doesn't mean it will remain in the dung forever."

Dharmaji Master came to see Akka, accompanied by a friend. The Master wore a wristwatch and both were continuously looking into it. They kept telling each other the time and deliberately used words like minute hand, second hand, and so forth. Probably they were just showing off. Govindadada got angrier by the minute.

Finally Akka got married and went off to her in-laws' family. Whenever she visited us my two brothers teased her, "Tell us, do you really count your bites when you eat?" which would make Akka furious. But at the same time, she would narrate tales, grinning from ear to ear, of how her brothers-in-law kept pieces of bhakri hidden in the roof, and how they stole each other's hidden food. Govindadada had a grudge against her because she did not marry the boy from Mumbai related to his family. He used to tease her all the time by mimicking "second hand--minute hand ... " She would get angrier and angrier and finally burst into bitter tears.

Baba wanted his daughters to work and be financially independent. Accordingly, Akka tried for a job and got it, too, in the mental hospital. They had staff quarters for their employees just outside the huge stone building of the hospital. There was a separate chawl for the Bhangis, which had some seven or eight rooms. Akka got a room there. Her husband was a teacher in Chiplun. Baba had thought that Akka's parents-in-law would come and live with her. But her father-in-law could not leave the duties that his village had thrust upon him. Her sisters-in-law got married. They too found it difficult to travel from Mire to Ratnagiri on foot. Because of all these problems, Akka wanted to give up the job. That's when Baba decided to stay with her. He brought his luggage to her tiny room and helped her hold on to the job. He also put my two brothers Achyut and Krishna in a nearby school at Nivkhol. My other sister, Manjulatai, was quite small then. My brother Shahu and I were not born yet.

Akka wanted to leave her job again. The mad women in the hospital had come to know that she was a Dalit. A mentally disturbed woman was not willing to take food from her hands. She abused Akka because of her caste. Then Baba reasoned with Akka. He said, "In any case, they are mad people. But you are sane, aren't you? So behave like a sane person."

Baba was a very industrious man. He had a job and also worked as a bhat to carry forward the tradition of his family. In addition, he was an entrepreneur of sorts. In summer, he would take a contract of supplying mangoes. He arranged for the mangoes to be plucked from the trees, packed in cane baskets, and supplied to Lanjekar for sale. Aaye helped him as much as she could. She wove all sorts of cane things—big baskets, small baskets with closed tops, baskets for locking in hens, small baskets for collecting flowers, cradles—all sorts of things were grist to her mill. Besides, she also carried the baskets of mangoes packed by Baba to Lanjekar, for which she had to make an arduous journey, crossing the hills. Both of them saved bit by bit and built a small house with two small rooms and a tiled roof. The outer one served as a hall and the inner room was the kitchen. Later on, Baba constructed a verandah for people who came to consult the almanac with him. The verandah had a tin roof. He made the floor with soil beaten hard; it was polished smooth with dung.

Aaye erected a small shade in the backyard for stacking firewood and keeping her hens. In the kitchen she got a small platform built for the stove. She used to keep some sticks there and a hollow iron pipe to blow into the stove. There was another platform close by, about half a foot high, on which she used to arrange her water pots. Above this platform there was a wooden plank fixed horizontally on the wall, for keeping cooking vessels, brass jugs, bowls and glasses made of aluminium. Behind them stood four or five brass and aluminium dining plates. In a hanger above there was a small flat basket with a lid, just like a snake charmer's, used to keep bhakris, chapatis, or baked fish safe from the cats. On the side, opposite the stove, in the left-hand corner, there was a big square box, a common feature in almost all the households. This box could be used to keep rice, pulses, grains, and flour safe from mice and cats. It would also serve as a seat. Then there was a *vhayan*, a mortar, buried in the ground for pounding paddy or chillies. The grinding stone stood against the wall, and so did the small wooden stick and a tiny broom. The tool for pounding rice and, behind it, iron instruments such as a pounder, sickle, and a cutter were kept in another corner. Above these was a small alcove, made by fixing old wooden planks on the wall, on which useless things such as old baskets, tin containers, or strings would be strewn. Among those useless things lay a big implement called *kameru*, which was a big wooden stick fitted with iron teeth. Pressed against their hoods, it would pin poisonous snakes to the ground, making them immobile. Our mother and Bhai, my eldest brother, could easily kill cobra snakes with the figure of 10 on their hoods using the kameru.

A small transparent piece of glass was fitted in the roof to allow more light into the house. One could see small particles of dust, dung, and soil floating in the sun, streaking through the glass. Winnowing and cleaning would dramatically increase the number of particles floating there. In the middle room, Baba kept his tin trunk. It contained lots of papers, records of land, and some accounts written by him in the Modi script. Our covers and blankets would be neatly stacked on the trunk. On a string tied above the trunk would hang Mother's sari, folded neatly, along with our old clothes. There was a big alcove here and a cane ladder used to climb into it. In the verandah Father had kept a wooden bench for people who came to consult him. Near the bench lay Mother's stack of cane branches from which she cut out thin strips to weave her baskets. There would be plenty of light here. That is where we studied.

The houses of the Marathas and the Brahmins were at some distance from our house. Bhandari and Kulwadi women could drink water from their wells, but untouchable women were absolutely forbidden to do so. This was a permanent wound in Baba's heart. Therefore he had given strict instructions to my mother to allow the untouchable women to draw water from our well. The rope and bucket were permanent fixtures to the well. These were never removed.

Beyond the road, in front of the house, was Shirkewadi, where there was a cluster of four or five nice bungalows. In one of these, in a chawl-like structure, lived the daughter of King Thiba of Burma (Myanmar), whose name was Payagi, also called Faya. A man called Shivtarkar Sawant had married her.

When the British established their rule over Burma, they arrested King Thiba and kept him under house arrest, first in Madras in 1885 and later in Ratnagiri since 1890. In those days Ratnagiri was quite an obscure and difficult terrain, like the Andaman-Nicobar Islands. It was a sort of punishment posting for teachers. Water was quite scarce. The British had constructed a nice little bungalow for the king. Though he was a prisoner, he never forgot the fact that he was a king. He used to hold darbars in Ratnagiri in royal style and showered gifts on the poor.

Occasionally, my mother went there in the hope of receiving a gift. She told us that they could not walk upright before the king. They had to bend down and almost crawl like a child while entering through a very small door to approach him. Then they would catch the silver rupee or some other coin which the king threw at them and had to return the same way, without turning their backs on the king. Whatever allowance the British gave the king was quite inadequate, as most of it would go into organizing darbars, generous gifts, and offerings. Later the king sold off his gold, jewels, costly possessions, and even his furniture to meet the expenses. He counted his days in the hope that Burma would become independent one day and he would be able to go back to his own country. Finally, he was in dire straits. He died in Ratnagiri and was buried there.

The king's daughter, Princess Payagi, fell in love with a man called Shivatarkar Sawant, who was a private servant of King Thiba. She gave birth to a daughter who was named Baisu but called Tutu. Sawant was already married, with children; so the love story ended right there. In the final days of her life, Payagi became mentally deranged. She received a government pension, and a woman was appointed to look after her. Sawant got Tutu married to a man called Shankar Pawar, a mechanic for the state transport buses. Tutu lived with her husband in a hut on Nachane Road. Payagi would sit in the door the whole day, whispering to herself. She could not follow what was going on, but the moment she saw her son-in-law going to work, she would begin to shout at him, "Hey, you, Shankar Pawar, look after my daughter well. Don't beat her, please don't." Though she was mentally unhinged, the heartrending words of a mother would bring tears to the eyes of the passersby. The women in the royal family were completely ruined. After Payagi died, she was buried in a grave near her father's. I was just two then. Tutu was younger than my mother by some four or five years. They were good friends. Tutu's children, Pramila, Digambar, Chandu, and Baby, studied with me in the same school.

"You were the first one to sleep in the cradle in our house. You were just two months old when we came to live in this house," my mother would tell me. Till then we had lived with my older sister, Shantiakka, in her house. Her children, Jija, Shivaji, Prabhakar, and we two or three children of our parents were born within a space of one or two years. Akka used to come home to breastfeed her children on her lunch break. She would feed us also at her breast, which would be heavy with milk. Relieved, she would return to her job. Thus my siblings and I grew up on her milk as well.

When I was a couple of years old a strange incident took place in our house. Those were the days of the Shimga festival, also known as Holi. My father had gone to Phansawale for Holi with my elder brothers and sisters. Only my mother and I were in the house. One day we had an unexpected guest. My mother's father came to visit us from Mire. Hefty, fair, with a lean face covered by a thick moustache, he sat down without speaking. He was clearly quite disturbed. When my mother asked him repeatedly about the reason for his distress, he complained that his daughters-in-law did not give him food to eat or hot water for his bath, that his sons did not speak to him with respect. Then he burst into tears. He had complained like this a couple of times before as well, and my mother thought that this time too it was just like before. She never suspected it to be anything serious. So she uttered some soothing words to him, applied coconut milk to his body, gave him a good massage and bathed him with hot water. Then she cooked him some nice hot food and after he had eaten sent him to sleep on the verandah.

Sometime in the night she got up and went to the verandah to check whether he was sleeping well. But she found his bed empty. She waited for a while, thinking he must be somewhere close by, but when she did not hear any sound, she got terribly worried. It was quiet everywhere. The road in the front was also quiet. She was frightened. She ran to the well behind, which was full of water. But it was too dark there to see anything. So she picked me up and ran to my sister's house. She must have crossed a couple of compounds when her eyes caught sight of the peepul tree by the side of the road. My grandfather was hanging from the tree. My mother felt as if the solid ground beneath her feet had suddenly given away. Trembling violently, she reached my sister Shantiakka's house and told them what had happened. Shantiakka and her husband rushed out. My mother and my brother-in-law unfastened the dead body from the tree and brought it home.

People rushed to Mire to convey this message to my maternal uncles and aunts and to Baba who was at Phansawale. My mother's brothers and their wives blamed her for this tragedy. They charged her with deliberately not informing them about his mental imbalance. My mother was in a state of shock for a long time.

Immediately after Grandfather's death, one of my aunts who was married and lived in Sakhartar, contracted tuberculosis and succumbed to the disease. Her husband lived in Mumbai with their two sons. One of them left the house and never came back. This *mawshi* of mine used to earn her livelihood at Sakhartar by working as a coolie, carrying basketfuls of fish unloaded from the fishing boats to the hill. That is how she and her two sons had managed somehow to survive. Two of her daughters, Jana and Vitha, were already married off. After this aunt's death, my mother brought the mawshi's two sons to live with us. Our mawshi's daughter Sunder took charge of the cooking and the sons started going to school.

Around this time there was a terrible epidemic of plague and cholera. Poor people were dying like flies. Medicines were scarce. People who contracted typhoid and pneumonia died too, as medicines were not available. My eldest brother, Achyut, a twenty-year-old student in a college in Mumbai, caught typhoid and suddenly died. I must have been just a seven- or eight-year-old girl then. But I still remember the exact point in time when the warmth of the bed and my deep sleep were shattered by my mother's heartrending sobs, which gradually percolated deep down to the unconscious, shaking me to the innermost core of my being.

"Oh my child, my heart, when shall I see you again? My baby, where have you gone? Where will I ever find you?" She cried in a rhythmic sing-song voice every night, ceaselessly grieving for her son, as if she were singing an *ovi*, pushing her fingers down her throat to bring out the vomit of grief suppressed inside. In the morning her crying would wake us all up, like the alarm of a clock. We would jump out of our beds, quickly fold the covers, arrange them neatly on the string and start doing the morning chores. We crushed a tiny piece of coal between our teeth and brushed them with the dust. We stared at the yellow flames in the stove. while drinking tea without milk, occasionally ate stale bread with tea. My elder sister would fetch water from the well in the backyard, a brother cut firewood for the stove, a cousin sister would go to the river with a bundle of clothes to wash, children went to school on the road in front, villagers stumbled onward to the market and returned as if in a frenzy! Our mother, however, was completely oblivious to these things happening around her. She went on mourning the death of her son, sitting in the courtyard, her fingers frantically, ceaselessly, weaving baskets, winnows, and other stuff, one after another, stricken with suffering. My mother's usual appearance: her tall slim frame, light complexion that had the glow of wheat, thin long face, blood red kumkum on a green tattoo mark on her forehead, the mangalsutra around her neck, woven in ordinary thread, a few green glass bangles around her wrists and the *khut khut* noise made by the thick silver toe rings on her feet ... gradually dissolved in my memory to be replaced by another image of a tear-stained, thin, bare face without the red kumkum mark ... and a thin, skin-and-bones body withered in grief after my father's death.

My father died when I was in the third standard, in 1954. He was just fifty-eight. I remember him quite well. Had anybody asked me to draw his portrait, just two colors, black and white, would have sufficed. He was thin, short, and dark. He would be dressed in a white dhoti, white kameej, or long shirt and a black coat. He would also wear a white Gandhi cap. He had large, protruding black eyes and very white teeth. No other colors! Whether it was raining or not, he would always carry an umbrella in his hand. There would also be an almanac in the pocket of his coat. People used to come to us from various villages around to consult him, some to get his help about something they had lost and were eager to get back and some, possessed by ghosts, to get exorcised. He would consult his almanac and recommend various remedies. Sometimes he would collect the ash from the stove, whisper some chants, tie it up in small packets and give it away as a remedy.

Ghosts generally possessed more women than men. Once a woman from our village called Tulshi was possessed by a powerful ghost. She was a childless woman. Her husband was going to marry her sister. Once she went to the market to sell firewood and came back smoking a cigarette. She was also speaking English, saying, "Yes, No." People were astonished. They started telling each other how Tulshi was speaking English in a way that would put even an English sahib to shame. Then they brought her to our house. Her once tall, hefty frame had now become emaciated, as she would not eat anything. Her face was drawn and her hair tangled. The sari she was wearing had not been changed in ages. Baba made her sit down on a wooden plank and spoke to her for a long, long time. Then he took some rice grains rolled in ash and threw them on her body, all the while chanting something like,

> Bismilla rahema, rahim bajar bajr kaya,
> Hanumant jati lanka, aap bandh par bandh,
> Jakilsakil ki dadh bandh,
> Tambyacha coat nawi ki body mastak rakhi,
> Peeth rakhi,
> Khapri beirang,
> Jahangir ki janardan ja hamare dil,
> Hanuman dilme rakhawale hein.

This made her suddenly go quiet and she quietly went home. Many such possessed people would come to our house. Baba also went to various villages to treat possessed people.

As a priest Baba conducted all kinds of ceremonies for our people: marriages, *puja,* even death rites! Most of the time he was not at home. But when he returned, he brought bundles containing rice grains, new clothes, and coconuts. When our Aaye untied those bundles in front of us, the children, he kept a sharp eye on us. The rice bundles contained slivers of dry dates, coconut, almonds, walnuts—and what not! We kids would just grab such things. One of us would pull the new cloth and want to have a new dress or kameej made out of it. When many such pieces accumulated, we got new clothes. Of course, the dress would not be uniformly colored! The kameej had many colors, the sleeves having a different color each. The rice grains would contain loose change—one paisa, two paise, or anna coins. When we began snatching them, Baba placed a resounding smack on our heads and shouted, "Rascals, does the money belong to your father?"

Baba was a very stingy man. He never spent even a single paisa on himself. He never went to a hotel even for a cup of tea. He would get angry even if we asked for money to buy a pencil. When he was angry he looked like a monster, straight out of the pages of *Chandoba,* a Marathi children's magazine. When he was home he would behave as if torturing us, the children, was great fun. At night he would make us read books in the light of a hurricane lamp till our necks ached. He would scold us if we so much as moved. He would also make us drink castor oil. In those days, a powder called *chinapood* that was supposed to have a Chinese provenance was sold in the market as a remedy for worms. He would mix that powder in molasses and roll small round tablets of the mixture. His eyes shone with a strange light while he rolled them. Even a look at those tablets would be enough to kill not only the worms but wipe out their whole families. On top of it, we had to drink castor oil in the morning.

Once I could not swallow the chinapood tablet. I started hollering. Baba got up and placed a sharp kick on my chest. I collapsed backward, and the tablet slid down my throat. Then he started laughing. I used to get terribly angry at him. When he went out, I always prayed that he would not return.

There was a Maruti temple near our school. Whenever I felt like giving school a miss, I would go and sit in this temple, with books and all. I used to pray, "God, please don't let him return home." And that's what finally happened.

After my brother's death, my mother involved herself in weaving baskets, and Baba took on a lot more work. He was prone to jaundice. Once he was bedridden. Aaye said, "His blood has turned to water in his stomach. In the hospital, they took out water by the tubful." When I went along with Aaye to the hospital, he was covered in a white sheet and was almost invisible while he lay in the bed. His stomach had swollen like that of a pregnant woman. When we went near him, he wept like a child. He told Aaye, "Educate the children."

On that day I felt that he must not die but live. He had great hopes for Shantiakka's education. But she never liked school. I had a great impulse to go and tell him, "Don't worry. I'll go to school. I'll work hard and study. But please don't die." But he died nonetheless. That was a Friday night. His body was kept in a sitting position against the wall the whole night. People kept coming and sat mourning, praising his qualities. The next day was a Saturday. We had morning school. I don't know why but I packed my school bag and asked Aaye, "Shall I go to school today?" She just turned her face away. I do not remember having shown such enthusiasm for school before or even afterward.

On that day we carried Baba's body to his village in a big doli, like a palanquin, crossing the hills and valleys, mourning all the way. Several garlands of white champak flowers had been strewn over him. Baba was the priest of our community. He would be given *samadhi*.[3] The custom was to bury the priest close to the burial ground in the village and construct a samadhi or shrine over his grave; even Phatiakka had been buried the same way, and Baba was buried near her. Even today these samadhis stand intact in the village.

Aaye's morning ritual had been to mourn for Achyut, her son. Now she added Baba's memories to her rituals. Her hands started weaving still faster. She never visited the village after returning to Ratnagiri, not even for festivals. We kids rarely visited the village for the Gauri and Ganapati festivals as it would be the rainy season and the rivers and streams on the way would be flooded. In our entire neighborhood we and a couple of other houses would celebrate the Ganapati festival at home. Everyone would flock to our house for singing religious prayers and bhajans. The house was full of girls and children during the day. At night women, especially those visiting their parental home for the festival, would gather in our front courtyard and play various games. These married girls would share with each other stories of their married lives, crying and laughing over their sad and happy experiences.

Women worked very hard to prepare for the festival and earned a little extra money by selling more grass and firewood bundles, which they saved for the festival. They bought new clothes, bangles, necklaces, and such things for their children. They would also get tattoos on their and their daughters' foreheads, arms, and hands from tattooing women. If someone did not get a tattoo, they scolded her saying, "When you face God after death, He will ask you, have you come with a tattoo or without one?" They swept their houses clean; polished the floor, walls, small alcoves, corners of rooms—all dirtied with constant spitting—with cow dung, went to the river to bathe, dressed in new saris and blouses, and got all decked up, wearing cheap ornaments bought from the bazaar shops. They would catch a string in their teeth, take it backward over the head and tie their hair in a tight bunch. They would roll the string several times around the gathered hair, so tightly in fact that the roots of the hair rose in pimples and their faces would get a pimply border. All this preparation was for the program at night when they danced and played various games like *zimma* and *phugadya,* in front of the Ganapati. But some came for the program straight from work, with the same old dirty clothes and tired bodies. They nudged each other, urging their friends to dance. They sang many songs, dancing in circles, bending forward and backward, snapping their fingers to keep rhythm. The songs reflected their hard lives. Someone with a good voice sang and the others repeated the song after her,

> Girija sits down to pound some grains.
> She sits and pounds and stands and stops.
> Girija holds back her tears, O how she does!
> O how she endures and asks whoever she sees,
> Where do you come from, tell me O Friend.
> Where are you from, to whose family do you belong?
> Please take a message from me to my brother.
> He should come and take me home for the Gauri festival.

The next lines continued with what happened after this message had reached her brother:

> Girija's brother has come to fetch her home.
> Girija washes his feet with tears, O how they flow,
> Her brother asks her, "Why do you cry sister, why do you cry?"
> "I've eight brothers-in-law and nine sisters-in-law;
> How do I endure their torture? For how long?"
> "Don't worry sister, here I have come
> To take you home, sister, to take you home."

The women sang this and many such songs in singsong tunes. Sometimes they remembered their own brothers and sisters and wiped the tears in their eyes.

I always remembered my cousin Susheela at such times. She was married to a man in Partavane. He was a drunkard and Susheela's mother-in-law was a tyrant. Both beat her up mercilessly at the slightest pretext. They would drive her out of the house with her young children even on stormy dark nights. The poor woman would take her children and cross the hills and valleys at night, her face broken, body swollen, bleeding and aching all over, and reach her mother's house at Phansawale. When she came like that, and if Baba saw her, he would bark, "Who's that? Susha? All right, give her something to eat and send her back the way she's come. She must stay with her in-laws!"

Baba had tremendous power over the household. Everybody was so scared of him. Anybody who dared to contradict him would be sent back, with an aching body and an aching mind. I sometimes felt so mystified. He was the one who insisted on our getting educated, "Let the girls go to school. They have to stand on their own feet, be independent. They must also learn to ride bicycles." But the same Baba behaved so irresponsibly in Susheela's case. He never confronted her parents-in-law about their treating her so inhumanly. He never gave her any support. Later she died a very untimely death in Partavane. Did he believe so firmly in the diktat that a girl has to live with the family she has been married into? Was his sensitivity dead as far as she was concerned? Or was it because he wanted to take revenge on her mother, my aunt, who had falsely accused him of "beating her son till he shat blood" and cursed and created a scene before the whole village? Baba had sounded so balanced when he told Shanti, "The patient in the hospital believes in caste because she is mad; but why do you when you are sane?" Then why did he behave in such a way? How could he nurse so deep a grudge in his heart against his widowed sister-in-law, a helpless and illiterate woman, and her children? Or did he also suffer from the same malady that is typical of Konkan—family feuds? Whatever it was, I felt very bad about Susheela. Even today I do. Nobody sings those songs anymore, but the tune is deeply entrenched even today in my heart, inextricably entwined with Susheela's memory.

Govinda and Babi, my cousins, were several years my senior. They were almost as old as our Shantiakka. Their education did not progress much beyond the third or fourth standard. They were barely literate; that is, they could just read and write. They managed to somehow survive on the meager earnings from the land, which they had inherited, and their priesthood, which enabled them to conduct ritual worships, consult the almanac, dispense holy ash, and do all the other things that a priest was supposed to do. My father himself had initiated them into priesthood, by accepting them as his disciples in a ceremony, and tied the black string of a priest on their arms. This ritual was very important because one could not become a priest unless this initiation ceremony had been performed. Baba used to perform as a priest in Kelya Mahal and another priest, Bhikaji Sagardas Gosavi, would perform in the entire region, up to Rajapur.

Baba had married off his nephews well. Govinda was married to Parvati who came from a poor family. Babi's wife, however, came from a wealthy family. Her father was a contractor who undertook roadwork. She was from the village Karbude, supposedly quite developed. But the girls from that village were famous as "forward"! There was an interesting story behind this. In the Konkan region, the only form of entertainment was *khele*. But sometimes *tamasha* groups from Kolhapur and Satara would also come to perform. Some of these performances would be quite erotic, and women were forbidden to see them.

Once a tamasha party visited Karbude. All the men in the village went to see their performance. Since no woman was taken along, they got together and decided to perform a tamasha by themselves. They gathered at someone's place and began dancing to the beat of the *dholki*., a drum. Meanwhile a man happened to return to the village as he had some work to do. When he saw what the women were up to, he went back and called all the other men from the tamasha show. The men were furious and they beat up the women. From that day on, people from other places would be rather wary of marrying their sons to the daughters of Karbude. That is why my aunt Thoralibay did not approve of Vitha as a daughter-in-law. But she was scared to say anything in front of my father. Maybe she felt guilty for making false allegations in the ratamba incident. She must have felt that she was responsible that her sons did not get education and became drunkards. She must have had the nagging feeling that, had it not been for her misdeed, her sons too would have become educated like her brother-in-law's.

Everybody would call her Ghareen, the mistress of the household. All she would do is cook, but she was amazingly good at it. Whatever she cooked would be tasty. She was just like my mother, tall, lean, with the same longish face and fair complexion. She wore blackish gold earrings and, around her throat, a thick thread with a couple of keys strung in.

She used to wear a small piece of sari around her waist with a short *pallav* draped on her head. She also wore thick silver rings around her wrists and in her nose a hooked nose ring, which looked like a cockroach. I never remember my mother fighting with her. Maybe they had their own differences of opinion, but never a big fight. And she loved us, the kids. Babi died before I was even born. But my cousin Govindadada and sisters-in-law, Vitha and Parvati, always loved us.

We would wait for them eagerly at the time of the Shimga festival. We were impatient: when would they come and take us? They would come, invariably, and take us away. They would even carry us if we were tired. I was quite plump then. "You fatso, don't you come with us!" they said. "You won't walk. You'll become tired and want us to pick you up! You'll break our bones." Then they would laugh. Vitha had three children and Parvati had two daughters who were born after Vitha's children. We loved to play with them.

Parvati was the elder daughter-in-law. A short, thin, light-skinned woman, she was not really old, but her face was wrinkled and her cheeks hollow. She chewed paan or betel leaf constantly so her mouth was always red, with big white protruding teeth. All women who carried huge bundles on their heads had thin, split hair, especially on the top of their heads, as if nibbled by mice. She wore her nine-yard sari, actually a piece of a sari, quite short, tucked between her legs, leaving the thighs uncovered. She had two or three pockets around her waist, in the form of pleats tucked in, where she kept a tiny bag of paan, *adkitta* to cut the betel nuts, lime box for the quicklime, a couple of coins, sometimes a small pack of sweets for the children, and a bundle of bidis for her husband. She looked thin, but was actually quite strong. Every day she carried huge bundles that were too heavy even for a man on her head to Ratnagiri. She did all the household chores—brought water from the river, swept the house and polished it with cow dung, cleaned the panes, patted cow dung cakes, ground grains—all by herself. Besides, in the farming season, she got busy with everything, from farming vegetables to cleaning paddy. I do not remember her husband ever talking to her. My sister Akka would say, "God knows how they got their children!" Yet her *sasu*, mother-in-law, always barked at her.

The younger *vahini*, Vitha, was comparatively better off. She was a hefty woman with a round, fair face, albeit a little sunburned. She wore her sari as if she was wearing bermudas. Parvati's legs were thin, but Vitha had nice shapely calves. With her pallav, the loose flowing end of the sari, on her head, she also wore a *bormal,* a chain of small gold beads, around her neck, and thick silver bangles on her wrists. After her husband's death, she and her children started living separately. Her brothers were a great support to her, which made her mother-in-law a little wary of her.

Both of them would lovingly invite us to the Shimga festival and coax Mother a lot to send us to them. We too would be impatient to go. First Mother would say no. But she relented after we, particularly I, threw a lot of tantrums. So we began our journey with them on foot. They came to the market and took us with them on their return journey. We were not used to walking so much. The hot burning sun in the west would scorch a side of our face. The soil under the feet would be blistering hot and the rocks would be as hot as the griddle on a stove. Like the village women, we too felt like bursting into abuse against our ancestors, but remembered the dictum at school, "Never speak bad words!" So we just put up with the blistering pain and, when we could not endure it any more, rushed under the shade of a tree and cried.

The women were used to this singeing, and the skin of their feet was very thick. But they patiently waited for us. They would draw us close and wipe our tears with their palms, coarse and rough like wood and dry hard fingers. We would avert our faces to save ourselves from that rough touch of their fingers! They would rush us, saying, "Come on kids, how will the road come to an end if you keep on stopping like this?" Sometimes one of our sisters-in-law took pity on us. She put down the basket on her head and plucked huge leaves of the kumbha or palas tree, wrapping these around our feet. Then she broke off a longish stick, pulled off the bark, and wrapped it around the leaves on our feet, taking it around the toes and ankles. Then, pushing her hands through our armpits, she made us stand up and said, "Come on kids, now take care of your *chappals,* your 'sandals,' and try to catch up with those who have gone ahead. Come on, get going."

The leaves around our feet looked like socks. We would drag our feet through the rocks and stones with those "socks" on. But we were not used to chappals. After some time small stones would get inside the "socks" and prick us hard. Finally, after some more time, the leaves would be torn to shreds, our feet would get entangled in the bark string and we would just fall flat on our faces on the hot path in abject surrender. The women laughed. Sometimes they would sympathize. And sometimes they would just pick us up and carry us for some distance, though they were so thin. This made us very much ashamed of ourselves, even at that young age.

Somehow we managed to cross the hot path halfway, seeking shelter in the shadows of the trees and dipping our feet in the cool waters of the rivers on the way. By the time the sun went down, the burning paths were cooler. But there would be blisters on our feet. Somehow we managed, dragging our feet, to reach the sati temple. Then a new surge of enthusiasm washed over us with the thought that home was now close. We did not have the custom of sati. So there was no knowing who in our community had committed sati there. By the time we got there darkness would have spread through the trees and bushes, enveloping everything, as if someone had thrown a whole lot of coal powder down from the hills. This was the place where the young children would be desperately waiting for their mothers. An elderly aaji would also wait there with her wailing infant grandchild, cursing her *suun* for being so late. Young snotty children would run to their mothers when they saw them coming. Then the women picked up their young ones to their breast, holding the elder ones by hand. Children went on demanding various sweets from their mothers till they reached home. Then we walked eastward on a path that took off from under the jackfruit trees and went on.

There was a hill to the eastern side of the village, with a river flowing at its foot. On one side of the river were two small hills, in the midst of which our wadi was situated. Our house was close to the river, so close, in fact, that my mother would say, "I'll put the bhakri on the hot griddle and return with water from the river in time to turn it over before it burns!" Some houses were in the eastern and some in the western part of the village. So the words *ugwat* (east) and *mawlat* (west) were commonly used. The way to our house was from the western side. We turned and walked on while the women living nearby entered their houses. On the right-hand side were the samadhis of our ancestors. We rubbed our foreheads on these and walked on. And then we reached home.

Our house was a big one in the wadi and had a tiled roof. There was a small pandal in the front courtyard. Crossing that we reached a longish narrow verandah on the right, off of which was a small room for storing grains, followed with a small platform by the verandah, about two or two and a half feet high. On crossing it, we entered the gods' room on the right-hand side. Images of several gods were kept on a platform, hidden under plenty of hibiscus flowers, now wilted. Some five or six unshaven coconuts, similarly covered under hibiscus flowers, were erected against the wall. The gods' corner was crowded with many colorful stones, each in the name of a god, copper plates, spoons used in worship with long handles, tallish brass and copper *surayas,* slender jugs, eating plates, black *dhoopatanis* or wooden incense burners. We would again touch the platform with our foreheads. Then we would enter the inner part of the house called *majghar,* the middle room, generally used by women for resting and household work. In this room was a grinding stone near the window and a stone mortar buried by the side. A crowbar would stand against the wall in the corner along with a pestle for husking rice. The kitchen was on the left.

There were two big stoves. A raised earthen platform behind them contained two smaller openings to cook on—all polished with dung. A small black earthen pot of salt, covered with a coconut shell, was kept on a stove. On another, an earthen pot with ambeel, the thickened sour gruel made from rice grains, would be covered with a coconut shell. Near the window a pitcher of water was kept. Behind that were kept three or four yellow bundles of paddy tied with the *shumbha* rope, made of coir—too big to be held in one's arms—covered with sacks and blankets sewn together from old clothes! A bamboo hung horizontally on a wall on which old clothes, torn blouses, dirty towels and children's old clothes were flung.

Behind the majghar, three or four steps led to another *padavi,* a long narrow verandah, in one half of which my younger sister-in-law lived with her children like a tenant. There was a small wooden plank over the padavi supported by some stakes fixed to the ground. It was covered with many pots and pans, along with water pitchers and earthen pots. There was a hen house as well, around which light rice grains like *wari* and *harak* were strewn and a hen picked at them constantly.

There was a small courtyard behind, polished with dung, beyond which lay the pen for cows and buffaloes. On the right stood a big stone stove with a big copper water pot, completely blackened with smoke, for heating bathwater. A small bath stone lay nearby, with a small german silver pitcher with holes, lying around like an abandoned orphan. Only women bathed here in the wee hours of dawn or sometime late in the night, behind the curtain of darkness. The men went to the river. In the rainy season they had a quick bath under the rainwater flowing down from the eaves of the house.

When tired and exhausted, we dropped onto the front courtyard of the house, Govindadada and Babidada's children came and threw their arms around us in welcome. All our tiredness just vanished. Govindadada, dressed in a loincloth and a short-sleeved *bandi*, a jacket, would be sitting in the padavi, his legs hanging down from the raised sides. The light of the hurricane lamp would be sufficient for us to make out the joy on his sunburned face, though we could not see it wholly in the semidarkness. Happily grinning, he would welcome us. "Best thing you've come! Good your mother gave permission! But she never comes herself," he muttered under his breath.

In the door of the majghar, Thoralibay stood, looking at us lovingly. We could see only her feet in the light of the lamp. She would say to Govindadada, "Why, it's their own house. And their mother will certainly come one day." Then coming forward, she tenderly stroked our faces with her palms and kissed us, saying, "My poor babies are tired. Go children. Wash your feet and then drink the ambeel on the stove."

This ambeel was cooked in boiling water with a little salt. Extremely tired and exhausted from the long journey on foot, and awfully hungry, we washed our feet with the lukewarm water in the copper pitcher and went to the stove. The ambeel was cold and a little off too, as it had been cooked in the morning and had stood on the stove in an earthen pot the whole day. Thoralibay served it to us in earthen pots, using spoons made at home from coconut shells fitted with thick sticks. The putrid smell of the ambeel gone sour assaulted our senses, but we would be completely impervious to that. We just poured it down our throats, since hungry tummies would be howling for food by this time. In the moment of joy at meeting the people we loved, the ambeel actually tasted sweet.

The younger sister-in-law went to her room in the padavi and her children followed. Then the elder one emptied her basket before her sasu. She took out the small packets of dal, molasses, and fish bought in the afternoon, which had begun to smell by this time. The fish would be bundled in the bark of the betelnut tree. The house cat, excited by the smell of the fish, mewed incessantly, brushing itself against her feet, its tail bobbing up in the air. Bay would get angry at him, "Come on, come on," she said, "this is for you only. Go away, you bastard! Go out, out … out. Hey kids, pick him up and throw him into the river!" She went to the stove to cook rice and we tried to shoo the cat away by clapping our hands and stamping our feet. But it stuck around.

The elder vahini would then take the fish in a pot and wash it clean at the stove in the backyard. The cat would follow her. It would get under her feet, meow from the pit of its tummy, as if its tongue would hang out if it did not get fish now. Vahini would sit down, place the blade between her feet, and clean the fish by removing the scales, head, intestines and tail, and threw these to the cat. But the cat would be so impatient that it would not wait till she had thrown all the pieces at it. When she threw the head at him; it would rush madly and catch it, hold it in its mouth and polish it off in no time. Once again it meowed, running madly to catch the heads thrown at him. It would be terrible if another couple of cats and dogs joined the fray: fierce fights ensued, upon which Vahini would tell us, "Children, go in. The dogs might bite you." But she needed water from the pitcher to wash the fish, and one of us had to get it for her. She washed the fish and handed the pieces over to Thorlibay for cooking. Immediately afterward she went to the grinding stone to grind the spices. She washed the stone first and ground red dry chillies, coriander seeds, turmeric root, a few cloves of garlic, and a little piece of coconut together for the fish curry. We were amazed by her stamina. We wondered why she wasn't tired after having carried a heavy burden to the bazaar and walked back such a long distance! Actually she was the main source of energy in Govindadada's house.

The younger vahini brought something too—leftover mutton pieces, legs, head, brain, lungs, and so on. Her son Shantaram cleaned them in their "house." Her elder daughter, Babi, would prepare the spices. She roasted dry coconut pieces and onion in the stove, and ground it on the stone with some readymade red garlic paste. The rice would be already cooked and ready by the time her mother returned. Once they had prepared the meat, the meals were ready. Someone came to invite us to eat. We would be sitting in the padavi, chatting in the dim light of the hurricane lamp. We were hungry, and it was a real testing time for us.

Because Vithavahini lived separately, Thoralibay, and Govindadada were angry with her. If we went to Vithavahini to eat, they would be upset. On the other hand, if we did not eat with Vithavahini, she would be very hurt as she really loved us dearly. When she coaxed us, we had to go. Govindadada would return after having had a few drinks. When he sat down to eat, he invariably asked, "Where are the children?" Bay would tell him sarcastically, "Oh, they are meat eaters, they don't like our fish! Go on, you eat." But Govindadada would sit on his haunches till we came. We had to, once again, eat off his plate after having eaten at Vithavahini's. Only then would he feel happy. His daughters, Tai and Kamal, would also wait for us to eat.

In all this Parvativahini had no say. She continued working like a maid in the house, doing everything except cooking. She had no power at all. She could not even help herself to the sour ambeel if she were hungry. She would bring the earthen pot of the ambeel outside to wash and would quietly drink the remnants in the pot, pouring it into some other receptacle. She was the last to eat and sleep. But, young as I was, I never realized the worth of her work, her endurance, and the deliberate indifference of the others toward her. Instead I treated her with an insolent indifference because of her big knee caps, thin bony legs, torn sari, unkempt hair, and cracked feet—all of which were obviously a result of walking with a huge load on her head on a regular basis. I always maintained a distance with her, so much so that when a classmate of mine, Shyamala Chavan, asked me, "Who's that woman in your house who looks like this?" I replied, "Oh, that woman? She's our maidservant!" when I ought to have told her that she was my sister-in-law.

Shyamala passed along what I said to Vahini. One day she came to visit us. I was at home. She asked me, with a smile, "So Vimal, I'm your maidservant, am I?" I was taken aback by her question. I thought she was going to be angry, complain to my mother, and abuse me. But nothing of the sort happened. She just kept smiling at me and nodding her head. I did not understand the range of meanings packed in that smile at that time, but when I grew up I did.

She had not dared to ask me, confront me as to why I had said that. Her eyes had reflected so many things—helplessness, vulnerability, defenselessness! As I grew up I came to understand that look more and more. After that I tried in various different ways to make up for that insult. When she came to Mumbai for Tai's marriage, I took her all over Mumbai to show her the city. Now I was no longer ashamed of her inadequate sari. Actually it fascinated me. But my efforts toward a rapprochement were terribly inadequate as my guilt never ended; instead it became more pronounced.

This incident changed the way I thought and made me more humane. Now my sister Shantiakka's sister-in-law, Hiriakka, who was like Vahini, thin but very loving, came very close to my heart. She had returned home for good only a few days after her marriage because she was ignorant about sex and terribly scared of her husband. But she had managed to conceive in the few days spent with her husband and later gave birth to a daughter. She lived in the padavi of her mother's house, without becoming a burden to her brother, earned her own living and lived with self-respect. When she visited us, she would bring basketfuls of fish or oysters. But she never accepted any money or other things in return.

I knew how difficult it was to get down the path between the two hills, Mirya and Sakhar, into the creek to collect oysters, mulefish, crabs, and so on. I had gone with my maternal uncle's daughters a couple of times. In the early hours of dawn, at the time of low tide, they would say the sea is drying up and rush out of their house with big and small baskets. They climbed down the hills in a great hurry and went to the creek. Carefully placing their feet on the dry areas, making their way through the shapeless undini trees covered in mud in the seabed, they reached the middle of the creek. The water there would be very shallow now. They thrust their hands into the sand, or dug in with their sickles, then pushed their hands deep to collect the variety of fish there. They picked the shells fast and quickly threw them into the baskets around their shoulders. They avoided red shells and round shells as these would be tasteless and went on looking for a different, tastier variety called *tisrya*. When they thrust their hands into the sand, their nails often got pulled apart from the flesh. The sand entered the nails and it hurt. Their fingers often got bloodied and their backs ached with the strain of constant bending. Their feet went to sleep.

But that was not all. Women who were more adventurous climbed on top of the rocks, hunting for oyster shells. These would have to be practically dug out of the rocks and were called *bochane*. Some went toward the sea and collected the white salt accumulated in some of the pits for years. Other women hunted for crabs or crawfish in the cracks in the rocks by pushing their hands inside. They got drenched in the waves dashing against the rocks. Their hands and feet would be cut by the sharp edges of the rocks and salty seawater stung the wounds.

Gradually the tide would flow in, water rising from all sides. Then they yelled warnings at each other, hurried one another, swiftly cut off huge pieces of rock with oysters in it, filled their baskets, trying to collect as much as they could. In the hurry sometimes novices would simply pick up rocks thinking they were oyster shells. When the water rose to their knees, they would hurry out of the water, balancing the heavy basket on their heads. Some women lost their lives because they didn't notice the water rising. My maternal uncle's daughter Lakshi was saved from drowning by some people. But they could not save the two other women with her who drowned.

Once on the shore, they would spread the oyster shells on it, cover these with dry leaves and twigs, and bake the oysters. They would also carry a matchbox for a specific reason. When a crab tried biting one's fingers, they lit a match under its claws. Else the crab would not let go of the finger, even when the rest of its body was cut off. The matchbox was essential. They would gulp down the dry pieces of bread they had brought, along with the baked and cooked oysters, in the scorching sun. To me the women appeared as shapeless as the undini trees, covered from head to toe in mud.

At the same time, they constantly worried about various problems. "My daughter is sick, let me give her a little bread with these oysters; let me see if that brings back her appetite."

"Oh yes, my old woman must be waiting for me to come. When she was young, she collected basketfuls of crabs and shells! But the poor thing is really old now, can't lift a finger."

"And these days those Bhandari and Daldini women do not leave anything in the rocks."

"Remember, my friend, their menfolk go with them! Our men go to the toddy shop. That's why we are reduced to this state!"

They returned from the sea, chatting about such things all the way. How the Bhandari and Daldini women had grown rich on fishing, how they were decked out in gold ornaments, how much wealth they had amassed! When they reached the top of the hill, their waiting children gathered around them like big ants.

Every time I saw Hiriakka standing in front of my office with a basket of crabs, which she had managed to collect with such infinite labor, my eyes would fill with tears.

Every village would celebrate Holi on different dates of the Marathi calendar. The Shimga, which some people celebrated on the third day from the moonless night in the month of Phalgun, was called Tersa Shimga.[4] The custom was to eat sweet chapatis made of molasses and *arhar dal* on Shimga Day, and the next day was known as Dhulwad,[5] which is generally celebrated by eating mutton *bondas,* large meat and potato balls.

Tersa Shimga, according to the calendar, comes much before the real Shimga Day. So those people who celebrated Tersa Shimga were called gluttons, as they had moved the date of the Shimga ahead for the love of food. Some villages, taking inspiration from the Tersa Shimga, started a new custom of celebrating Holi on the eighth or ninth day from the moonless night in Phalgun. This came to be called Sayama's Holi.[6] The rest of the village, however, celebrated Holi on the fifteenth day, that is, on the full moon night, as was the true custom. This would be the real common Holi. But some people celebrated Holi even after this. This was called Bhadrecha—auspicious—Shimga. Poor people, who felt sad to see others celebrating various festivals till the full moon day, would celebrate the Shimga after everybody else had done so. So this last Shimga was supposed to be auspicious for them. This is what Govindadada and the other elderly people would tell us. Thus Holi was celebrated in many different ways.

In our village it was customary to celebrate Tersa Shimga. On the hill beyond the river of our village there was a huge rock known as Chandaki Devi's rock. The young men of the village would cover the rock with dry leaves and grass a week before the festival. On the day of Holi all the old and young men and children in the villages would go to this rock on the hill, playing in a band. There they would put turmeric and kumkum on the covered rock, worship it, break a coconut, and then set it on fire. They would pray, "Lord, please keep our children happy." Then they would bellow, beating their palms against their mouths. This would be followed by obscene curses and shouts that could be heard for four to five villages around.

Who knows why it was called Chandaki's Rock? It must have been the symbol of a mother goddess. But it wasn't clear why it was burned. Women would say, "Once they set fire to Chandaki's Rock, our problems too are burned off." After setting fire to Chandaki's Rock in the morning, young men would go to the forest to collect wood for the village Holi. There they would already have identified huge trees for burning during Holi. It was an honor given to the Mahars to deliver the first blow to the tree. The task of carrying the huge trees down the slope of the hills to the Shambhu Temple in the village would make people froth at the mouth. Then the huge trees would be made to stand in front of the temple where Holi would be celebrated. People from the Maratha, Bhandari, and Kulwadi castes would just touch the tree in name, but the real tough labor would be for the Mahars to perform: they would have to lift the heavy tree trunk and make it stand. But once the Holi rituals and celebrations started, the Mahars would be simply ignored. They had no place in them.

At dusk the Marathas, Bhandaris, and Kulwadis would worship the Holi and then set the trees on fire. This done, they would start praying loudly. This ceremony was called *garhane*. It featured lots of prayers for the village's well-being and averting calamities. But, funnily enough, they also prayed for diverting the calamities to the Mahars. Then the ritual of howling and cursing began. Again terrible curses would target the Mahars. But the Mahars dared not lodge a protest against this.

On the contrary, the young Mahar boys, poverty-stricken and destitute, would drink liquor and get intoxicated. They would try to forget their toils, the labor spent in cutting the trees and carrying them down the slope to the temple. Fires of hunger would rage in their stomachs and they would try to quench these flames by pouring glass after glass of liquor down their throats. They would beat the drums and the *tashe* in frenzy. The upper-caste men who had prestige would dance around the Holi, matching their steps to the drumbeats. They would be the ones to carry the palanquin of the god, decorated with tassels, on their shoulders. They would push it like a he-buffalo on each other's shoulders, jump four feet high in their dance. Each man from the upper castes would give his shoulder to the palanquin and dance till he was exhausted. All except the Mahars! None of the Mahars would be allowed to even touch it. With dust flying from the dancing feet, *gulal* thrown around, it would be difficult to recognize people. Taking advantage of this, some Mahar boys would run to take the palanquin on their shoulders—and some even succeeded. Then somebody would notice the deception. All this would invariably end in quarrels and fights. Our young men would have carried sticks with them in anticipation.

On the Holi day, the Marathas and Brahmins would make sweet stuffed chapatis called *puran poli,* and in our houses we would cook lentils called *pavata* or *varana.* This was the crop that would be ready around Holi. We ate dal and rice with cooked pavata lentils and gathered in front of the Shambhu Temple in the evening to see the dancing of the palanquin. We carried old blankets to wrap around us in the cold and jute sacks to sit on. We wore necklaces made of sugar coins and kept on licking them with wet and sticky mouths, staring at the scene before us, fascinated.

When fighting began over the issue of Mahars touching the palanquin, we would quickly run away with the jute sacks, only to return after things cooled off and squat in the dust again. Many of the Mahar boys, beaten up in the fights, intoxicated, would lie down on our sacks, whining, crying in pain from the wounds they'd received. Their mothers would try to take them in their arms, soothe them, pat their faces, but the boys would ramble incoherently, their eyes swollen and red with liquor. They would curse and try to go to the palanquin again and again. Their mothers and sisters would try to stop them. This drama went on for quite a while, until the play, the folk drama, *khele,* started.

Some twenty to twenty-five actors, dressed in swan-white barabandi,[7] turbans, lined with delicate silver fringes on their heads, entered the stage in a group. They wore cymbals around their necks on long strings and beat them rhythmically, singing the ritual songa "Payala Naman" (meaning the first *namaskara*), the salutation, to mark the beginning of the play. Their bodies would move backward and forward in unison. Then two more characters would enter, with *mridangas,* their fingers beating the rhythm in a frenzy on the mridanga, and present a dance. Actors wearing masks of mythical characters like Ganapati, Sankasur, and Tumbaru would appear and dance. Then a humorous dialogue between a guruji (teacher) and a student would ensue. The teacher asked, "What's your age?" The student answered, "Two hedges around my house." The guruji asked, "Show me your slate." The student showed him his basket for collecting dung. All this would make us roll with laughter. Then this humorous interlude would be followed by the much awaited *wag* or play about King Chandrasen.

The open skies above, the furiously burning Holi beside, the temple behind the glittering *deepmal*—multiple lamps on a stand—Petromax lamps blazing all around, the team of actors on the stage, and the cold night with the bright moon in the sky—the entire atmosphere would be charged with magic. Then somebody would break wind, obviously a result of the lentils eaten in the evening! Women would cover their noses with their pallav and burst out, "Who did that? Who's rotting? May God burn him!" or "May God burn his rotting arse!" This made everybody laugh.

Soon King Chandrasen entered the stage in his shimmering clothes. Many kings would follow in splendid gowns, sparkling with decorative spangles, wearing scintillating golden crowns, shimmering armbands, sparkling jewels, dazzling necklaces, flashing rings, decorative shoes, and gleaming swords in their hands. The Sutradhara would sing and narrate the story, "This is the great King Chandrasen. The sun and the moon are his servants. Yakshas and Gandharvas come to put him to sleep!" and so on. Leelavati, the beautiful young daughter of King Chandrasen, appeared, to capture the hearts of young men. And the prince, whom she would choose and to whom she would offer the garland in her *swayam-wara*,[8] was so handsome that he conquered the heart of every young girl! So much so that, had he asked me, I would have just jumped up and followed him blindly. This story would be followed with dances. Actors in different roles danced gaily, and the magic spell of the prince could not be broken. Gradually, our eyes grew heavy with sleep.

Suddenly there would be deafening beats of dhol and tashe, and sleep would evaporate from our eyes. There would be excited cries everywhere! Women would shout, "Wake up kids, wake up. See, Ravana has come with his army!" "Look, look, there he is! Ravana! Ravana! See how he's dancing." They would hurriedly pull out the jute sacks from under our bodies. The beating of the dhol and tashe would reach such a crescendo that our tiny hearts started beating faster and faster, till they were ready to jump out of our mouths. Ravana would hold us mesmerized; our eyes would be glued to him, all agog. Everybody stood up. Someone would pick us up so as to help us see Ravana better. Ravana would be a huge, hefty fellow. He would come dancing, with swords in his hands, balancing his crown fixed to a wooden plank on which lay the nine heads, raising a cloud of dust in his wake. By this time it would be daybreak and we walked back homeward.

We would see King Chandrasen, his marriageable daughter, and the Prince Charming, also on the road, but without the glamour and glitter of the night; their faces carried garish traces of makeup, their heads were shaven and bare. Seeing the prince in broad daylight sans his glamour could not destroy the magic spell cast by his image at night.

Despite staying awake throughout the night, the women would still be charged with energy. They would be excited and eager to go to the houses of the upper-caste Kulwadis, Marathas, and Brahmins to beg for the festive food. Someone would say, "Last year I managed to build a compound around X's chilli crop, all alone. At that time the bitch didn't even piss on my hands.[9] But I won't spare her today. I'll demand food to last

me three whole days." All of them had served the upper castes in different ways throughout the year. Someone had labored in the fields, woven
baskets of various shapes and sizes for them. They would ask to be compensated for their work. Especially houses that performed the customary
Mahar duties, such as beating the dhol, disposing of dead animals, delivering messages would go to beg as a matter of right.

Our sisters-in-law, Vitha and Parvati, would also go begging, along
with other women in our community. They would carry baskets on
their heads to collect the leftovers that might be given to them. Now
ours was the priest's family. Besides my father was a schoolteacher. Food
was never scarce in the house. On the contrary, on the next day, Dhulwad, we cooked plenty of mutton and chicken and a big potful of rice
in our house. Thoralibay would make plenty of vadas of chickpea flour.
Yet her daughters-in-law would go begging for the festive food. But if
Baba came to know of this he would get mad and shout, "These stupid
women! When will they cease to behave like beggars? Go tell them, don't
go begging! At least don't bring any such food to my house. And don't
ever show your faces to me again!" But both of them would stand, leaning against the door, holding their pallavs in their mouths, trying to hide
the amused laughter. They would tell us, "Go kids and tell your father
that *you* want to eat sweet chapatis. *That's why* we are going to get them
for you." It was another thing that they never got sweet chapatis. All that
they brought back with them were stale pieces of bhakri or rice.

Some women would go to far-flung houses. They would carry with them
separate containers and pots for collecting various dishes. But the Kulwadi
women who gave them food would pour everything together in their baskets. Whatever they wanted to give—dal, vegetables, *kheer*—would all be
poured on the rice in a mixed mound. Women would bring back basketfuls
of rice in which many things were mixed. Not wanting the remaining rice
to go rancid, they would put it into a basket and hold it against the running water in the river. Shaking the basket against the flowing water, they
would rinse it till only the clean rice remained in the basket. Sometimes,
they would wash the rice at home. They poured the insipid, cooked rice
in an earthen pot and put it on the stove on low heat. Their entire house
would survive for two days on those leftovers. In some houses the flesh of
dead animals would be eaten. But that was forbidden in our house.

Holi was also the season for mangoes, corinda berries, cashew bulbs,
and many other local fruit. There would be nothing in the house except

rice and bhakri. So we would love to eat cashew bulbs. We also loved to make wine from them. In the morning we would polish off the ambeel or bhakri made from rice flour and run off to the hill beyond the river, called Chandaki's Hill. There would be hundreds of cashew trees there, all laden with cashew bulbs. Some of these trees were protected, inside a compound, whereas some were in open spaces. We would climb the trees and pluck many golden bulbs and big green cashew nuts. Our clothes got stained, but such things never bothered us. We would collect the nuts in our long skirts and feast on them to our heart's content, bringing back whatever remained.

Then we would steal the equipment—a glass, a bottle with a tight cork, a piece of cloth, the torn border of sari or string—required to make wine behind the cow pen. We would dig a deep pit in the ground, squeeze the cashew bulbs and collect their juice in the glass, and pour it into the bottle. Sealing it well with the cork and string, we would bury the bottle in the pit, cover it up well, make sure we were not being watched, and keep a stone on top as a mark. Hardly four days passed before we impatiently went back to the place to dig the bottle out, our excitement at its peak.

Once the bottle was unearthed, we cleaned it and the cork was opened with a harsh *plock*. A sharp rancid stench assaulted our nostrils. We saw some froth on the top. This concoction would be simply undrinkable. But we would all collect it in the glass and sip, smacking our lips loudly. Then we would pretend to be dead drunk, like Govindadada or other drunkards in the neighborhood, and imitate their walk, talk, and so on, with peals of laughter all around. This drama would have the drunkard and his cursing, nagging wife in the main roles. Very often we would come across empty bottles of hard drinks, kept by Govindadada in the room in the padavi that was meant for storing grains. We would make sure he was not around and pour the drops from the bottom of the bottle into our mouths, on the tip of the tongue. Suddenly there would be a stinging sensation on the tongue, and after some time we felt intoxicated. Who knows if we really were!

Once we had collected cashew bulbs and were busy squeezing the juice behind the cow pen. Some were furiously digging a small pit to bury the bottle in. Suddenly we heard people talking loudly in the cow pen. Hurriedly, we hid all our things under a torn jute sack and peeped in through the holes in the walls of wattled sticks to see what was happening. Govindadada and a couple of villagers were standing there, near the bullock, along with a couple of others with rings on their ears and wrists. The bullock was tied down. He was terrible when set free. He would indiscriminately charge at people, aiming his horns at them. He would even charge at the other cows and buffaloes in the neighborhood. Women returning from the river carrying pitchers filled with water would be in mortal fear of him. The very sight of him would terrify kids like us. But that day I realized that the rope was not taken off his neck. He was tied. Someone in the cow pen gave him a resounding pat on the back and scratched his neck. The other man tied his front legs together. Then they pulled the bull toward them and made him lie down on his side. Once his back touched the floor, the man wearing a jacket and earring said, "Take hold of his hind legs and part them wide open." Two men did accordingly.

We kids were watching through the holes in the wall, fascinated. I thought that they were going to cut him open. Scared, I said, "Let's go in. I'm afraid of blood." Shantaram was the oldest amongst us. He laughed and said, "Don't be silly. They are not cutting him, they're crushing him." He walked around the pen and went inside. The rest of us followed.

Dada blew his top when he saw us. He shouted at us and drove us out. We resumed our positions behind the wall near the holes.

The guy wearing the pearl earring held a couple of long wooden batons in his hand. Two men held these around the balls of the bull and pressed hard. The bull gave a deafening roar and kicked his hind legs with all his might. We froze, petrified. The two chaps holding his hind legs collapsed. After a while they got up and sat on their haunches, asking, "Did you hear? Did you hear the sound?"

"No, not yet."

"What do you mean, not yet? Of course! I heard it. It was like fingers snapping." The guy with the earring replied.

"Yea? Really? But I didn't!"

This went on for quite some time. For a long time, they went on saying, "Yes, yes" and "No, no." The bull was breathing hard through his nose, pushing his horns deep into the floor; the pain must have been horrible. In the meanwhile, my sister-in-law came in with a small earthen bowl. She had brought butter from the Brahmin priest's wife and mixed some turmeric powder in it. She applied this mixture on the bull's genitals. Then Dada untied his front legs. The bull struggled to his feet and urinated. While he was urinating, the men began to file out of the cow pen. One of them gave him a resounding pat on his back and said, "Roused so hard, weren't you? Now take that! How do you feel now? Go, go, there is a cow outside, waiting for you. Want to go?" They all went out laughing, fit to burst.

Next day Vahini once again went into the cow pen with the medicine. As usual we followed her in procession. She tried really hard to avoid his kicks while applying the medicine on the bull's genitals. His organ was swollen red, and one could see the crushed blood vessels inside, all black and blue. It looked like a huge *ramphal* hanging from the tree. Whenever I read about rape cases in the newspapers, I would often remember the huge swollen balls.

Two

Baba suffered from an ulcer and, after my elder brother Achyut passed away, started falling ill frequently. Sensing that he was not going to live much longer, he arranged the marriage of my other brother, Krishna. He was eighteen or nineteen at that time. We lived in the chawl of the Bhangis. He chose a girl called Sushila, the daughter of one Devji Kamble, who lived in the same chawl and worked in the mental hospital. Sushila was a fair-complexioned good-looking girl. I would always remember a popular Marathi song when I saw her:

Bring me a sister-in-law, brother,
As fair and delicate as a flower.

She was in school, studying in the sixth standard. Baba agreed to the marriage on the condition that the girl remained at her father's home after marriage and passed her final school-leaving examinations; after which he would bring her home. This condition was accepted, and the marriage took place.

I must have been just seven or eight then. The reason why I remember this wedding is that I was chosen as one of the five virgins called *muhurtawalis*. These girls were supposed to observe a strict fast till the marriage took place, which created an enormous problem for me. Hunger was not a thing I could cope with.

The pandal was erected in front of our house, and the villagers had decorated it with neem twigs.Bunches of mango leaves, considered to be auspicious, were hung in between. A banana plant, heavy with clusters of bananas, was placed at the front door. A pole cut off from the shewari tree was planted in the middle of the pandal, as it was held to be auspicious too. It was colored red and yellow, using kumkum and turmeric. A betel nut and one paisa coin with a hole in it were tied in a piece of yellow cloth in a knot and hung from the pole in the pandal. A ceremonial lamp, called the *laman diya,* hung next to it.

A day before the wedding, a ceremony, keeping the *timte* in the pandal, was performed. A few women gathered a newly married couple and us, the five virgins. We were taken to the river with some rice grains in a basket, which they wanted to wash in the river as part of the ritual. They warned us again and again not to eat till the wedding took place. We vigorously nodded our heads in acquiescence. Then a band started playing, leading us ceremoniously in a procession to the river. A woman with the basket of rice on her head walked in front of us, behind the band. When our procession reached the river, we sprinkled some kumkum and turmeric in the water and the woman washed the rice. We were brought home in a procession. We felt very important. Everybody had their eyes glued to us. And when women started admiring and making much of us because we were the important virgins, I felt quite puffed up. The women colored the wet rice grains to be used as the *akshata,* that is, thrown on the bride and groom at the time of the marriage.

At night Baba and Aaye put a coconut on the platform behind the stove and kept a small mango branch near it. They made a lamp of dough, lighted a wick in it, put it in front of the coconut, sprinkling turmeric and kumkum on it. The mango branch signified that our family deity came from the mango tree. Many families had animals as the household deity. In such cases dough figures of the respective animals would be placed before the coconut and worshipped.

Those who had the pig as their family deity were respected tremendously. The story went that Lord Shankar had once taken the form of the pig to save somebody from our caste. So it was an unwritten rule that pigs could never be killed. Some people would not even utter the word. Who knows why. But it was something similar to the Muslims never doing so.

Women sang songs all the time: while sweeping the front courtyard and polishing it with dung, at the time of husking, sifting, and cleaning rice grains and putting them into containers.

> The peepul tree at my door, how in the wind it sways,
> Under the peepul tree, my young Krishna plays,
> The mother watches the baby, engrossed in his play,
> My boy is a jasmine bud, the proud mother says.

There were so many songs that they would sing while various rituals were being performed:

> Look it is dawn, the guns have just been fired
> Wake up, dear hostess,
> So many things need to be fried!

Or

> We have filled up the Ghana
> With rice grains one and a quarter *khnadi*.[1]
> O bridegroom, this is in honor
> Of you and your family.

In the morning, they made Bhai, the bridegroom, stand up and tied *mundawalis*[2] of wild white rui flowers on his head. Women from all over the neighborhood ran to apply turmeric on him. The music to their songs was provided by the band. Women just burst into songs, singing one after the other.

I tried to remain with the other muhurtawalis, and we roamed around together. Everybody kept reminding me, "Remember, you are fasting! Don't eat anything!"

I was quite all right till the bride arrived at the pandal and took her seat in the appointed place. I kept telling myself that I was not supposed to eat anything. But by the time Bhai was given his ritual bath and stood on the tiny pieces of shewari bark, with his rui flower mundawalis, and the remaining holy turmeric was sent to the bride, I started feeling restless. Now the bride was being given a ritual bath. The songs started playing again. I felt that on the whole the entire program—the bride's bath, her wearing the yellow wedding sari, her being brought to the pandal—was going on at an inordinately slow pace. I also began to get terribly impatient. I thought I should go forward and drag the bride, who was walking ever so slowly with the others, fast inside the pandal, so that the marriage could take place immediately, and then I would be able to eat something.

Finally, the bride and the groom arrived, took their places, and people began to sing the ritual *mangalashtakas* as a blessing and shower the akshata on the couple. I stood behind Bhai with the holy *karha*—jug—in my hand, with mango leaves and a coconut. But my feet trembled all the while. The weight I had put on since the day before began to shed fast.

The mangalashtakas never seemed to end. They went on and on. Though it was others who sang, it was my throat that got more and more parched. Finally, the last of the mangalashtakas were sung, the final *sawadhan* was shouted and the dhol and tashe exploded with such force that my heart virtually leaped out of my mouth. It was said that some young girls, especially brides, would often faint because of the noise. Many women held the bride, my new vahini, and sprinkled water on her eyes. Probably she too was affected similarly. But I was in no mood to pay any attention to her. I only waited for the feast to begin. I kept a close watch if anybody was going toward the corner where the *patravalis* or leaf plates were kept. The other muhurtawalis were standing in a group with some women, laughing and guffawing. I felt so angry with them: how could they laugh when hunger raged in their stomachs?

Why did they have to make a public spectacle of the sari they had bought for the bride? Wasn't it enough to show it only to her, since she was the one who was going to wear it? But no! One of our relatives took the sari, spread it on his left arm and went all over the pandal, exhibiting it to all and sundry, "Look at the sari, the sari ... look at the bride's sari," he went on piping, and everybody said, like an echo, "That's good, that's good!" raising their hands, as if they were giving benediction! The fool took the sari outside the pandal to show it to somebody! By the time all this was over, lunchtime was long gone, and the sun had traveled to the western horizon!

In the meanwhile, I had handed over the auspicious karha in my hand to someone nearby and paid a visit to the backyard where dal was cooking on the stove and the already cooked white rice grains were spread on blankets. I cast a hungry glance on these food items and returned to the pandal once again.

Now the sari display was over, and it was time for giving *aaher*, the ceremonial gifts. Suddenly a relative of ours got up and shouted, "Wait, wait, see what is being given as *aandan*—the dowry! Go on, declare what you Shiragaonkar people have to give." He began to reel out, "Elephants, horses, army ... ? Come on, tell us what you will give your daughter." Then the women from the bride's family came forward. They picked up various utensils that were being offered as aandan, such as a large brass dish for mixing flour, a copper pot, *kalashi,* or jugs, a *samai,* tall brass lamp, and raised them for all to see. "See the aandan!" they said laughingly. All the guests were happy to see these vessels. They nodded their heads and clapped to show their appreciation. Poor people who could not afford to give anything would declare that they had offered a mango tree or a cow or a calf. Some really would give such things, but some would get permission from the Panch people to get their promise canceled. While I was standing there looking at the bride's aandan, Aaye came like a ferocious cow and tugged at my hand, "What are you standing here for, fool? You want to starve? Come and eat."

I followed Aaye, climbed the high *ota,* the platform, and came into the majghar. The four fasting girls and the new couple sat on a blanket. They had green plantain leaves spread in front of them, on which small heaps of rice were covered with lovely fragrant *amti.* They stared at me with large round eyes, without saying a word, as if they were teasing me. I rushed forward and sat down beside them. Then Aaye and five *suwasisnis,* or married women, came forward. They put kumkum mixed with oil on our foreheads. They took fistfuls of rice grains and pressed them against our foreheads. Some rice grains fell down into the rice served on the leaves. I was so impatient; I wanted this ritual to end fast so that I could eat. Each woman was pressing grains against my forehead so hard it was as if she were trying to push the grains inside my skull. What's more, everyone was joking, saying that since I had loitered for so long in the pandal I must have eaten something. After this, many weddings took place in the village, but I never dared to become a muhurtawali again.

In Bhai's wedding no traditional rituals like the breaking of bidis or vessels (in upper-caste weddings, this would be the breaking change to biting of *vida* or a paan) or the opening of fists in which a betel nut would be hidden took place. Nor did the couple play any games that were usually played in our community at such times. Shantiakka opposed these customs, saying they were all traditional, outdated things and ought to be given up. Even Baba opposed such practices. But in the weddings of other people such games were played, the reason why they went on for four or five days.

The last ritual of the wedding was *saptapadi*, meaning taking seven steps. Seven heaps of rice grains would be arranged on a wooden plank. The bride would step on each of them and scatter the grains. Once this ritual was over, the marriage ceremony would be concluded. Then a ritual for naming the bride would be performed. She would be made to take the pallav on her head and be given a new name. Next the *bashingas* or head coverings on the bride and groom's heads would be taken off and tied to the roof. The women would take charge of the newly married couple and begin to play games. Gradually, even men would join in. In the first game, women put kumkum mixed with oil on the foreheads of the bride and groom. Then they would press rice grains into it. The bride and groom had to rub their foreheads against each other to remove the rice grains. This was probably a practice session, suggesting that the couple would have to beat their heads against one another in their future married life.

There was a game that taught the groom how to deal with his wife. The bride would be given a pot to carry water on her head and also a small jug and sent away with four or five *karavalis* or girl attendants to some distance. Then the groom would be made to sit on the threshold at the back door of the house, with a stick in his hand. They would teach him the lines he would have to tell the wife when she returned. When the bride came back with the water, he would strike the ground with the stick and demand an explanation, "Why are you so late?" The women would help the bride to come up with answers such as, "I was late because the cows muddied the water, so I had to wait till the water cleared," or "The rope fell into the well and I had to wait till it could be brought out," and so on. Then they would make her swear that she would never be late again.

There was a game for the mother-in-law as well. The women would throw some very tiny black beads into the bride's hair. Then the sasu would comb the bride's hair with a phani—a lice comb. She would show the black beads on the comb to all and say, "Oh, look at this! See how her head is infested with lice! What a dirty girl this one is!" Then she would laugh loudly along with the other women and admonish the bride, "I will not tolerate such filthiness in my house!"

In such games, even the *sasra* or father-in-law would participate. Once the couple returned from the bride's place, where a ritual for washing off the *haldi,* the turmeric applied at the time the wedding, was performed, the sasra would hang a small bundle from a stick and threaten to go off to Kashi. Then the new couple would plead with him, "Please don't go to Kashi; don't leave us. We will serve you well."

All these games were basically intended to control the bride and keep her in check. But when they were being played, everybody laughed and had a good time. These were happy occasions in their lives.

Bhai got a job at the age of eighteen at Lucknow in the railways. He went off to live there. We, the three young siblings, went to school. Though Baba used to consult the almanac when advising people, he had never prepared our horoscopes. Aaye would say, "He wrote the futures of other's children but forgot to write that of his own." Had Baba made my horoscope, he would, most certainly, have predicted that I would be a cowherd, looking after the cows and buffaloes owned by others and carrying heavy bundles on my head.

I was enrolled in the preprimary school, known as *bigari,* long before my right hand could touch my left ear over my head, as they say. I was really too young. Somebody sued to engage the preprimary class in the verandah of the house of one Gandhi, which was just four houses away from ours. This was the house where they would also organize a *jatra* of Sadanandaswami. For a couple of days I attended school, jumping gaily across the compound in between the two buildings. One day I soiled my pants while crossing the compound, and that is when I realized the real meaning of school. I just did not go back to that school again. Later I was enrolled in the first standard of the Damle School. On the first day we were let off after prayers. I went home. My sister asked me, "What happened in school?" I answered, "Nothing." She burst out laughing. For the next three years I studied only because I was afraid of my father.

Then Baba died. At first Aaye appeared to be so defenseless. I was happy. I thought, Good, now I can do as I want. But I was soon disillusioned. My father had told Aaye before his death to educate the children. She soon became firm. In fact, she became more rigid than ever. The money Father would bring in had stopped. My brother used to help us, but it was Mother who had to manage the expenses. Earlier she would work to support Father's income. Now she started toiling hard. She would sit under the vad tree in our courtyard, weaving her bamboo baskets till late at night. That was the last thing our eyes, heavy with sleep, would take in before we went to bed. And when we opened our eyes early in the morning, she would be sitting in the same place. In between she would go to the stove to do something. In the past it was my father's hands that worked, now it was hers.

Aaye changed. Earlier she was thrifty, now she became sordidly stingy. The village women or our cousin's wives occasionally came to borrow a little money. But now she never parted with a farthing even when she had any. She would send Manjula to sell the eggs our hen produced. Earlier, she used to grumble. Now she became combative. The slightest thing would provoke her. It could be anything: the slightly late arrival of the man who fetched the bamboos for her in his bullock cart, the fare charged by him, the quality and number of the bamboos. Then Shahu would get up and go to help her. They would tie the bamboos in bundles of four or five each. Women from the surrounding villages would come to buy them from her. She would fight with them too. She would argue with the customers who came to place orders for her baskets of many sizes and shapes, her aaydans. Earlier, she would scold us, now she started cursing us. The husband of my elder sister, Shantiakka, used to say jocularly, "You want to know who my mother-in-law is? Go straight on until you arrive at the crossroads. You will hear a woman cursing loudly. That's my mother-in-law!"

I was the youngest child in the family. Yet I was never indulged. In fact, I was an unwanted child because I was a girl. When I was born, my cousin Govindadada wanted to throw me away onto the dung heap. When I grew a little older, many would beat me. The largest share of these beatings came from Aaye, for skipping school. She seemed to have extra strength while thrashing me. Her tired body became so agile then! But if I fell ill or had a high fever, she was so gentle and kind! She took me in her arms, put strips of cloth soaked in salt water on my forehead. Her touch felt so good. But even as she cared for me, she would be restless somewhere deep inside. She would constantly mutter, "God, I have to weave the basket, got to finish that one!"

Sometimes she promised home delivery to her customers. That is when she would lovingly call me the Little One. The moment I heard her calling me by that name, I knew I had work waiting for me. I hated doing it. Some of the people she sent me to never allowed me to enter their houses. They made me stand at the threshold; I put the baskets down and they sprinkled water on them to wash away the pollution, and only then would they touch them. They would drop coins in my hands from above, avoiding contact, as if their hands would have burned had they touched me. If the house belonged to one of my classmates, the shame of it was killing. So I used to ignore Aaye's calls, even when she called me repeatedly. And then her temper would rise and she became abusive. It was not just Aaye, even the women who came to the well to fetch water, and her friend Tutu, abused me as well. I resented this very much! Fine, let Aaye abuse me, but why should Tutu? On top of it, she said, "Give this girl the job of a cowherd. Otherwise marry her with my Digya." Digamber was the name of her son. Then she guffawed. This really would get my goat.

Tutu wore a long skirt and a long blouse that reached till her waist. She was a plump, short woman with a yellowish complexion and a wide mouth. How I wished our dog would bite her! But that stupid dog would bark at me when I told it to bite her. Tutu had amazing fingers. She made paper flowers, sprinkled some shiny powder on them, and took them to the market to sell. They sold like hot cakes. The village *mamis* who came to the bazaar at Ratnagiri bought these to put in their hair, tied in a bun on their necks. Even when she came to visit Aaye, she sat at a distance from us on the steps in the courtyard, her fingers busy making flowers, while she chatted with Aaye. If she were thirsty, she would go to her own hut to drink water. Something common between her and Aaye was the speed with which their hands and mouths worked simultaneously.

Aaye had another friend from the Chambhar caste. Her son was in my brother's class. But I do not remember them ever drinking water in our house. In the Konkan region, it is rare to find a separate Chambharwada. And Dhors or Mangs are rarer still.

Aaye got hopping mad if I refused to make home deliveries for her. She made such an infernal din that finally I had to agree. I retaliated by refusing to go to school!

As I came back after delivering her things, Aaye would know that I wanted something in return. She promised to give me a paisa coin for buying mollases or chana. But these were all empty promises. No money ever parted from her hands. But I would miss school anyway to go and sit in the Maruti Temple. "This will teach her a lesson!" I'd say to myself.

The nomadic Komti people usually camped close by. Their children often came to the temple to play.

The Brahmin priest of the temple bathed the idol of Maruti and worshipped him. He also gave us the holy *prasad*. I liked him very much. He was very fair, with a face that looked as if it were carved out of marble. His earlobes and feet were a lovely pink. He was always dressed in half pants, with a *janeu*, the sacred thread, around his bare white torso, and wore a red vertical kumkum mark on his forehead. And he had such a sweet smile!

Once we were playing outside as usual. The priest was busy with his puja. But he did not come out as usual to give us the prasad. So we sat on the stairs patiently and waited for a long time. Yet he did not come out. After a long time the door opened and a Komti girl called Ulgawwa came out, her face wet with tears, in a terrified state. Then the priest also came out, but he left without giving us any prasad. Suddenly I was frightened of the priest. I wanted to ask Aaye why Ulgawwa was crying but could not do so. My secret would have been out.

I used another trick when I felt like skipping school. I hid the only frock I had to wear to school. But Aaye knew me. She would tell me, "That's the school bell ringing! Go, eat some dal and rice and go to school." The school was close by. But even if it had not been so, she would have heard the bell nevertheless.

Once I had hidden my frock behind the stone mortar. Both my mother and brother started looking for it. My brother was getting late for school, yet went on searching for it. Finally he found it behind the mortar. He pulled it out like some precious jewel from Alibaba's cave and showed it to Aaye. My mother and brother gave me a couple of blows each, and my brother literally dragged me to school. He dragged me to the door of our class, pushed me in and strode off.

Herlekar Guruji was in the class. He was like our father, in another form. Had Baba worn pajamas and a shirt, he would have looked exactly like Herlekar Guruji. Herlekar Guruji was a little taller and had bloodshot eyes, which could make one wet one's pants in fright. He practiced stringent discipline, and half of that was directed at me. Aaye had given the teachers full permission to beat me up because she firmly believed in the principle "spare the rod and spoil the child." Baba had taught her that education was impossible without punishment. Besides, I too had endorsed the idea by gaily singing out a poem in our textbook that expounded the same philosophy. I was a frequent target for Herlekar Guruji. He always made me do the dirty work, like cleaning the board, the class, collecting the dirt and disposing of it. Besides, our school verandah was used as a sort of toilet by buffaloes and cows. Students in every class took turns cleaning it. When it was the turn of our class, I alone was forced to clean the entire mess. The reason was simple. We had a cow called Kapila at home. True, she never yielded any milk. But thirty-three *crores* of Gods resided in her stomach! At least that is what Aaye believed. She had brought Kapila from the village for the express purpose of worshipping them. Guruji firmly believed that it was our cow who was the culprit.

One day Guruji asked me to clean the mess. It was not even the turn of our class. Still he told me to clean because I was late. It was so humiliating that I refused even to budge. Guruji ordered me to clean up once again. But I did not move from my place. My friends—more foes than friends really!—turned to look at me and laughed. Guruji got up. I could feel the heat waves of his anger. Aaye used to tell me that if one comes across a tiger or a python, one is paralyzed with fear. I felt just the same. Guruji came close and slapped me hard. Then he told me to get out. Howling, I ran home.

Aaye was sitting in the courtyard, weaving baskets. Her hands stopped as her eye fell on me. "What's happened? Why are you crying?" she asked. By this time my face clearly showed why. It had swollen and carried the deep imprint of Guruji's palm. Aaye was enraged. She said, "Let's go to your school." Now I very much wanted her to confront the Guruji, but I did not want her to go to the school because, frankly, I was ashamed of her sari, which now was reduced to rags, her bare legs and uncombed hair. Aaye stopped the work. She asked me, "Why did Guruji hit you so hard?" I replied, "Because I refused to clean the school verandah. Guruji says it's our cow, Kapila, who dirties it."

No sooner did Aaye hear this, than she began to boil with fury. "Show me that Guruji of yours," she exploded, "Point him out to me when he passes by! I'll show him! As it is, life is so difficult!" Here she quoted a proverb! "When it is the widow's son's turn to receive alms, the giver gets a boil on his palms!" Everybody else can get education, but when it's the turn of my child, it turns out to be a big problem." She went on muttering like this for a long time, her hands furiously cleaning the bamboo strips with a small sharp knife. Suddenly she got up and applied a concoction of turmeric and ginger on my cheek as a salve and once again got busy with the weaving. I grew sleepy.

It was evening. The bell rang and school was over for the day. I saw Herlekar Guruji coming out from school, behind some students. My heart began to beat fast, thumping against my chest and I just managed to utter, "Aaye, Guruji!" Aaye sprang up like a female cobra. Then patting the pleats of her sari straight, she called out from the courtyard, "Hey you, Guruji, wait a moment!" Guruji looked at me and asked rudely, "Yes, what is it?"

"My girl studies in your class, Guruji! What did she do today that you beat her up so much?" She pulled me toward him and showed him my swollen cheek. I did not dare to look at his face. He flushed crimson and said, "Your white cow shits in the verandah."

"Our white cow? She shits there, eh? Why, did you see her doing that? Guruji, you are so educated and yet you speak so foolishly? Look, I am a widow; my life is ruined. Yet I sit here, under this tree and work. Why? Because I want education for my children so that their future will be better. And you treat my girl like this? How dare you?" Aaye was speaking in her dialect in a voice loud and ringing. Then she thundered, "Let me see you laying even a finger on my girl again and I'll show you! Let me see how you can pass this road if you do so."

"Sure, sure, see … " Guruji mumbled something and took to his heels. By this time many onlookers had gathered around us, intently watching me and my face, swollen like a monkey's.

Guruji did not beat me again. I started going to school on time. And, most important of all, I started considering my mother a great support.

I was in the fourth standard. The year had, somehow, dragged itself toward the end. The examination results had not been announced as yet; today would be the day. My mother was far more worried about my results than I. "Today you will get your results, go to school early," she kept telling me. Finally I reluctantly dragged my feet to school. I had never studied well, so my heart was racing. When Guruji came to the class with the result sheet, I had eyes for nothing else. He began to announce the results. He would read the name, the roll number, and then shout Pass or Fail so loudly that probably even the surrounding villages heard our results. There was another problem. The classrooms had tin partitions; sometimes the voices of different gurujis, declaring results on either side of the partition, got mixed up and one would hear Pass instead of Fail or vice versa. We would sit, literally with our souls in our ears, praying to the thirty-three crore gods to allow us to hear the results right.

The moment a student heard the word *pass*, he jumped in his seat and rushed to the guruji to receive his progress card from him. Students kept returning to their seats, triumphant, brimming with joy. Looking at them made me feel more scared than ever. Will I pass? Crouching low in my seat, I sat frozen with fear awaiting my turn. I was desperately praying to God, begging Him to pass me so that I would be able to escape the clutches of this monster, our Herlekar Guruji. Two students before me had passed, but two had failed and were now sitting like squashed mice in their seats.

Finally, Guruji called out my number. I was all ears. My heart thumped loudly in my chest, my legs turned to jelly. I somehow managed to scramble up to the Guruji's table. He stared at me furiously and kept on staring till I had reached his table, his eyes boring holes in me. Then he placed the progress card in my hand with a flourish, as if he were bestowing some honor on me, shouted my name and announced, "Fail." The other students began to laugh. As I turned and started returning to my place, he fired the parting shot, "Show that progress card to your mother!"

He went on to speak at length. A dark pit had opened under my feet into which I began to sink. The word *fail* reverberated in my ears. I heard nothing else. The thought of sitting in Herlekar Guruji's class for yet another year petrified me. It was far more overwhelming than the fear of facing my mother at home with my progress card. Tears choked me, but, desperately trying to hide my tears, I somehow returned to my place. I wanted all students after me to fail. I sat down, watching the faces of students who were declared to "fail" and in the same boat as me.

Finally Guruji finished reading out the list. He made an announcement about summer holidays, and all the students ran out of the class, shouting in chorus, ready to enjoy their holidays. I came out slowly, trying to avoid Guruji's sharp eyes. I lingered in the verandah for a while, trying to find other students who had failed like me, but they had vanished.

My face must have shown my utter desolation. I wanted the earth to open up and sink in it. I did not know where to go. I did not want to go home. I kept on walking listlessly on the verandah. Then I saw a man called Subhash Desai, a friend of my brother's, passing by the school. He happened to notice me. Coming toward me, he asked me, "What, have you failed or something?"

I simply nodded my head.

"Which class?"

"Fourth."

Now I began to cry.

"But why should you cry, you silly girl?" He said. "Look at my sister Kamal. She fails in each class at least twice. But she never cries like you. On the contrary, she begins her studies once again, enthusiastically." I knew Kamal. What he said about her was quite true. She was far more interested in new fashions. Her hair would always be stylishly done! I often found her in Dhekane tailor's shop, discussing new fashions in clothes. She always wore frocks, when all the girls of her age wore saris. "You also do the same thing," Subhash went on. "You can take the scholarship examination. Believe me, you will certainly pass. Don't cry. Go home." He patted me on the head and went off.

His words provided immense comfort to my tormented soul. My tension lessened to a great extent. So I stopped worrying about how to show my face at home and instead reached there like a seasoned person, with a straight face.

Aaye was sitting in the courtyard, weaving baskets as usual. But she had an eye on the road, waiting for me to appear. The moment she saw me she stopped work and stared at me searchingly like a cat. I was about to escape like a frightened mouse but my elder sister standing at the door demanded to look into my progress card. One look at my face was enough for her to know the result. "Show me your *regress* card," she said. She always called my progress card my regress card.

Silently I held it out in front of her. She glanced at it and went in. At that moment, Shahu, my brother and self-appointed caretaker, arrived and announced my result to Aaye in a voice ten times louder than Herlekar Guruji's. Aaye's eyes became round, like saucers. "Failed, eh?" she said and began a verbal abuse directed at me and at herself as well. My loving brother then said, "You think words will have any impact on her? Take a stick and thrash her," and immediately translated his words into action by hitting me hard on my back. He looked at me with murderous rage! Now I was really frightened. I thought Aaye was going to get up and really pick up a stick to beat me. But she sat quietly, drinking all her tears, and looked just like a student who had failed. I stepped into the house, resolving to study hard.

Often, women dropped into our courtyard, like reporters flocking to the newspaper office, with loads of news. They came with huge baskets on their heads as they would be on their way to the market. Aaye would be sitting outside in the courtyard, ceaselessly weaving her baskets, boxes, and other stuff. They would pour out all the news from the village, bazaar, their homes, and goodness knows where else before her! Aaye listened to the news, crisp like fresh fish from the net, without pausing in her work. We would invariably linger in the courtyard to catch the latest.

Sometimes it would be a daughter-in-law on her way back home from the market. Drawing water from the well, she would first wash her face and feet. Wiping her face with her pallav, she approached Aaye to complain, "Could I tell you something Aatoji? You know my mother-in-law harasses me a lot. She suspects I'm having an affair with her husband, my father-in-law! Now my husband works in Mumbai! But this woman keeps on sending him letters and all kinds of messages ... why? Of course, to poison his mind against me! Now you tell me, is it right? Could you please tell her something, reason with her?" Then her voice would drop and grow huskily secretive as she whispered, "You know what she did today? Don't tell this to anyone please, all right? This morning, we were coming from the village. On the way, my sasu saw a cock; it belonged to the Kulwadi woman nearby, you know! She pounced on the cock, rushed to the market, and sold it off. Now if that Kulwadi woman catches hold of me, what am I to do?" After breaking this sensational news, she tried to fathom its effect on my mother's face by casting furtive glances at her. But Aaye's face remained impassive and her hands flew over her weaving like a machine. She did not utter a single word. The daughter-in-law got up and left.

And if the suun came, could the sasu lag far behind? No way! She also hurried to my mother. Dumping her shopping near Aaye, she too went to the well to drink some water and returned. Then she began to fire questions.

"So, the shrew was here, wasn't she? My suun?"

"Yes. She was." Aaye replied in a dry and neutral tone.

"What did she tell you?"

"Nothing! Why, what's happened?"

Satisfied, the sasu squatted near Aaye, took out a piece of stone-dry bread from her basket, and pushed it into her mouth. Noisily crunching it under her teeth, she burst out with her complaints: "How that slut has made my life hell! My poor son works himself to death in Mumbai and look at this slut … enjoying herself to the hilt! How she goes around making eyes at men … how she giggles with them … how she goes from village to village, swinging her hips, to see khele! And you know something? She sells large firewood bundles but keeps all the money to herself … eating whatever she fancies! And ask if Madam does any chores in the house? Not a chance! Now if a woman decides to become a slut, what can you do? Not even the king will be able to stop her!"

The mother-in-law let out her steam for a while like this. After her catharsis was over, she would get up and leave.

Some of these news bulletins used to be routine stuff! But there would also be some really sensational items, deserving an editorial or a column! Even today some of it is quite fresh in my mind.

Aaye would sit in the courtyard, thus, weaving her baskets, absorbing all the news that came to her, occasionally responding with a grunt, a word, or a sentence at the most. But she kept her thoughts to herself. She never passed on the news to others, nor did she ever use it for setting people against each other. Maybe that's why women found in her a safe place to unburden their hearts. Had the baskets been recording instruments of some kind, they would have revealed the agony and ecstasy in the lives of those toiling women.

While Baba was alive, Aaye had contacted diphtheria. Some three or four small knots had grown around her throat. There would be pus, high fever, and terrible pain. I remember, once Baba had brought a vaidya from a village called Dingni to treat her. He took a betel leaf, dipped it in ghee, and put it on the knot. After this he took a turmeric root, the length of a finger, put it in the stove till it was fiery red, pulled it out, and put it straight on the knot. A burning noise and smoke was followed by a terrifying scream! Aaye screamed with intense pain. Her screams explode in my brain even today. The vaidya left after giving her some medicines and praising his own method of cauterizing the knots. Every time she was cauterized, Aaye screamed as if she were dying, her hands and legs flaying wildly. She burned with fever. Pus and blood flowed from the knots for days together. She was almost dying.

Aaye continued to suffer even after Baba's death. Then she began to get terrible abdominal pains, like postpartum pains, and suffered terribly. The pains would sometimes be on the left side and sometimes on the right. Then Manjulatai or Shahu would give her the water jug treatment, which was like this: first some dough would be kneaded and patted into a small round shape, to be placed on that part of the stomach that ached. Then a small mud lamp would be lit and placed on the dough. The jug would be turned upside down and some pressure applied on it. Gradually, as the lamp burned out, the skin on her stomach would be pulled into the inside of the jug, along with the gas inside the stomach. Gradually the pain subsided. The attacks would come any time. But Aaye rarely stopped working. Pressing a rod or pestle into her stomach to lessen her pains, she would continue with her weaving. When the pain became unbearable, she threw herself down on the ground.

Manjutai must have been sixteen or seventeen then. Somebody once advised her, "Take your mother to Miraj, to the hospital at Wanleswadi. Some foreign doctors treat patients there, and they are good. She will certainly get well." So Tai took her to Miraj.

When Aaye left for Wanleswadi, she was just skin and bones. With her skin pale and taut like the surface of the tabla, nose like a dry stick of wood, lips parched dry and eyes sunken hollow, she looked as if she was on the threshold of death. When she sat in the state transport bus, her eyes swept over all of us. Everybody felt that they were seeing her for the last time. All of us were crying. Crying, by itself, was nothing new. We cried as a ritual even while bidding farewell to a casual guest. But this was different. I, my sister Akka, Shahu, my uncle, my mother's brother, all of us shed bitter tears.

My brother-in-law went with Aaye to the hospital. But once he had admitted her to the hospital, he returned. It was Manjulatai who stayed to nurse her. She had to stay in a tiny, dusty room meant for patients' relatives. Bandicoots, rats, and mice kept her company all through the night. But she stayed there with quiet determination. She cooked food on a stove and nursed Aaye. When Aaye came home after a month, she was completely cured; she had even put on a little weight! Her eyes were shining and she was laughing when she stepped out of the bus. I threw my arms around her neck in sheer happiness, crying, "Hurrah, Mother is back!" At such a tender age, my sister had nursed Aaye like a child, becoming her mother.

I was a bad child, though. After breakfasting on stale bread and tea without milk, I used to collect my "toys": coconut shells, bottle lids, tin boxes, and various things like that. I would set up a stove, first with three stones, and then push small twigs under it. Then I kept a coconut shell full of mud on the stove; that was rice being cooked. In another shell, I squeezed juice of green leaves crushed with stones; that was amti. I gathered the residue of the green leaves in a lid and that was the vegetable. Food was ready! Now I needed people to eat this food. So I would go out scouting for diners. There were some families who lived as tenants in the house of a lawyer called Mr. Kapdi. It was to their heap of garbage that I went to gather bottles, broken limbs of dolls, or pieces of discarded toys. These I cleaned, blowing away the dust, ash, and dirt. At such times, if anyone inquired about me, Aaye would tell them, "The waste pits! That's where the donkey must be!"

After the waste pits, my next stop was the compound of our house. A tailor called Dhekane used to throw all his leftover rags into our compound. These rags would serve as clothing for the broken pieces, my dolls. My dolls looked like scarecrows, really. But I decorated them with the red petals of *pangara* flowers and served them "meals" on the plates of pangara leaves. Sometimes Kunti, Changuna, Bayo—girls from the families of laborers working in Shirkewadi, which was nearby—joined me in play. Sometimes we would play the game of husband-wife. Kunti was much older than us. She became our husband and made us do all kinds of things!

In those days, I was so taken up with playing like this that I was completely impervious to other things. While playing games like *thikrya, lagorya, sagargote, langdi, khokho* with my friends, I forgot everything else. My mother used to be ill quite frequently with fever, stomachaches, or diphtheria. Then she had to lie down in bed. She would lose all taste for food. At such times she could eat a couple of morsels only if there was some pickle or fish to go with it. The fish market was quite far away from our house, and nobody would be willing to go there. Then Aaye would send me off with a couple of paisa coins to the "Pandit" family to buy some pickle from them. They lived opposite us, across the road.

The memory of their mango pickle—hot, fiery red, with raw mango pieces floating in oil—made my mouth water. I would dash across the road to their house for the pickle, tightly holding the coins in my fist. Taking care not to touch, or even let my shadow fall on things lying around, I would reach the cement steps of their house. The crescent-shaped steps looked like a sort of pyramid from below. I had to stand at the lowest step. The pyramid would make anyone standing at the bottom feel really low. From there I tried to peep into the house, trying to see if anyone was around. But it would look quite deserted from where I stood. Then I had to shout, "Hello, anybody there? I want some pickle, worth two paise." After I had shouted three or four times, someone would peep out and ask,

"What do you want?"

"Pickle."

"Which?"

"Lime."

"How much?"

"Two paise."

The face would disappear from sight. Peace reigned again. Then I would have to begin calling out again, awkwardly, "Hello, I want some pickle." As if I was a thief or a beggar! After a long time, Pandit Kaku would peep out and the same questions and answers would be repeated. Then she would disappear behind the door.

Their pickles used to be in *sowale*, that is, in a state of ritual purity. It was said that she did not touch the pickle without bathing. My brother always used to say, joking, "Why don't you follow the *kaku* into her house? Before she comes dressed in her sowale sari, you might just go ahead and dip your entire hand into her pickle jar. You can tell her, "Oh, you took so long! And I'm getting late. So I am helping myself!" Since you would have polluted the jar, she would give away the entire jar to you!" We would conjure up the picture of the commotion that would have ensued if I really did some such thing and laughed heartily.

Anyway, after some time, Kaku would bring some fiery red pickle on a plantain leaf, the lime pieces covered with yellow rai dal and oil, and keep it on the second or third step. Then I kept my coins on a step, which the kaku collected, but only after she had sprinkled water on them to cleanse them of pollution!

Meanwhile, Aaye would be desperately waiting for the pickle at home, her plate of rice covered with a cane corn sifter. She abused me for being late through no fault of mine.

Dada Lanjekar was a mango merchant in Ratnagiri. He had loved my father like his son. If Aaye's illness continued for a longer time, he would call on us to say that we must feed Aaye on food collected from his house to make her well. Their food would be so tasty. The plate would be filled with rice, dal, two vegetables, salads, pickles, poppadams, curds or buttermilk, and a desert like shira or shrikhand. The rice would have ghee as well.

I loved to go to the Lanjekars to collect this food. His daughter-in-law was a very kind lady. She never looked upon me with contempt. On the contrary, her face glowed with the joy of giving. She filled the plate with fresh hot food and, like a mother, patted me on the head and advised me to take it home safely. And this was not only for a day or two. They gave us food every day till Aaye got well. Actually Aaye ate only a little, it's I who polished off everything. It improved my health better than Aaye's, and I began playing with renewed vigor.

One day Aaye was taken ill. She had no appetite at all. She could not find anyone to go to the fish market. So she called me and gave me an anna to buy a variety of small fish that was very cheap. At any other time I would have hated to walk so far. But that day I was willing to go, not out of sympathy for Aaye, but for quite a different reason. There was a Radhakrishna temple near the market. (It stands there even today.) Right from the first day of Shravana—mid-July to mid-August—to the eighth day called Goklulashtami, a festive day, *kabaddi/hututu* competitions were held. This was a very prestigious competition and many renowned clubs from all over Maharashtra participated. The winners got attractive prizes. The winning team would get a silver shield. Naturally, the competition was tough, and players tried to do their best. Huge crowds went to watch the matches as well as performances by individual players. It would be very difficult to enter the crowd, which was rather thick. People did not budge an inch, even if it rained hard.

Many famous teams participated in this competition. For instance, there was a team called Ranoddhar Sangh from Mumbai, having a number of renowned players such as Ganpat Kamble (he was a cousin's brother-in-law), Madan Pujari (brother of the famous singer Dasharath Pujari), and many others. Since Ganpat Kamble was a close relative, I always got a chance to stand in front of the crowd, near the players. They would talk and laugh with me. Naturally, this was my chance to show off. And if there was anybody from our school watching me in that state, I would be in the seventh heaven. Sometimes my brother also went to watch the matches.

Now, that day the Ranoddhar team was going to play. Most probably it was the final match. It was a bad day, since Aaye was ill. Besides, it was also a school day; so watching the match was a difficult proposition. So when Aaye told me to go to the market to buy fish, I jumped at it.

I set off toward the market with some money and a bag. I wanted to go and see the match first. But then I reasoned, suppose I went to see the match first, there was a chance that all the fish would be taken by the time I reached the market and I wouldn't get any. So I decided to buy the fish first and then watch the match for a while before I returned home. With this excellent logic I went to the market.

In the morning the fish market would be more or less empty. It would be crowded in the afternoon when the village women came to the market with their varied seasonal wares— boiled seeds and flesh of jackfruit, ca-shew nuts, mangoes, cucumbers, bibbe nuts, wild fruit like chibud—and bartered them for various kinds of fish like *chadwa, mushi, shingte,* and *wagli.* Barter was still their preferred way of trading.

The market was empty when I got there. The fish sellers created a rack-et the moment I arrived, calling out to me loudly. They began thrusting their hands into their baskets and pulling out various kinds of fish, shout-ing to attract my attention. There were women selling all kinds of fish who stopped me on my way and clamored, advertising their goods. When I managed to escape this throng of creek fish, I was surrounded by the Bhandarni women who thrust their shellfish under my nose, shouting, "Here, buy these mule, they are cheap; a *payli* for just an anna." "No, no, you buy this *kurlya*" (they were quite alive in a net). "Look at them, caught on a moonless night; they are so tasty!" Small girls, as young as me, sat next to the women with their *kalwe,* looking at me with hope. Some of the women, hastily warding off the hoards of flies on their plates of tiny live prawns, began to coax me, "Why not buy these small fish? Very tasty they are!"

My eyes, however, kept flitting to the tall platform where big, fat, and rich fisherwomen, Daldin women as they were called, sat with big and expensive fish like *saranga,* pomfret, *modwasa,* and *surmay.* The women were laden with gold. They wore thick gold bangles, heavy necklaces, long mangalsutras with many chains, a number of earrings (their ears would be pierced at seven or eight places, at least), including the hang-ing heavy *zhumke* and thick gold rings on their fingers. They looked so imposing with their display of wealth that onlookers were simply floored.

They also wore a silver box tied like an armlet from which they took out tobacco powder from time to time to brush their teeth. They looked and sat like majestic queens, decked up in glittering jewellery. Children like me, or poor people, did not dare go near them because, first, we could not afford the fish and, second, the women nearly took it as an affront if we even approached them.

Once a poor village woman, a mami, went to one of them and pressed a fish with her finger while asking about the price. This simple act incensed the Daldin woman so much that she thrust her knife into the poor woman's hand. Blood spurted out and she howled in pain. Finally there was a police case. I shivered involuntarily to see the huge knife in a Daldin woman's hand.

Suddenly I found myself in the grip of a Daldin woman. She was holding onto my bag with one hand and sprinkling water on her fish with the other. "Hey, how much money have you?" she asked me.

I opened my fist and showed her the one anna coin. She pounced on it and threw eight *bangda* fish into my bag. Eight fish for one anna! Wow! I was happy! I had got them so cheap! I smiled at her happily. She took out a silver tobacco box and started polishing her teeth with the tobacco powder as she smiled back at me.

When I reached the temple, the match had already begun. The Ranoddhar team was going great guns. There was a huge crowd. I walked around, trying to find a gap through which I could enter. But that was impossible. So I tried climbing on a gallery nearby, but even that was bursting with people. They were all engrossed in the play—shouting, clapping, stamping.

The commotion around gave me an intoxicatingly heady feeling. I was now dying to watch the game. I managed to climb down from the gallery and tried to enter the crowd once again. Suddenly I found a gap. A player charged at the other team, in attack. His opponents, who had formed a chain, encircled him. They suddenly moved back. People standing close to the ground had to move back too and I rushed through a gap and reached the ground, where a player, our Ganpatdada, was sitting. He had been declared "out." When he saw me, he smiled and called me. I was elated. I glanced at the crowd and was thrilled to see some familiar faces there. On a regular day I was a nobody to them. But today I thought they were admiring me. Showing off in front of the crowd, I sat close to Ganpatdada and began watching the game. I had totally forgotten that Aaye was sick at home, waiting in bed for the fish. That I had bought fish for her and had to take it home flew completely out of my head.

The game went on for quite some time. In the end, the Ranoddhar team won the match. There was thunderous applause from the audience. Ganpat Kamble and other players began to jump and dance. None of them noticed me now. Suddenly I remembered why I had come to the market. How would I explain the delay? My head reeled with the very thought. Galvanized and tense, I sprinted homeward.

When I pushed the door open, I saw Aaye lying in bed. There was a plate near the bed with some dry rice still sticking to it. So she had somehow managed to eat a few morsels! Without making any noise, I tiptoed in. She did not hear me, but the smell of the rotting fish must have reached her. She opened her eyes and, rotating them madly, began hurling abuses at the poor players and myself.

I was completely mystified! How did Aaye come to know my secret? That is when my brother came out of the kitchen, wiping his hands. The answer came to me in a flash. And so did a resounding blow from him! He hit me hard and said, "Just a while ago you were jumping up and down happily, watching the Ranoddhar players; so why are you standing here with such a crestfallen face? Now you eat these rotten fish!" He snatched the bag of rotten fish from my hands and threw it on my face, turned, and left for school.

I recoiled as the rotten fish hit my face and the horrible stench assailed my senses. I stood rooted to the spot like a statue. I'll never behave like this again, I thought. I'll never cause trouble to Aaye again, I resolved. But Aaye went on abusing me and the Ranoddhar team as well, for a long, long time afterward.

Akka's children were almost the same age as us. Although we were uncles and aunts to them, the relationship was more like that of friends. We would spend most of our holidays at Akka's place. I loved being with them so much that even if my mother had tied me to a post, I would have escaped and gone to Akka's place. Akka had shifted her house from the Bhangi chawl to a more middle-class neighborhood. Akka's neighbors, all hospital workers, would celebrate the Dasara festival in a great way. They would make huge bundi ladus and distribute them among people.

I remember the Dasara also for its festive atmosphere. The huge ladus we were given, the *gudhi*, or decorated pole, that Akka erected at the door (she saved the new *choli* piece specially for the gudhi instead of stitching a blouse), the decoration of flowers and sugar rings around the gudhi, the wonderful puranpoli Akka made, the procession of colorful *tabuts* of Moharram which we watched along with the crowd, the molasses rings tied like a watch on our wrists that we licked happily, the colorful "sky lamps" we made for Diwali, sitting out late at night—all of these things provided a bright dimension to the drab and dull routine followed in our house.

We often found Akka taking some ten or fifteen patients out of the hospital. Dressed in white saris, worn a little short, and loose blouses, their hair woven into tiny tight plaits, falling on their backs like scorpion tails, they followed Akka quietly, in a line, heads bent downward. They looked like a herd of sheep, really. Akka would tell us where she was going to take them. Sometimes they went to hear a public speech, sometimes to an exhibition, or even to a movie. We were highly envious!

One day somebody had the grand idea of seeing the hospital from inside. I think it was Manjulatai! So, one fine morning, all of us—I, Tai, Vahini, Akka's children, a cousin called Bhagubaya—went with Akka to see the mental hospital from inside. There were separate wards for men and women, and entry into the ward of the opposite sex was prohibited. Akka took us through a beautiful garden, cultivated by the mental patients themselves, to the women's ward. The huge gate was locked. Akka opened it and we entered. Sane patients were moving around, doing their jobs. In the verandah of a building we found some women who were completely naked, without a stitch on them. They were grinding *jowar* grains on huge grinding stones. The sight of us had upset them. They started waving their hands at us and hurling abuses in a foul language. We were petrified with fear. If they were mad, why were they not locked up in their rooms? Why were they given this work? We didn't dare go on.

Then Akka said, "Don't be scared. They are quite harmless really! This work is part of their treatment. It is not necessary to lock them up." Immediately after this we received a demonstration of what Akka had said. There were a few rooms locked up. We heard insane shouts and cries coming from these. We tried peeping into a dark room through the bars of a window. Suddenly, a woman, completely naked, her hair falling in thick tangles, rushed from the dark recess of the room, screaming hysterically at us and gesticulating wildly. It was evident that she was not aware of the windows being barred. Shockingly enough, we too did not realize this! We ran for life. After this I often saw mad women going to the theater, following Akka in a line, but never again did I envy them, not even in my remotest dreams!

Later on, Akka was transferred to the Civil Hospital at Kudal, and I lost my place to play. During the summer vacation, I would somehow manage to cull a little money from Aaye to go and stay with Akka. People there spoke Malavani, which made me feel awkward, because it was so different from our language. One day a woman came to the hospital for delivery. Akka told her to move her head to the other side. But the woman told her that that was what she had already done! Akka was quite confused till she realized that the word for "head" was used to mean "legs" in Malavani! Akka's children declared snootily that they would never speak such a silly language! But in a year they picked it up so well that they started telling us how sweet and spicy the language was! Not only that, they also started making fun of our Bankoti dialect, which is spoken in the Rajapur-Mumbai belt. Not that they were wrong! Bankoti is a spineless dialect, with no pep and vigor in it! Even people fighting in it sound tame, like the insipid vegetable made with *aloo* leaves! The speakers of this dialect did not have the guts to counter the upper castes, in spite of the deliberate insults repeatedly heaped on us. Of course, when people got together at night in the wadi, everybody would be full of bravado and frenzied discussions followed.

I remember an incident well. The savarnas in the Konkan were very resentful of Dalits leaving the Hindu religion to become Buddhists. They deliberately tried provoking the Dalits in many ways. The Dalits were supposed to collect drinking water from a particular part of the river. One day, early in the morning, people from the Maratha community deliberately took their buffaloes and bullocks to the designated part of the river to wash them. The Dalit women from the wadi had to wait for a long, long time before the muddied water settled down and they could collect some clean drinking water. So the Mahars held a meeting to discuss this issue. One man got up and said, "How can they make our water dirty? Just think about this deliberate affront!" Everybody began to speak simultaneously and nothing could be heard properly. So one man shouted, "Why are you all speaking at the same time? Take turns and speak one at a time!"

"All right! We will shut up! You speak!"

"Anyway, it was only animals drinking the water! How were the animals to know that they were drinking from our part of the river? If they were able to speak, they surely would resist drinking from the Mahar part of the river."

"Shut up, you! Don't talk rot! We are not talking about animals! It is these Marathas! It is their animals who made the water dirty!"

"Bah! As if I don't know that already! You think I'm mad? Don't talk to me like a *Baman* priest! Now, those Marathas are powerful! Tell me, will you be able to impose a fine on them? Do you have the guts?" That effectively silenced everyone! That was how spineless they were, without any resistance! And they spoke the same language!

I still remember another incident that took place the last time I went to Akka's house, which was also on the way to the bazaar like ours. Many Dalits from the surrounding villages would come to her house to drink water or just sit for a while. Akka continued in the footsteps of our father in this respect. Akka's husband was a teacher at Kudal. He too used to help poor people in their hour of need. Once when I had gone to stay with Akka, a poor couple came to see them from a village called Anaav. They were sitting on their haunches in the verandah. The husband had wrapped a loincloth around his waist. There was a huge gaping wound on his bare back. His wife sat crying, wiping the tears with her torn sari. It seemed that in their village there was a ritual. An upper-caste man would inflict a big wound on a Mahar man's back and his wife had to cover the wound with some cloth and go on walking around, howling! Quite a ritual, that one! Dada, Akka's husband, was telling them, "You have to resist this custom! How can you tolerate it? This ritual is symbolic of some old sacrificial rites! The Mahar symbolizes the animal sacrificed! I tell you, get converted then this will automatically stop."

I did not understand what my brother-in-law was saying at that time! But now the import of his words is clear to me. Afterward Akka would say, "How are these people any different from our patients in the mental hospital?"

When I was in the fifth standard, we had a Brahmin teacher called Biwalkar Madam as our class teacher. Short and fair-skinned, she was always neatly clad in a silky nine-yard sari, a clean cotton blouse, hair rolled up in a bun. She was also a stickler for cleanliness. Somehow, she did not notice how dirty we were on any other day except Saturday. On Saturdays, however, she watched us with a hawklike eye, like a policeman.

First, she made us all stand in a line and closely examined our nails, fingers, teeth, eyes, ears, and nose with the same intensity as a doctor examining a patient. She also pulled down the shorts of some boys and examined their waist strings, looking for lice and lice eggs in it. The moment she came close, the boys pulled their shorts almost up to their armpits and held them tight. Some pulled up their running noses as well.

Clean students received a pat on their backs, whereas dirty students got scolded. On top of that, she rained advice on them. "If your nails aren't clean, you'll get an infection. Brush your teeth well, otherwise you'll get filaria." Unconsciously, her voice rose while she spoke. All students, who had not learned the lesson, in spite of being told repeatedly, received a terrific thrashing from her. She had a cane that she used freely. Needless to say, I was always among those at the receiving end.

Somehow, cleanliness was my worst enemy. Our mother would be too busy with her work to pay attention to us. That went in my favor. I would take a bath only at my sweet will. Most of the time, I went without a bath for two or three days; I would just wash my face, hands, and feet and go off to school. I played in the mud like a pig, and naturally my hair looked like an upturned bird's nest. I never knew how to keep myself clean or make myself look nice.

Once a week Aaye washed my hair with baking soda and very hot water. She washed my ears clean. When my hair dried, she applied oil to my head and combed my hair with a small lice comb. She also used a wooden spatulalike comb with four or five teeth and a long handle to remove all the lice eggs. Then she tied my hair into a plait, tight as a rope. When she combed my hair, I would see bright spots all around, it was so painful! As a ribbon, she used a piece of a torn sari border and tied it at the end of the plait. For a whole week the plait bounced on my back like the tail of a scorpion. All my friends dressed up their hair with nice satin or plastic ribbons and preened before the mirror. But if Aaye found me before the mirror, she would say, "Why look into the mirror? Look at the face of the person you are talking to. That's the best mirror."

I had only two sets of clothes, which I wore alternately for three or four days. It was not surprising that they looked extremely dirty. My clothes made Biwalkar teacher froth at the mouth. "Why are your clothes so dirty?" She would invariably ask me. We did not have the custom of washing our clothes every day. Every eight days or so, my mother or Tai or Vahini gathered all the dirty clothes and took them to wash at a faraway tank.

This, of course, I never told the teacher. She would have had a fit if I had done so. Still, in spite of all this, we never had skin diseases like *kharuj*. A well belonging to a certain Sarmukadam was said to have magical powers. Washing one's hands in it protected one from getting skin diseases. The water supposedly healed existing infections as well. Shahu explained to me that this was because of the sulfur in the water. He had read about it in a book. People traveled long distances to collect the water.

I had another bad habit, spitting. Somehow I had the notion that one should not keep saliva in the mouth. I did not know that spitting was a sign of bad manners or that saliva was necessary for digestion. I would spit anywhere. Since there were no tiles on the floor of our house, the ground absorbed the spit and it did not show. Even in school, the floor was nothing but beaten soil. But there I was scared of the teacher. So I would gather my saliva in the mouth and spit it out of the window, somehow managing to hoodwink the teacher.

I was an expert in spitting long distance. I did this with the *masheri*, burned tobacco, which we used as toothpaste in the morning. I always enjoyed brushing my teeth sparkling white with coal powder. Brushing and spitting would be great fun when I had a companion. We would have spitting contests. Like betel leaf eaters, we placed two fingers on the lips and spit through the gap. Our chatting would get more and more colorful with the masheri. Then, of course, Aaye would hit us so hard that our faces turned red.

In those days nobody considered spitting a bad habit in our community. Giving favored guests a good massage and hot bath was an established and honorable custom. They would be massaged with dry coconut chewed to a fine paste in the mouth; naturally a lot of saliva got mixed into it. This paste would be liberally applied on the guest's face, arms, and body and massaged well, followed by a good hot water bath. Had Biwalkar teacher come to know of this, she would have got lockjaw!

Aaye had a favorite aunt who lived in a village called Basni. Whenever she came to visit Aaye, she would be given this special bath of coconut paste. We, the kids, also helped Aaye in chewing the coconut to a fine paste. With such backing from home, my habit of spitting grew stronger still!

A story that Aaye told us once helped me to give up this habit completely. I began to find spitting quite obnoxious. One day Aaye had less than the usual quota of weaving. So she came to bed with us. Without getting up, I cleared my throat and spat long distance into the alcove. My sister, lying near me, screamed and my brother hit me hard on the head. Both were in high school and learned lessons in cleanliness. Because I had spit into the alcove, Aaye was reminded of a story, which she told us.

Once there was a thief. He entered a house at night in order to steal. He hid himself in an alcove, waiting for all the people in the house to go to bed so that he could do his job. The alcove was in the room of an old man. He got a fit of coughing. Clearing his throat, he spat all the phlegm into the alcove. This happened so many times that the poor thief was drenched. The thief got so fed up that he forgot why he'd come to the house and ran away in sheer disgust.

All three laughed at this. Then Shahu said, "We don't have to be afraid of a thief. We've got her to make him run away." They all laughed again at this, but I could not do so. I kept imagining myself in the thief's place, and it was extremely repulsive.

It was in high school that I learned for the first time about the various kinds of bacteria in the earth and air that cause infections and diseases. Shantiakka's schoolgoing children would tell their grandmother, "Bai, wash your hands before kneading flour for the chapatis. There's bacteria on one's hands." But she was never convinced. She knew stomach infections like worms. So she would spread her palms and ask, "Where are the worms? Look, my hands are clean. Why, are you making fun of me?"

Nevertheless, our Biwalkar teacher tried very hard to teach me clean habits. It was only when I was in the fifth standard and received the colossal sum of twelve rupees as the first installment of the scholarship that I knew I had passed the scholarship examination in the fourth standard. I myself was amazed that I had passed. Maybe it was because I was a repeater in the fourth standard and had sufficient practice! Or maybe it was because the government had decided to give scholarships to untouchable students without failing them, as I heard Biwalkar teacher telling a colleague. Nobody knows!

In any case, I got the scholarship. One day Biwalkar teacher walked into the class and called out my name loudly, asking me to come to her table. When I approached her, she gave me a form to fill in and handed over a ten-rupee note and two one-rupee coins to me. I rarely had a chance to see even paisa coins! When I saw all this money, I could not believe my eyes. My unsatisfied desires to eat a lot of things, which had remained dormant so long, sprang up with a vengeance. I so much wanted to hold two lollypops in either hand like red flags, and lick them; to buy the big juicy guavas in Khanolkar's shop near the school and eat them in class, even while the teacher was teaching; to buy berries and keep them in my cheeks to look like a monkey and chew on them. I wanted to eat ripe tamarinds, *amlas,* and make other girls jealous. Then I also wanted to buy the hot spicy bondas, like big cricket balls, sold in Pilankar's shop, and eat them without sharing with my brother. I so much wanted to tease him while eating them.

While I was listing all these things in my mind, the teacher asked me, "Now tell me, what will you do with this money?" And then she went on to answer this question herself. "Tell your mother to make two nice frocks for you. Your clothes are always so dirty! Now go and buy a good soap and start washing your clothes yourself. Understand? And, yes, start bathing every day."

There was laughter in the classroom. The boys stared at me. Now they knew that my clothes were dirty and I did not bathe every day. I died a million deaths at this humiliation. But, at the same time, the thought of buying new clothes also took root in my mind. I thought of nothing but the lovely clothes worn by the girls around me: their nice skirts, frocks, and balloon sleeves! I came home floating on a cloud.

Aaye was weaving her baskets as usual. She did not see me even when I crossed her and entered the house. Her face looked worried. She was engrossed in her own thoughts and her fingers flew over the basket. Going to her I told her about the scholarship and held the twelve rupees before her. Suddenly her face lit up with a sunny smile and her eyes sparkled. She stopped her work abruptly and said, "God is great. Now I can go to Basni and see my aunt. God knows whether she is alive or dead." My dreams crashed. I did not dare to tell her what my teacher had said to me. My plans of wearing new clothes were dashed. I was so angry with her! In the heat of the moment I resolved that I would make her get new clothes stitched for me. I decided that I would do anything to make her comply. I would throw tantrums, cry, stamp my feet on the floor, go hungry—anything! Then I got busy making plans.

There was an anticlimax the next day! Our headmaster, Mr. Desai, came to the class. He said, "Children, in a brief while, the *padayatra* of Vinoba Bhave will pass by our school on its way to the Congress Office. Do you know who Vinobaji is?" Then he went on to tell us all about Vinoba

Bhave: his Bhudan movement (getting landowners to donate land for the landless), padayatras, constant striving and simplicity. He told us about so many things! After some time Vinobaji's padayatra did pass by our school. All students went to see him, forming two lines. Vinobaji, dressed in a short *khadi* dhoti like Gandhiji, with his long beard and bare body, stopped near the temple for a brief while. Our headmaster got a huge thread ball from the grocery shop of Joglekar and made a garland by passing it forty times over his hand and put it around Vinobaji's neck. After some time the padayatra went off to the Congress Office.

I was struck by Vinobaji's bare body, coarse dhoti, and the equally coarse piece of cloth on his shoulder. His colleagues too were dressed in a similar fashion. Suddenly I felt, why should my dirty clothes offend the teacher? And gradually the thought of getting mother to sew new clothes for me, and throwing tantrums if she did not, evaporated from my head. I must admit, though, that Biwalkar teacher's advice on cleanliness did not fall on completely deaf ears.

Three

My classmates would always ask each other, "What have you brought in your tiffin box today?" Since I lived near the school, I went home during lunch break, but I would always listen to their conversation. I came to know so many new words! For instance, some said, "I have brought *poli* today." Poli? Then I came to know that they used this word for *chapati*. I was amused. When I heard someone say "dadpe pohe," I was quite intrigued. How can rice flakes be oppressed (*dadpe* means beaten or oppressed in Marathi)! Dasara was called Vijaya Dashami in our school, but I was so confused when someone referred to *bhakri* as *dashmi!* I had to quietly open the tiffin box of a girl called Sunanda Phatak—without letting her know, of course—to find out what this dashmi was! She brought dashmi every day.

When my brother Shahu returned from Mumbai, he would almost drool when he mentioned something called *srikhanda* which, he said, was supposed to be eaten with puri. He said it looked like the ointment we applied on skin infections. I was quite mystified. Ointment yet sweet? How can you eat such a thing? What did it taste like? Again words like *sandge, dhapate, khakre,* and *methkut* made me feel very curious

The upper caste girls always used words like *ladu, modak, puranpolya.* They brought such novel items in their tiffin boxes at times when we went on excursions. They would also bring such food when they played with dolls. But I never asked myself the stupid question "Why don't we make such dishes at home?" We were aware, without anybody telling us, that we were born in a particular caste, in poverty, and that we had to live accordingly.

We belonged to the Mahad-Rajapur belt, which forms the central region of the Konkan, and, compared to the north-south belt, this region is quite backward. I was born in a backward caste in a backward region, that too a girl! Since Father died when we were quite young, Aaye had to be very thrifty to make ends meet. Basically, she was a born miser, really! There is a saying in Marathi: imagine a monkey drinking wine, getting intoxicated, getting bitten by a scorpion, and then a ghost casting its spell on him. The point is people's traits intensify and eventually cause havoc in their lives. Her case was similar. Therefore food was always scarce in our house.

Coarse rice grains, bought from the ration shop, would be cooked for lunch. We ate this rice with *pithale,* a cooked flour of pulses called *kulith.* Sometimes we had some leafy vegetables, from our own backyard. Sometimes we had bhakri made of *milo,* that is, red jowar, a kind of millet, or, sometimes even of husk. This husk bhakri was so rough that it was impossible to swallow it. At such times, Aaye would encourage us, saying, "Eat it, eat it child! Only the person who can eat such food can achieve a lot of good!" We ate with the bhakri not any nice expensive fish but dried fish or small inexpensive fish, fried with onions, red chilli powder, and salt. We never got to eat fresh fish unless these were tiny and quite cheap. These tiny fish were called *chadu.* We would bake them in the stove. The poor women, the mamis who came to the market in Ratnagiri to sell mangoes, jackfruit, firewood, and such other stuff, often baked such fish on their way and walked as they ate it with their dry bhakris. Looking at them eating the fish would make me feel so hungry!

Aaye often cooked this variety of fish with the spice *tirfal* to make some sort of soup to go with bhakri or rice. In the rainy season she would just cook a plateful of *takla* leaves with a little salt and that was all! It gave her immense self-righteous pleasure to be thrifty!

In the rains, of course, aloo leaves were another vegetable that was liberally available. She would pick these in heaps and get us to clean them. Each leaf had a long stem. We had to remove the outer skin of these stems with care, which reminded me of the plastic ribbons my classmates tied to their hair. But I wanted to throw those purplish grey stems away, as they made our hands itch a lot!

Aaye would cook a potful of curry with these leaves, adding some *pavate* beans, salt, red chilli powder and amsul, dried ratamba fruit. She would cook only a little rice but plenty of curry. We hated mixing spoonfuls of rice in platefuls of curry, and our faces transparently reflected what we thought! Then we repeated a story Aaye had told us much earlier.

Once a son-in-law went to visit his parents-in-law. The mother-in-law had only a small amount of rice grains in the house. She cooked them and made plenty of aloo curry. She served him a little rice in the plate and poured plenty of curry on top. When he finished the curry and began to eat rice, she again poured plenty of curry on his plate. Then, to divert his attention from the curry, she began talking to him of many things. "Son-in-law, how many brothers are you?" The son-in-law, fed up with the curry, said, "If I survive this curry, four, otherwise, three!"

We recounted this story to each other and said, "If we survive this curry, we are five siblings, otherwise four!" We laughed so much that we never realized when we'd finished the curry. How could rich dishes like ladu, modak, and puranpoli dare come to our house when it had place only for aloo?

Aaye would tell yet another story of an obedient boy when we grumbled about the food. This boy was so obedient that when his mother gave him a piece of bhakri with an empty bowl, he pretended that there was some vegetable in the bowl and ate his bhakri with it. After hearing such stories, how could we ask for tasty dishes? So we learned to eat whatever was given to us without complaining. We could not say, "I'm not hungry now; I'll eat it later" for the simple reason that one would never be sure whether any food would be left over to eat later.

We never came across a doctor who asked us to eat plenty of fruit even when one was seriously ill. We ate fruits, but only those that grew in the Konkan region, like mangoes, jackfruit, berries like *karvande* and *torne*. We had to eat them before meals. If Aaye bought a jackfruit, she would cook even less than usual. She cut the jackfruit and gave it to us immediately before meals so that we ate less. That much food was then saved!

She made a curry using jackfruit seeds or served them boiled with salt. We would dry the seeds in summer so that in the rainy season we could bake them on the griddle and eat, sitting near the stove. They tasted so good and helped revive the taste buds.

Hapoos mangoes from Ratnagiri reached the Arab countries but never came to us. All that came our way was the ordinary mango called raiwal. Many students in our class smelt of hapoos. Their nails, cheeks, and lips carried telltale signs of the sweet golden yellow juice. My mouth watered even as I looked at them ... We had some hapoos trees in the village. But when they flowered, Aaye sold them off to the *khot* of the village for money. All that came our way were rotten mangoes that had dropped off the trees or were eaten away by birds. There was a story behind this too.

There was a man called Ganpat (Ganya to us). He was from Dabhol but worked as a watchman in the village. His job, of course, was to guard the mango trees in the village. He was a tall, thin guy, emaciated really, with a clean-shaven head except for a *shendi* or tuft at the back, an un-shaven face with a whitish beard and a loincloth around his waist. His most distinctive feature, however, was his black moustache, covered with green phlegm! It was quite an obnoxious and nauseating sight! He would work the whole day, guarding the mango trees in the village, and at night slept in our yard with all his belongings: two german silver pots, loincloth, and a *ghongade* (a blanket made from sheep wool), tied up in a bundle as a pillow. Aaye did not mind as the mango baskets kept at the door for sale were now guarded by default, free of charge. It was this man who brought us the fallen and dried-up mangoes. Many Muslim fish vendors in the fish market bartered such mangoes for small fish. Ganya could easily have earned a little for himself! But that poor man never bartered our mangoes for fish. When we took the mangoes from him, I always felt he was rich while we were paupers.

People traveling by boat to or from Mumbai stopped in transit at our house. Many of them were our relatives, while quite a few were simple acquaintances. They hotly debated the number of full and half tickets they had to buy, trying to save money. Once, just to make her look younger, the parents-in-law of a married girl, who must have been around seven-teen years old, made her wear a long skirt and blouse and managed to buy a half ticket for her. I still remember her sitting in our house with her face gone crimson and her body shrunk with shame.

The *chakarmani* guys left their bags, wives. and children in our house and ran to inquire about the boat timings. Some of them camped at the port or the busstop. People going to Mumbai carried bundles giving out a variety of strong smells: of mangoes, cashew nuts, and jackfruits. Travelers coming from Mumbai had bundles neatly tied with new strings. Relatives generally gave us things like chana, rice flakes, dates, which were a novelty for us! These people invariably left behind bedbugs that kept us company for a long, long time, keeping the memory of the visitors alive after they had left!

Near our house was a small teashop run by a man called Pilankar. He prepared *bhaji,* which were bondas as big as cricket balls. The lovely smell of these bhajis reached our house and set our taste buds on fire. We lied to Aaye to have the bhajis. We told her we needed to buy pencils and note-books and spent whatever she gave on the bhajis! We had even composed a song about them, borrowing the tune of a famous Hindi film song.

If a guest gave us a paisa coin, we spent it on the bhajis. Guests rarely gave us money as they would be as poor as we were. But when the relatives we loved visited us, it would be a festive occasion. A tiny cock in the backyard would be killed, and Aaye made wadas or balls of rice flour and chicken curry with plenty of water and red chilli powder! That curry awakened our taste buds, which had almost died with milo bhakri and rice.

Rice was our staple food. Special dishes for festivals were made from rice flour. Sweet kheer was made using rice flour cooked with molasses and coconut, *gharge* with rice flour mixed with shredded cucumber and baked with a little oil, and, for the famous Ganapati festival, modak with rice flour cooked with molasses and coconut! In our community, my mother was the only one who could make modak well. To do so, it is necessary to cook rice flour and knead it well. Small balls of cooked flour have to be flattened into small round shapes called *puri.* The puri has to be rolled in a round shape, with a spoonful of sweet filling inside made from coconut and molasses. Folding the puri into petal-like shapes to be joined at the end like a crown, without spilling the filling inside, is an art by itself! It is not at all an easy dish to make, but Aaye had mastered the art. She had traveled with my father on his working days, so she knew quite a few recipes. Not that she made such delicacies often. When Father was alive she would at least make kheer, but after his death she merely sat shedding tears. Nobody among our neighbors in the village even knew what a modak looked like. One of my cousins would tell us a story of a friend's modak experience.

Once a man from our wadi was invited to lunch at his friend's house. The friend's wife made beautiful modaks, which he liked very much. He saw how his friend's wife had boiled rice flour to make the dish. He came home, described what he had seen to his wife, and asked her to make it. She dutifully made the dish but when he sat down to eat, he could not see any modak in his plate. When he asked his wife, she told him to look into his bowl, which contained a mixture of hot water, rice flour, molasses, and coconut! Sarcastically he said, "Oh, excellent! What beautiful modaks!" She replied, "They would have tasted even better with coriander seeds! Only I didn't have any!" The poor woman had no idea of the recipe!

I heard another story of how shepherds were ignorant about various foods. There was a shepherd who once ate a *ghavan,* a sort of a pancake, which had a nice, netlike appearance, since the surface had many holes (good ghavan will always have holes like a net!). He was amazed at the dish and, considering what intricate work it must have been to make the holes, he bartered his buffalo in exchange for five ghavans! In other words, we were extremely ignorant about food. The menu hardly ever changed even at festive times. On Diwali Day, we ate rice flakes soaked in water with a little topping of molasses. Oh, yes: Aaye used to make a dish called *bore:* small round balls, made with rice flour mixed with black sesame and molasses and fried in oil. They were hard as stones, but we celebrated Diwali munching on them. Later on, when I went to high school, I observed how my friends prepared food in different styles at home and tried to imitate them. But Aaye invariably got furious with me because a lot of oil and sugar were required to cook food such as these.

It was during my visit with Akka for Diwali once that I learned about delicacies like ladu and *karanjya,* which were made specially for Diwali. She had learned the recipes from her friends. This must have been around 1950–55. Dalit homes in the city must have got acquainted with such delicacies by that time.

Aaye used to make a sweet dish called *bhanore* either at festive times or as a gift for relatives. This was a favorite dish of mine. It tasted like cake and was easy to make. Some molasses, coconut, and turmeric were mixed with thick rice flour and the mixture was poured into a pot coated with oil, kept on live coal pieces. Some of these would be kept on the plate covering the pot as well. It would cook slowly. Aaye usually made it during the night, and the beautiful smell permeating the whole house drove the sleep away from my eyes. Once it was cooked, the pot was turned upside down on a plantain leaf and the bhanore cut into pieces. It would keep up to eight days. People returning to Mumbai were sure to carry bhanore as a gift.

Besides rice, fish too was commonly available. The fish season started after the Dasara festival. Fishermen returned with abundant fish. Small fish would be sorted out, dried, and stored for lean days. Rich people stored the flesh of sode, tisrya, or mule; poor people stored the water in which these fish were boiled. The stock was boiled till it became thick like sauce and was then stored in bottles. This was called *kaat*.

When the menfolk went out and women and girls remained at home, they dined only on kaat. A small quantity was poured in water and cooked as a soup, with chilli powder, salt, and a piece of raw mango or amsul. This was called *saar!* Women ate their rice with this watery dish. Similar saar would be made with the stock of other fish. This was an extremely low-quality dish with no nutritional value. It would invariably upset the stomach. There was a song we used to sing:

> Hey what is that funny "dug dug" noise,
> What is the foul smell spreading all over?
> Well, what they cooked was fish water!
> Someone's had a bellyful! And how!
> She wears a short sari down to the feet now,[1]
> To hide what's trickling down from her butt!

This saar used to be the regular diet for daughters-in-law. The poor things ate it without a complaint and naturally faced the consequences. I too grew up on this saar; that is why my digestion is excellent.

Tasty fish like surmay, pomfret, and *halwa* never came our way. All that we could get were *mushi, wagala, shingta:* fish with a strong smell and thick skin, which nobody wanted. Yet another fish with a similar foul smell was the bull fish, so called because it had a horn like a bull's on its head. Only Mahars ate that. No amount of salt, amsul, or chilli powder could drive away the strong smell. We invariably complained. Finally Aaye gave in and bought small fish, which were not so smelly.

Among these small fish the most favored was a small finger-length variety. We made a tasty dish called *katyacha motla* with it. Such fish, or small river fish, were cleaned and then covered with a paste made of amsul, turmeric, oil, and salt. Next they would be wrapped in leaves of the kumbhi tree and tied up with thin long strips cut from the stems of wild creepers. The packet was kept in the stove under hot ash, sometimes even for eight days. These fish lasted long and could be taken out and eaten any time. This was a very tasty dish, and while it lasted our mouths kept watering.

I would, however, hate to carry such things in my tiffin box, either to school or on an excursion. Why, I would be ashamed of even talking about them. It always made me feel terribly inferior to the other children at all times.

My sister had a friend called Prabha Godbole. Her father offered tuition to school students. My sister went to him to be coached in English. I am not sure how much English she learned, but she certainly picked up their Brahmin habits very fast. One of these I came to know only after her marriage. But she had demonstrated another one immediately after picking it up. She cooked some *tur* dal, mashed it well, mixed some salt in it, and called it *waran!* Then she told us waran tasted wonderful when mixed with hot rice and a little ghee and a dash of lemon were added to it. She went on to add that if one mixed a little methkut—a powder of spices and lentil flour—in the rice, it became even tastier. Of course, this waran rice was no match for our food!

One day my classmates decided to cook a meal. They were discussing what everyone must bring: rice, lentils, and so on. I went up to them, eager to participate in the cooking. I found this idea of cooking by ourselves very good. But they wanted to avoid asking me to bring something. I asked enthusiastically, "What should I bring?" "Nothing," they said. "You just bring some money." They were going to cook at the house of a girl called Tarulata Sawant, as her parents were away. Girls like Sushila Dhumak, Kamal Chavan, and Sunanda Bhosale cooked a simple but tasty meal of rice, dal, and vegetables. They did not allow me to touch anything, though we all ate together. I really enjoyed the meal.

The next day I was horrified to hear that my eating had become the hottest topic for juicy gossip. Girls were whispering in groups about how much I had eaten. "She ate like a monster," someone said. Another endorsed it, "God, she ate like a goat." "She ate so much of everything! Awful!" It was so humiliating that I died a thousand deaths that day!

To earn a little extra money, Aaye had built two small rooms adjacent to our house. She rented them out to needy couples. Once a Muslim couple from Mumbai rented them. The man was called Mohammad and he was from a small place called Mazgaon, some six miles away from Ratnagiri.

Mohammad had sunken cheeks, as if he was sucking on a chocolate all the time. He had a long face and a lean body. His wife, Haseena, was an absolute contrast. She was very fair, with pink cheeks, coral lips, and a lissome figure. She looked so odd next to her husband! I heard him telling Aaye that she had eloped with him from Mumbai.

The couple had a small child called Abdul, suffering from a severe deficiency of vitamin D, with a stomach swollen like a pumpkin and rather tiny and thin limbs. Lying on the floor, he looked like a pumpkin creeper. He could not move; only his arms kept flapping weakly. His mother, Haseena, hardly paid any attention to him. She would move listlessly in the house like a string puppet, lost in her own thoughts. When Mohammad was around, he tended to the child. He would pick him up, bathe him, and change his clothes. Aaye had advised him to keep the child in the morning sun, as that was the best remedy for babies suffering from this disease, and he assiduously followed her advice. Every morning he would keep the baby in the morning sun and sat next to him.

Four or five months must have passed like this. One day they had some guests. Mohammad went to the bus stop to receive them. They were two girls, both my age. One was Haseena's sister Baby and the other her daughter Saida, who was a spitting image of her mother, with the same pink chubby cheeks, reddish brown hair, and large eyes with long lashes. Their arrival seemed to inject new life in Haseena. She revived and began to laugh and talk. She also started paying more attention to her child and began sitting in the morning sun with him.

The two girls became my fast friends. Ramzan, the month when Muslims kept a fast during the day, was on. The schools the girls went to were closed for the Ramzan holidays, the reason why they were visiting. After returning from school, I spent most of the time with them. It was fun listening to their gossip about Mumbai. Baby was good at telling stories from the movies. She acted out the dialogues as if she herself were the heroine, performing, emoting, winking, and making eyes at us. Sometimes she shed dramatic tears and sometimes she cooed and whispered the lines. She could demonstrate even the fight sequences. How time passed, as if it had wings!

They all spoke to each other in Hindi, and, listening to them, I managed to pick up a bit. Both of them made me work hard on a Hindi passage from my textbook, and I used to recite it with a grand flourish. It was a simple description of a morning, but it felt as if it were a description of something divine. I loved reciting it, and it lingered on my tongue like sugar candy. I presented it in my school. Boys looked at me with eyes full of admiration, as we look at somebody who speaks English fluently! Even the teacher was impressed. She would often call me near the table and make me recite the passage. I enjoyed the attention and felt proud.

Later on I came to know from Baby that Mohammad had been a servant in their house. Saida's father, that is, Haseena's husband, was in a Muslim country where he had married another woman. So Baby's father brought Haseena and her daughter, Saida, back to Mumbai. Haseena stayed with her father for a couple of years, where she conceived Abdul. That is when she came with Mohammad to Ratnagiri. But she was not happy here. She cried constantly, so Mohammad sent a telegram to her father. That is why Baby and Saida had come to stay with Haseena during their Id holidays.

Mohammad's relatives lived in Rajiwada, the part of Ratnagiri located in the land between the sea and the creek. The Muslim women in their locality sold fish door to door for a living. They used to come to our house as well. A couple of these fish vendors dropped by at Mohammad's place for a chat. The day Baby and Saida were through with fasting, the whole family wore nice clothes. A lovely smell of food cooking in their rooms wafted in the wind. Baby said they were making biryani. Later she gave us some, and I ate it with relish but Shahu did not. "It contains beef," he said. I felt repelled; but Aaye said, "So what! We have eaten even a dead bull!" Haseena wanted Baby and Saida to take some biryani to their relatives in the Muslim locality. When they asked me to go with them, I readily agreed.

We trudged through a narrow lane, crowded on both sides with dingy houses, along the marshy bank of the creek till we arrived at a big house. The outer wall of the house was dotted with fishing nets, baskets, bamboos, paddles, hooks, and other such paraphernalia associated with a fisherman's trade, hanging from pegs. Big fish were hung to dry on strings tied to windows. The houses around were no different. The whole atmosphere reeked with the salty, musty, stinking smell of fish and the creek.

A plump woman in a brocaded sari got up and walked out when she spotted us at the door. She was all decked out in heavy gold jewellery. When Baby took out the biryani container and handed it over to her, she frowned and said, "Didn't you find any other place? Why did you go and stay at that Mahar's house?" Baby must have found this quite embarrassing, because she pointedly said to her, "This is our landlady's daughter." The woman's face literally twisted up at this. Pointing at a bench, she said to me, "You stay there!" and signaled both Baby and Saida to follow her inside. They were there for a very long time while I kept sitting alone on the bench, waiting. The stink of fish was suffocating! I wanted to get up and walk off because of the humiliation. But I just sat there I don't know why!

Finally both Baby and Saida came out and, without even glancing at me, just said, "Let's go." I got up quickly and was on the street even before them. The fat woman called out loudly, "Tell Haseena Bibi to shift here, I'll make all arrangements. And tell Mohammad to come and see me." Both the girls nodded their heads vigorously.

There was hardly any conversation between us on the way back. They did not speak to me; they also walked at a distance from me. Since I had carried the bag with the biryani container on our way to the house, I offered to carry it on the way back as well. But Baby scowled and said, "No!" The fat woman had probably refused to accept it since I had touched it, because Baby said, "What a waste of time! Now who will eat all this?"

Who knows what the fat woman in Rajiwada had told them about me, but somehow they stopped talking to me from that day on. They began to behave like strangers. Before this happened I would return eagerly from school to chat with them; now I began to feel guilty, as if I had committed some grave offense. At the time of going back to Mumbai at the end of their holidays, they just said bye and left. How this hurt me! I wept bitterly.

Immediately after this, Mohammad vacated our house and shifted to Rajiwada. The Hindi lesson that I prepared so well with their help now lost all its charm. The sentences turned to ashes in my mouth. The incident weighed heavy on my heart for a long, long time, like a suffocating dark evening in the rainy season.

Four

After my father's death, the hereditary mantle of priesthood fell on my brother Shahu's shoulders. At that time he did not live at home; he had a job somewhere else. Shahu had undergone the ritual of *guru-mandali*. It was believed in our community that it was not enough to be born as a human being unless one received social sanction by belonging to a particular caste and religion. Else being a human was meaningless. Gurumandali was the ritual giving such a sanction. Each child born in the community, irrespective of its gender, was made to sit on the guru's lap as he whispered secret words in its ear.

There were two ways in which one could become a guru. Any man who had managed to walk up to Pandharpur and return alive or any man who came from a family of priests could qualify to become a guru. One of the major tasks of a guru was to drive away evil spirits that possessed people. From the tender age of twelve, Shahu began to perform religious rituals as a priest. To drive away the spirits, he too began reciting the magic chants the way my father did. He was a small guru of course. In order to drive away the really dangerous evil spirits, which were too strong for the small gurus, special gurus having adequate power to do so would be summoned. They also knew black magic and used witchcraft to make people vomit blood and die in an instant or be confined to bed all their lives. They knew how to drive away the "bayangi ghosts" as well.

Now the "bayangi spirit" was a class by itself! It could turn paupers into wealthy men in no time. People in the community believed that such a ghost lived in our house! My father had worked very hard all his life and, finally, toward the end of his life, had managed to repair his old house in the village and construct a tiled roof. Immediately, people in the wadi began to say that there was a bayangi spirit in our house. The funny thing was that the people in our house would say that such a spirit lived in someone else's house in the wadi. In each wadi there would be at least a couple of houses haunted by the resident bayangi spirit! Nobody knew whether this spirit worked all by itself or had other family members for assistance or whether it had appointed an entire office staff to carry out its commands! But the spirit was supposed to turn a pauper into a wealthy man in an instant. And all that it required in return was a yearly fee of a coconut and a cock. Not a bad deal, was it? But this fee had to be paid in time, otherwise it would just clear off everything in the house! It was as if it always carried a broom and a bottle of disinfectant!

Two months after Baba's death, my cousin Govindadada came to visit us with a couple of villagers. Aaye started mourning whenever anybody came to visit. Now she began weeping as well. Govindadada also began to cry loudly. In between his bouts of crying he told her, "Your house is on the borderline between two villages, Ratnagiri and Nachane. All the offerings from Ratnagiri have strengthened the bayangi's spirit and hence he is bent on wreaking havoc on you. See, it turned your husband's blood to water first, that's how he died. Then he claimed your son Achyut. There was no reason why he should have died. But he did. You brought the body of the grandfather in this house even when he had committed suicide by hanging himself! This is all because of this spirit." He talked in this vein for a long time. Finally he came to the point, "Sell this house and land and come back to the village with the children." He began to insist on this idea.

When he saw that Aaye was not willing to do what he wanted, he changed track, "I knew you wouldn't listen to me! That is why I have brought Someshwarbuwa along with me. He is a great sage, you know! Very learned man!"

The *buwa* was a silly fish-eyed man who had gone red. His hair and beard were overgrown and unkempt. He was dressed in a dirty dhoti and shirt over which he wore a black coat. To us he looked completely mad. For a long time, he sat on the verandah, beating on the floor with some five or six dry mango leaves.He kept muttering: "Give left." "Give right." Who knew what he was talking about? The rest of the program began in the evening.

In the evening, Govindadada pounced on a young clucking cock, sprinkled gulal and *abir* on it, and disappeared with the buwa and the villagers, who accompanied him. When they returned, the dead cock hung upside down in his hand and they were all dead drunk. After dining on chicken curry and rice, the buwa went out of the house. When he had walked some thirty feet, he began to dig. Then he put his hand into the small pit and brought out a lemon with a few pins stuck into it. When cut and squeezed, blood-red juice ran out from the lemon. Then he sat on his knees and once again thrust his hand into the pit. He asked someone to hold his other hand. After this he made as if someone down there in the pit were forcibly pulling him into it as he struggled with a spirit. To the onlookers it appeared as if a great struggle was on. Finally he pulled out some seven or eight lemons from the pit. I did not know what effect this had on the adults around, but we children were petrified. Our hearts literally jumped into our mouths. We just wanted to run away to Govindadada's village. I did not leave Aaye's side the whole night.

The incident had a completely different effect on Aaye. She started to mourn Baba's death still louder. "My lord, my master, why did you leave me and go away? Why have you deserted me? Now see, these people are plotting to take your land. You had told me never to trust Govinda! That's exactly right! See what they are doing … !" When Aaye launched such a frontal attack on Govindadada's real plan, all of them, including Govindadada, could do nothing but get out of the house.

All such things—ghosts and supernatural experiences—stopped abruptly after the conversion ceremony took place. That was later, of course! In truth, we hardly had an idea of what conversion meant, nor did we know who this Dr. Ambedkar was who had asked us to convert to Buddhism. Activists like Nathuram Kamble from Shirgaon, Haribhau Aire from Partavane, Bandya Chawekar from Kele, and Gopal Mastaar from Mire played a great role in this respect. They guided people in different matters, including those related to the government, by discussing and explaining things to them. Despite holding full-time jobs, they spared a lot of time to help us.

It was these people who first brought the news of Dr. Babasaheb Ambedkar's sad demise to us. They had heard it on the radio. That day is permanently etched in my memory. It was evening, and I had gone home limping because I sprained my ankle while playing at school. When I reached home, a strange sight met my eyes. Everyone in the house was weeping. Nathuram Kamble sat sobbing uncontrollably on a bench in the verandah. Aaye, Manjulatai, Shahu—everybody was weeping. I too began to weep, since they all were. After a while, Nathuram said that he would go to Mumbai the next day for the last *darshan* of Babasaheb and left. Gradually I came to know who Babasaheb was, and then the conversion happened quite suddenly.

Crowds of people from the surrounding villages marched to the grounds of Gogate College in Ratnagiri until it resembled a sea of humanity. We went there too, along with Govindadada and the other villagers. Several instructions were being issued from the loudspeakers hanging overhead. Then came the reverberating sound of *Buddham Saranam Gachchami*, and we too joined in the chanting of the crowd.

After the ceremony, we went home. Govindadada and the villagers collected the idols and various pictures of the gods and goddesses adorning our walls, which Aaye used to worship every day, and threw them into a basket. I was expecting Aaye to remonstrate with him, but was amazed to see her dump some of the idols as well. After the death of my father and, later, of my brother, she had removed the idols from their seats in fury and put them out of sight. But they returned after a few days, and she began praying to them to protect our lives. But this time it was quite different. Now she appeared to have permanently done with the gods. We followed Govindadada to the village with the big basket.

A meeting was held in the village the previous night, in the light of petromax lamps, asking people to discard the gods. Since ours was the house of a priest, there were all kinds of idols in our house, made out of silver and brass. Baba had obtained them from distant holy places like Benaras. Besides, there were many vessels—copper plates, spoons, brass jugs, jars, incense holders, and many others. We put all of them in a basket. In fact, the silver and brass would have fetched a tidy amount if we had sold the stuff. But we had firmly resolved to discard the gods with all the accompanying paraphernalia. So we went to the river with the other people, the young children in tow. On the way, people chanted the same traditional invocation, but with a completely different set of words:

> O ye Gods,
> Yes, that's right, Maharaja,
> Go back to your own place.
> Yes, that's right, Maharaja,
> You never did any good to us.
> Yes, that's right, Maharaja,
> Now our Lord Buddha has come.
> Yes, that's right, Maharaja.
> Now we aren't scared of anyone.
> Yes, that's right, Maharaja.

Soon our procession reached the river, shouting slogans like "Long live Ambedkar," "Long live Lord Buddha." We walked right up to the point of origin of the river where there was a deep pond. We threw all the gods and vessels into the pond and returned home. After a few days, we came to know that certain people from the neigborhood had fished them out and sold them off, thereby earning quite a tidy sum to warm their pockets.

My sister's son Prabhakar, however, did not like the gods being discarded. He shed bitter tears. He remains a Hindu even today. Now he has got his caste changed to Maratha and had it registered as well. But people who know him still recognize him by his previous caste and make it a point to disclose it to people who do not know him. I do not know what he achieved by this change on paper!

After conversion, Govindadada hung a portrait of Dr. Ambedkar on the wall in the gods' room and kept a Buddha idol in the place vacated by the gods. His daily prayers had stopped. Activists from our wadi went from door to door to teach people the Buddha Vandana, the invocation to the Buddha. Now the people of our community went around with a feeling that there was no reason to pray to god for comfort, as if all comforts were automatically delivered at their doorsteps. The activists organized the Buddha Vandana every evening. This was something new to us, so there would be a lot of confusion when we tried to sing it. The tune went wrong, words changed their order, and lines got mixed up. This made us erupt in gales of laughter. But gradually we all learned it well.

Now activists began to travel across several villages to spread the word of Dr. Ambedkar among our people. Ambedkar Jayanti, or Ambedkar's birthday, Buddha Jayanti, the Buddha's birthday, Nirvan Din—Dr. Ambedkar's anniversary of death—would be observed on the designated days. One important fallout of this was that boys who usually played truant gradually began to return to school. Also, the older rituals performed to mark birth, marriage, and death were given up and new ones gradually came to be finalized, according to the Buddhist religion.

Our Baba had gone to school in Partavane. He had lived with his sister there. Her daughter was called Bhikiakka. She was a beautiful girl with a fair complexion when she was young. Later on, all her hair went white and most of her teeth fell out well before she grew old. She had a great affection for us, her maternal cousins. Her stepson's marriage was the first performed according to the Buddhist conventions that I witnessed. We, the children, went to Mirjole to attend the wedding. This was the first Buddhist marriage that I attended anyway. The activists had warned all the women in the community not to perform any of the older rituals such as applying turmeric on the bridegroom's body, tying flower mundawalis around his crown, tying a mangalsutra around the bride's neck, and playing instruments such as dhol and tashe! All of these had to be dropped! The women were furious over this. Everybody wanted the marriage to be performed in a way that matched the affluence of the bridegroom's family.

Both Bhikiakka and her cowife, the mother of the bridegroom, worked in a mill in Mumbai. Their husband was employed as a jobber. His word carried a lot of weight in the village and also in our community in Mumbai. The husband and his two wives lived in a small one-room-apartment block in the B.D.D. chawl, on Delile Road, with their seven or eight children and a couple of tenants. Often they had visitors staying with them too. Though the house was small, the husband's ego was inflated because of his job and two working wives who served him as well. He lived in style, drank heavily, and had affairs with several women. Bhikiakka was his first wife. In spite of begetting two children by her, he married a woman from the *ghat*, the hilly Western Ghats' region. She produced some five or six children, out of whom four survived. After he came back from work in the evening, the husband perched in comfort on the bed with his second wife, munching on delicacies like almonds and dry dates. Poor Akka would be made to slog in the house. She would be constantly cooking, cleaning the children, feeding them, washing utensils and clothes, and doing a thousand household chores. Yet there was no peace for her in the house. At the slightest pretext, the husband showered blows and kicks on her. Sometimes he even whipped her. The other wife abused her with dirty words. She did not survive, though, for long.

Everybody called Bhikiakka's husband Jobber or Mirjolekar. When he visited the village, he invariably came to visit us. My mother hated the very sight of this man. "The bastard has ruined my niece! It's because of his beatings that she has lost all her teeth!" she used to bitterly complain behind his back. But she spoke to him civilly, fearing he would use it as a pretext for beating Bhikiakka in case she did not.

When he came to visit, he would tell us ghastly stories about beating up his wife and violent things like murder. His throat had gone hoarse permanently, perhaps because of excessive drinking. He always spoke in a rasping, harsh voice. When he guffawed, his whole body shook like a sack. His stories would be broken, piecemeal, without any proper beginning or end: for example, he would say, "Beat the wife with a rose, she pouted. Beat her with a whip, she laughed!"

Another story of his virtually sent shivers down our spine and made us worry for the very life of Bhikiakka. "Once a guest came visiting ... he saw a white bundle hanging from the roof ... blood dripped ... drop by drop. Wife's murdered, the guest screamed." (Here the bench he sat on shook violently with his obscene laughter.) "Her head ... cut off ... tied in a bundle ... hanging from the ceiling ... blood dripping ... the wife was alive. There was a watermelon hanging in the bundle. Ha, ha, ha, ha. What is dripping? Blood? Or watermelon juice? Confront the wife. What is this guest to you? Whipped her with a hunter! Shall I cut off and hang your head?"

The story would proceed thus, featuring fill-in-the-blanks-type sentences. All that we children understood from the story were two things. First, watermelon juice looked like blood and, second, Bhikiakka was a lost soul. However, ultimately it was he who became a lost soul! His addiction to drinking got so bad that he lost all control of himself.

When he retired from his job, he squandered away his own as well as his wives' money making merry. He decided to spend whatever little remained on his younger son's marriage. The son had no other qualifications except a house in the village, a farm, some mango trees, and a room in Mumbai. On the basis of these assets, the son earned himself a beautiful young wife. The marriage was to take place in the evening. The bride's people came with their relatives to the groom's village. My sisters-in-law from Phansawale, Parvati and Vitha, also went to attend the wedding. We too came from Ratnagiri.

We were very keen to see the new rites by which the marriage would be performed. The bride had already arrived and was staying in a house nearby with her family and guests. There would be no *haldi* ceremony, where the bride and groom were rubbed with turmeric before their baths, and the village women were forbidden to sing the usual marriage songs. So they were quite upset. They kept dropping in to see the kind of preparations that were on. Some of these were just like traditional marriages. A big pandal covered with coconut leaves was erected in front of Akka's house, over the courtyard, the floor polished with fresh cow dung, a *rangoli:* designs with white rice flour paste drawn on the green floor. The rangoli was partially spoilt, stained by streaks of greenish cow dung. The pandal was decorated with colorful *patakas* or paper flags. All of these things were the same as before. But the table and two chairs arranged in the courtyard were certainly new. Finally one old woman, quite mystified, asked, "Why this table and chairs? Is the school teacher coming to perform the marriage?"

Many women gazed at the mike set up in front of the table with candid curiosity. They were intrigued by the loudspeaker, which looked like the trunk of an elephant. And when it began blurting out songs, their jaws fell open with amazement. Slowly guests began to assemble.

Bhikiakka was all decked up today in a brocaded nine-yard sari. She wore a golden bormal round her neck and gold-plated copper bangles around her wrist. She used to have many ornaments, but most of these went down her husband's liquor bottle. Her husband, dressed in a dhoti, shirt, and cap, kept walking around, intimidating people by moving his bloodshot eyes. The house was packed with guests. Her elder son, his wife, daughters, sons-in-law, other relatives, and many other people had come to attend the wedding.

The villagers did not have to do much except enjoy the marriage feast. The white-robed Buddhist priest conducted the wedding single-handed, right from shopping to performing the marriage rites. He first covered the table with a milk-white piece of cloth, placed the photographs of Dr.

Ambedkar and the Buddha on it, garlanded the photographs, and offered some flowers to the Buddha. Next he lit five candles, dropping molten wax on the plate in which to stick the candles. After this he took a glass made of brass, filled it up with rice grains, and stuck some lighted incense sticks in it. Then he took a branch of the peepul tree, put it in a small mud pitcher filled with water, and dipped the end of a white thread in it. The preparations were complete. Now he asked people to send the white sari bought for the bride to her. The groom's sisters, sisters-in-law, and aunts departed to do the job.

Some women minutely observed each movement of the Buddhist priest. Their evident interest in what he was doing made him feel all the more important. He would knock the mike occasionally to see whether it was working and also to make people aware of his importance.

After some time, the groom, dressed in a white pajama, shirt, and white cap, arrived and was made to sit on the chair. The bride came draped in the white sari. Again the priest tapped on the mike and said "hello, hello." Some of the women cracked jokes at this, but some of them took it as part of the new marriage ritual. The priest would not let anybody except the bride and the groom come forward. All instructions were given on the loudspeaker and broadcast to the entire village.

Before commencing the rituals, the priest asked permission of the president and all other members of the community to go ahead with the marriage. Someone seconded the proposal. Then the *Panchasheel* and *Trishsran*[1] were recited and the bride and groom exchanged rings. They had to take twenty-two oaths, which the priest made them repeat after him. Next they put garlands of marigold flowers around each other's necks and we showered petals of the same on them. Since they were standing at a distance, most of the petals we threw fell on our own heads. When the mangalsutra with black beads was brought in for the bride, the priest rejected it and admonished the relatives to bring one with white beads. But since it was difficult to get white beads at the eleventh hour, he was told to make do with the black beads and the matter was sorted out. In those days many girls were given mangalsutras with white beads at the time of marriage, but later on the white beads were quietly replaced with the traditional black ones.

After the ceremony of exchanging garlands and tying the mangalsutra was over, five married women were invited to apply the haldi-kumkum on the bride and offer her toe rings. Everything proceeded quietly, without the usual cacophony, the bride trembling like a leaf when the ear-shattering drums were played and at the deafening outbursts of tashe! In fact, most people thought that the marriage was a drab and dull affair. Many women were openly critical and dying to sing the usual marriage songs, but they were strictly forbidden because the songs included the names of gods!

Many of the guests proceeded to give presents to the wedded couple. Their gifts began to be publicly announced on the mike. "XYZ has given a brass tiffin box." … "So and so gives five rupees." The husband received many brass utensils and more money than the bride. She got only a small brass jar and two rupees. The public announcement of gifts encouraged even those who had no intention of giving any to come to the mike with at least eight annas or a rupee. Once this part of the program was over, arrangements for lunch began. Plates made from leaves were arranged in the pandal and children, and some adults too, took hold of the mike to create an ear-splitting racket till somebody removed the mike from their hands and stowed it away. People sat down to eat in the light of petromax lamps and ate well. The helpings served were generous, which was something unusual. Usually, servers just pretended to put a lot of rice on the plate when only a few morsels fell on it. The families were poor and could not afford to serve lavishly. So the guest would have to be satisfied with whatever little he got. If anybody asked for a second helping he would be called a glutton. Poor families would serve simply hot water, made sour with leaves of the mango tree, to go with the rice. Our poor hungry people would relish even that.

Once I went to attend a wedding at my sister-in-law's place, along with two of my nieces. When we three stout girls sat down to eat and began asking for rice again and again, the cook got angry. "Whose daughters are these anyway?" He burst out. "They are eating like monsters." Then someone answered him, "They are from our Sushi's family! Daughters of Arjun Master!" On hearing this, the host came forward. "Oh! Are they? All right … all right … let them eat as much as they want! Serve them well!" The cook returned with more rice. But being called a monster was not easy to digest, and we politely declined.

Here, however, it was different. Though the house was on the brink of a financial disaster, they did not want to make it known. The Jobber himself lurched all over the pandal in his drunken state, urging people to eat more.

After dinner, children were asked to sing songs. Since I was an urban, schoolgoing child, they clamored for a song from me. So I sang a poem from a textbook of mine about a boy called Shravan. It was my favorite poem, and I sang it with gusto. When I began singing it, an old woman said, "At least sing it with the groom's name in it!" Immediately I substituted the groom's name in the place of Shravan. Shravan was a poor child devoted to his parents, whom King Dashrath killed by mistake with a bow and arrow. No one knew that the poem had such a tragic meaning. I did, but I turned the poem into a song and had no qualms about replacing the word Shravan with Janardan, the bridegroom's name! The joy of singing a song with the groom's name in it outweighed everything else. Eventually, I recited this poem not only at this wedding but also at many more!

Five

I enrolled myself in Shirke High School in Ratnagiri in the eighth class. My older brother Shahu was a student of the same school. He had received first-class marks in his matriculation examination the previous year and went to Mumbai for further education. He got himself enrolled in Siddhartha College and found a room to stay in the hostel in what was Dr. Babasaheb Ambedkar's bungalow, Rajagriha. But Mumbai simply overwhelmed him. There was nobody to guide him. Insensitive co-students in the hostel, a terrible feeling of homesickness, the usual familial fights between Bhai and his wife, and his own addiction to tobacco and cigarettes—everything made life difficult for him. He would go to college and come back with a mind as blank as an empty shell. He did not even know what a syllabus meant! So, finally, when he failed in the first-year examinations, he came back to Ratnagiri.

After coming back, however, he got a job in the office of the Ratnagiri Jail. He also got himself enrolled in Gogate College at Ratnagiri. The principal, Professor Javadekar, helped him tremendously, and somehow the sinking ship of his education was afloat again. There were some people in the college who behaved as if they were doling out the scholarship money for backward-class students out of their own pockets! Kulkarni, the head clerk, was very sympathetic to the backward students and took a lot of trouble on their behalf. He would himself copy out, in large letters, circulars about the dates of submitting applications for a free studentship or scholarship forms for students and pin them up at various places inside the college so that students would not miss them. He would meet students and counsel them. He helped several students this way.

Shripat Kamble, a friend of my brother's, began to call Shahu by the name Shyam, and it stuck to him. We too began to call him by that name. He would have changed his name legally, but later on he came to know the great work of Shahu Maharaj of Kolhapur and gave up the resolve to have his name changed.

Shripat had lost both his parents. He lived with his brother who was employed as a sweeper in Ratnagiri. An ordinary, dark-skinned person of average height, he usually went quite unnoticed. But he had a winning smile and a beautiful, melodious voice (he sang like Mohammad Rafi), which instantly endeared him to everybody. No school program would be complete without him. His classmate Asha Jog, who also sang very well, was called Asha Bhosle's "duplicate." The two sang duets and songs from Marathi plays together. Later, when Asha got married, her husband told her, "From now on you will sing only for me!" That was the end of poor Asha's singing. Shripat stopped his education halfway and went to Mumbai. Later, one of my nieces got married to a cousin of his and he officially became a member of our family. But even before that he always loved us as his own family, and the situation has not changed a bit even today. He is the only man I know who is very happy to participate wholeheartedly in the happiness of others.

Once I went to his house, with my sister-in-law and a niece, to meet his brother's wife, who had received a telegram about her father's death. The grieving woman was literally singing her grief. Her words came out in a singsong manner, in varying rhythms and different speeds. She cried for some time and then took a break. Words dropped out of her mouth as if in slow motion:

"O ... h ... d ... e ... a ... r ... f ... a ... th ... e ... r, ... wh ... e... r ... e ... h ... a ... v ... e ... y ... o ... u ... g ... o ... n ... e?"

Then suddenly changing track, they would tumble out of her mouth at a literally breakneck speed! "WherewillIseeyouagain?" It was astonishing!

She went on and on like that, wailing/singing his praises in that singsong way. It was so funny! But we could not laugh aloud. We turned our faces toward the wall and tried to control the rising laughter so hard that our stomachs ached with the effort. Finally, we simply gave up and the laughter just tumbled out. But we took care to keep our faces averted. Any casual observer would have taken us to be such sensitive women ... weeping so hard for her poor old father! Later on I told Shripat, "Why don't you ask your sister-in-law to teach you music? She's so good at it!" He smiled mischievously. Shripat followed Shahu to Mumbai. We thought he would join All India Radio as a singer, but he got a job in some company, and that simply killed the singer in him. Occasionally, he sang the typical sad Rafi songs at the birthday parties of our children! That was all the music he got to sing.

Meanwhile, my school started and so did the days of an excitement that was difficult to define, which set my heart aflutter. I did not know what it was that made me feel so. But I could feel my eyes repeatedly turning to look at the boys in my class. I blushed without reason. The silly boys of yesteryear, with runny noses and shorts that threatened to slip off, had suddenly blossomed into school heroes in nice teri-cot, mixed synthetic fiber and cotton, uniforms. The same boys who used to jump around, laugh, and speak so freely had suddenly become quite shy. Their young voices went hoarse, the down on their lips grew darker, and they looked more like "men." Their faces were not the innocent, bold sort that they used to be; a new stealth had crept into their eyes. Even while pretending to speak to a friend, their eyes would stealthily roll in the direction of the girls. They had begun to tease us a lot.

Who knows what kinds of things they said about us, but we, the girls, certainly discussed the boys quite seriously. Girls would report with long faces how some boys followed them to their homes, tried to borrow their notebooks, make them laugh, and so on and so forth. The discussions would invariably end with, "But I am not like that, of course!"

I used to envy these girls so much! Such things never came my way. I do not know how I had offended the boys. I felt so left out. I was so different from all those traditional girls! I was very active! I participated in every program the school organized. I had resolved not to remain behind in anything. Cultural program, drawing competition, sports; not a single event in the school happened without me! I felt no stage fright. I was a very good mimic, and the audience would be in splits to hear my mimicry. I would even mimic our teachers without any inhibition whatsoever! That's probably why students called me Aga, a well-known comedian of ample proportions, from the Hindi films of those days. I was quite plump then, which is another probable reason why I was called thus! The moment the boys saw me approaching, they would shout, "A ... g ... a ..." This would get me very incensed.

Once I came to school as usual. The instant I passed through the gate and entered the school campus, the boys began their chorus—and who knows what happened to me?—but I also shouted back at the top of my voice,

> I don't give a damn for you,
> May someone shit in your mouth for you!

There was a stunned silence! The windows in the teachers' room flew open, and the teachers craned their necks to see who had the guts to retort thus! The boys teasing me disappeared into their classrooms like mice startled out of their wits. From that day on, nobody dared to call me Aga. The boys used to be a little wary of me—because of my boldness, plumpness, or caste!

I liked boys a lot. I was especially keen on some of the boys in our class, like Avinash Torgalkar, Prakash Kode, Anil Dhumak, and Shantanu. But all of them, except Shantanu, were so standoffish! They gave themselves such airs! Shantanu looked like a popular hero of the Hindi films called Bharat Bhushan, save that the former was more handsome. A creamy complexioned boy, he had a beautifully carved face with proportionate limbs. In *Swayamwar*, the famous Marathi Sangeet Natak, Rukmini, Krishna's beloved, describes the beauty of her paramour Krishna, saying, "He is so beautiful that whichever part of his body I look at, my eyes simply stay glued to it." The same thing happened to me when it came to Shantanu. But this O-so-beautiful boy was nothing but a meek vegetable! Had someone slapped him, he would have said, "Thank you" and turned the other cheek! He would not participate in any program or competitions! He would talk to me, but every time he opened his mouth I thought I was talking to a baby.

Another extremely important topic among us girls was "menses." We called it the touching of the crow.[1] By the time girls reached their eighth class, they would have come to know the real meaning of this expression.

Everybody would be "touched by the crow," but few were willing to admit it. It meant that we were no longer children; we had grown up and become women. Nobody wanted to admit that. It was more or less a shameful thing! We would all hide our real ages, using as tight a bra as possible so the bust would not show. Some would even smash the pimples on their faces in order to make their faces look immature.

It was known that the beginning of menses marked the imposition of restrictions on girls who had them. "Don't do this, don't go out, don't stay out for long …" There was no end to the no's that we had to listen to. All the girls would be curious to find out who had started her period and who had not. But everyone would keep her period a closely guarded secret. It would be a hot topic of discussion when someone was found out. The girls would point and whisper, "Hey, watch that smarty's skirt; yeah, the one with the stylish braid! Isn't there a red stain behind?" Or someone would whisper, "You know what? I went to that XYZ's place the other day. Do you where I found her sitting? At the back door, with her plate, bowl, and clothes! And how she shows off, as if she has not yet started!"

"But what about you?" I would deliberately ask.

"Oh, no! I haven't! I'm just thirteen, you know!"

"But doesn't everyone start by thirteen?"

I would try to be smart and pry.

"Ah, then you must have started already!"

She would be smarter!

"Oh no! Ain't I as young as you?" I would lie smoothly. Actually, mine had started the year before.

When I remember the day my period started, I am amused. But that day, when I found my skirt stained all red, I had burst into tears. But Aaye had laughed. "Come on, what are you crying for? Every woman has to go through this. Good. At least now you will have a little more sense! Now don't cry. Change your clothes, take a pad, and go sit at the back door." This made me cry harder. As it was, people in the class kept me at a distance because of my caste. Now because of this even my own people in the house would keep me away! My sister came in. She had been through all this. She said, "There is no need for you to sit secluded. Behave naturally, as usual, in the house. There is nothing like sin or merit in starting your periods. It is just a natural thing to happen to a woman!" She went on explaining in this vein for a long time. Maybe it was because of her friends like Prabha Godbole and Manda Rege that she knew a lot about such things. However, neither I, nor my mother, understood much of it! My sister managed to silence Aaye. I bathed, changed my clothes, and did not sit secluded. But I found walking a little difficult and awkward.

Why should only women have to suffer like this? Why are men free? The questions bothered me for a long time. One day Bhikiakka was mighty amused as she told me a story: "In olden times, it was men who used to get periods, but that would be in an underarm. One day Parvati saw the menstrual blood flowing out of Shankar's underarm and said to him, 'My Lord, it doesn't look very nice! So what you have in your underarm, give it to me in my underbelly.' Since then women have had to endure this." I was so angry at Parvati! Why did she have to feel so much for her husband? Well, if she loved him so much, she could have spoken only for herself! But why punish all women?

But there was something odd that happened. When my sister or sister-in-law had their periods, they had to sit at the back door, secluded, whereas I could move anywhere in the house. The temple was an exception, though. I used to be afraid God would punish me and make me blind. Once, a friend asked me, "Why aren't you coming to the temple?" I answered, "Oh, because we are Buddhists now. Why should I?" But that was only for the sake of giving an answer. The underlying psychology had hardly changed.

Now, with these physical changes in me, I noticed something else. Though the boys in my class or school did not pay me much attention, the boys in our family and community started frequenting our house. Their behavior had subtly changed too. They tried to attract me with promises like "I'll give you berries," "Let's go to the village and swim in the river," "Let's go and pluck tamarinds or amlas from the trees," or "Let me give you champak flowers!" They would be eager to offer all kinds of things.

At such times, I would remember what the girls told me when we discussed things in school. A girl had said, "My stepbrother sits on my sister's stomach and has threatened to do the same thing to me if I told anyone." Another one said, "My maternal uncle plays dolls with me and pretends to be my husband, drags me into an alcove, and presses me hard."

Recently one of my friends told me that their neighbor comes to play with her daughter and pinches the young child in particular parts of her anatomy. Every girl, I think, goes through this experience.

There was a small piece of land around our house. Aaye grew a little paddy there for us. A farmer called Sanagare came to till that land for us with his tiller and bullocks. Once Aaye sent me to his house to call him. When I reached his place, he was going somewhere in his bullock cart. But when I told him that Aaye had called him with his tiller, he put the tiller in the cart and asked me to jump in. Since he was going to our house, I did so. He whipped his bullocks and they sprinted off. But the cart did not stop at our gate. So I shouted, "Stop, stop. Aren't you coming to our house to till our land?" He whipped his bullocks again and said, "I'll till you instead!" I was so frightened that I jumped down from the running cart.

However, I did not tell any of this to Aaye. I was certain that that she would have simply torn him apart. And yet ... I was so ashamed, that I simply could not bring myself to tell her.

Of course, in spite of all this, I had a keen desire to mix with boys. But Aaye would keep a close watch on us, like a policeman. If she suspected anything, she showered curses on the boys and drove them away. Then she would give me long lectures.

She would tell me the weirdest things. "Once you start your period, if a man so much as touches you, you'll be pregnant." She would also tell me that if a woman accepted things, like water, flowers, a leaf bowl, and so on, from a man, she would be pregnant. Then many mythological examples would follow. Karna was born out of an ear, Brahmadev from the navel; the mothers of Ram and Lakshman bore them because they had eaten rice touched by Dashrath! She had listened carefully when Baba had read the scriptures aloud! Initially, I too used to believe all this! I was curious to know where exactly babies came from. Once when I saw my sister-in-law delivering a baby in our house, the scales fell away from my eyes. Besides, our physiology-hygiene teacher explained things at length in the class with the help of diagrams of animals and plants. His examples used to be so strange! Once he told us that flowers were the genitals of plants. For a long time after that a glimpse of a flower would make me go red in the face. Poor Aaye had no idea how our knowledge had expanded in school. She would keep trying to scare me by telling mythological stories. However, after all this, I found it very difficult to behave normally with the boys who came to our house.

If this was my problem at home, a very close friend of mine called Sunanda was troubled by something else. She was my classmate and neighbor too, as her house was very close to ours on the road. We always used to be together; we were inseparable. Sunanda was a beautiful girl. She resembled Baby Nanda, a popular actress of the Hindi movies then. She would comb her hair like the actress, put a large *bindi,* a kumkum mark like a dot, on her forehead, and even smile and speak like her. She was a hot favorite among the boys. Even the male teachers in our school would ogle her. Our thin, emaciated-looking drawing teacher was absolutely mad for her. He would chide us if we did not bring our own colors to the drawing class, but brought his own tubes of color for her. She could not even draw a single line straight; but he would urge her to become an artist and promise to coach her individually for the GD (General Diploma) Arts course. He was literally wasting away for her. But she either failed to notice it or chose to ignore it because her heart was otherwise occupied.

She had a secret, and as her closest friend only I knew it. She was in love with a young man. All that had happened between them was no more than a glance, that is, he had glanced casually at her just once. She mistook it as a sign of his love and since then had been moonstruck. This probably was the result of seeing too many Hindi films. Both of us had mastered the art of giving false notes from parents to the teachers. We would regularly miss classes to go to Hindi movies. Sunanda lapped up the stories of rich heroes and poor heroines and I yearned for a marriage with some lame, blind, or disabled guy. It was sad that there was none of that sort around!

Sunanda's affair was totally a one-way street. The man she loved was born with a golden spoon in his mouth. He was extremely rich and never traveled except by car. He had a big shop dealing in spare motor parts in the market, where he would go every morning. She knew the times when he would go to and return from work by heart. She then would thrust everything aside and make herself up nicely. She would stand in the courtyard like a film heroine, waiting for her beloved. Half her soul would be concentrated in her ears, eager to hear the sound of his horn, the other half in her eyes to see him. He reveled in this attention. He would turn to look at her, favor her with a brief glance, and throw a smile at her. Her sister and I used to watch this exchange. Sometimes we would tease her so! But the affair did not proceed even an inch beyond this. However, she refused to go anywhere during those days for fear of missing even one chance of seeing him. His passing by had become a part of her life, her very life force.

The fresh glance would be the theme of our chat. Naturally I would get bored to death listening to her. But I could not avoid the chat as she was the only friend I had. I yearned to have a relationship of the sort myself so that I could talk to her about it. Since I had nothing of my own, I had to discuss somebody else's affairs with her. Engrossed with such affairs, we would endlessly keep walking the road between our house and hers. Finally, in sheer exasperation, Aaye would throw a stone in our direction, and that would end our talks.

Once we were returning from school on a day "the crow had touched me." I was aching. Sunanda was constantly talking about "his look." I was trying very hard to pay attention so as not to hurt her. Finally, we reached our house. But she went on and on. And then suddenly she stopped and said, "Who's that man in your tenant's house? Look, there he is, in white clothes." I turned to look. He was a slim young man. I quickly entered our house, put away my school bag, and had a wash. No sooner did I come out, Aaye handed me a cup of tea and said, "Go, give this to the young man in Vasanti's house."

"Who's he?"

"A friend of Khedaskar, Vasanti's husband."

"So?" I was really surprised. Vasanti's husband was much older. How could this man be his friend? Aaye had accepted Khedaskarbhau as her "son."

She went on, "He and Khedaskarbhau worked together in an office in Rajapur. Now he has been transferred here. He has come with a note from Khedaskar. Since Vasanti has her period, she asked me to make tea for him. Take it. Go, give it to him."

I could not help smiling at this. I was in the same state as Vasanti. The moment I went with the cup of tea to Vasanti's place, she said, "This is Vimal, our landlady's daughter."

"Yes, I know," he said. "I've heard a lot about her from Khedaskarb-bhau." The young man said, staring at me. He was a dark man with a fresh-looking face. He had a wide forehead, amber eyes, straight nose, thick curly black hair, nicely trimmed moustache, and smiling lips. Somehow, I was tickled inside. At any other time, I would have been naughty enough to ask, "And what have you heard from Khedaskarbhau about me?" But I was tongue-tied. I blushed and handed him the cup of tea.

"Which class are you in?" he asked, taking the cup from me.

"Eighth."

"Hum … nice!" What was nice about it?

"So you draw well ... participate in all programs ... win many prizes ... don't you?" He went on to say.

He appeared to know quite a lot about me. I realized he was interested in me. Excited by his words of praise, I began chatting with him. Soon I found myself telling him all kinds of silly things about my school.

Aaye realized that I was going a bit too far. She called me home on the pretext of some work. He too got up to go. "All right, I'll leave now," he said. "I have to attend the office here from tomorrow."

"Have you any arrangement for your lodgings and meals? Otherwise we can provide you with the meals," Vasantivahini asked him from the back door. She had a special style of speaking. She would always use verbs in the plural form to describe herself. She was from Kolhapur where they spoke the language used by the royal families of the higher-caste Maratha community. Many women from poor Kunbi communities in the Konkan may also be found using this verb form, perhaps because a lot of them had worked as bondmaids in the royal Peshwa households and probably picked it up from there.

"All right," Harishchandra replied. "I am staying with my friend." He gave the detailed address, looking at me. Then he turned and left.

I entered my house. The stomachache and pain in my calves had disappeared and a sweet yearning was coursing through my blood. Is this what Sunanda means by her "deep something"? I asked myself. Whatever that may be, I was happy for another reason. Finally I had something of my own to tell her, and the thought brought a glad smile to my lips.

I wanted the young man to visit Vasantivahini's house more often. I liked chatting with him. I also noted that he had enjoyed being with me and wanted it as much as I did. It took me more than a couple of years to realize that we loved each other. Harishchandra had the habit of repeating anything at least twice—and with the same enthusiasm. Everybody in his village, Bhirwande, was said to have this habit. People from that village were jocularly called "the Bhirwande books."

There was a story behind this. Some Marathas in this village had fought bravely in the British army. As part of the ruling class, they carried great prestige. Among them were four khot families, living on four different wadis in the village, held in very high esteem. Many programs in the village could take place only with their permission. One of these would be the reading of holy books in the temple in the month of Shravan (mid-

July to mid-August). The Brahmin priest would read holy books in the temple, and the entire village flocked to listen. The Brahmin priest would begin the reading with the permission of a khot present on the occasion. But after the bhat had read a little bit, another khot would come and angrily object to the reading, asking how it could have begun without his permission. He would make the bhat read the story right from the beginning. The third khot would arrive a little later, then the fourth. They would again raise objections and make the bhat reread from the beginning. Thus people got into the habit of saying the same things again and again, without proceeding further. Harishchandra kept repeating this story to us, again and again. He would come, eat with us, and go away. He stayed with one of his friends called Mohan Girap and had his meals in a small hotel. Everything was normal, as usual. However, once I asked him a question that I should not have asked. Who knows why.

It happened like this. I had started reading popular romantic writers in Marathi like Kakodkar. I lingered on many words in these novels. The heroine would always flush pink or blush crimson. I too wanted to experience some of these shades. Once I came across the word *nitamba*, which meant buttocks. I had gauged the meaning of the word from the context, which was really crystal clear. But I wanted to be naughty. It was a good thing I had not noted the word *uroj* (breasts) then!

One evening, Harishchandra came home to visit us as usual, after his office was over. We had a small room as our study. He would sit there. I had just returned from school. Tai, my elder sister, was not yet back from her office. Aaye was busy doing something at the back door. I brought a jar filled with water and a glass and kept them on a table nearby. Then I sat in front of him on a chair. As usual he started inquiring about my school and studies. I got up and, pouring water from the jar into the glass, pretending to be hesitant, asked him with an innocent expression on my face, "There is a word that I cannot understand. Could you please explain it to me?"

Looking at me with his piercing eyes, he replied easily, "Sure, which word?"

My tongue refused to utter the word, but I forced it, "*Nitamba!* What does it mean?

For one moment he was dumbstruck! He had extended his hand to take the water but, changing tack midway, he suddenly threw both his arms around me and showed me exactly what the word meant. This was so unexpected that the shock sent both my arms flying around his neck. The water spilt all over him, and he was drenched. And, like a typical Kakodkar heroine, I flushed pink, blushed crimson, and ran into the house. I really had not expected him to do anything of the sort!

After this, we would sit chatting for long hours. We also began meeting secretly. In those days, any girl who had fallen in love would be considered "fast." I remember a man in his forties called Sawant and his young *mehuni*, his wife's sister, standing at the gate of the Zillah Parishad office near the mental hospital, talking to each other from eleven thirty in the morning till late afternoon. Sometimes the chat would go on till the evening. They would stand there chatting, rooted to the spot. People passing by would look at them scornfully or mockingly. But they would be completely impervious to such looks, beyond caring. The meetings and chat stopped only when they got married. Both must have got spondylosis after all those days spent standing and talking. I always used to wonder, "How can they be so shameless? What must they be talking about?" I got the answer when our clandestine meetings started. Then I realized that such parameters did not apply to lovers!

Everybody in our family noticed that Harishchandra came to our house frequently and that we sat chatting for hours. They had no objection to his coming as a friend. But nobody wanted us to be married. He was only an SSC-pass and worked as a simple clerk. My sister wanted my husband to be at least a graduate. My brother in Mumbai wanted me to marry a man who was more educated than me and equal to us in status. And my mother considered my age, sixteen years, as quite dangerous. So when Harishchandra came visiting, she kept me occupied in some work. She often threw veiled suggestions at him to come less frequently and leave sooner. She also told Vasantivahini about this. Moreover, she had instructed Shahu to spy on me. He would always be on my track, a huge stone in hand.

There were just two spots near our house in Ratnagiri where one could go for a quick chat and return in a short while. Harishchandra and I would meet there. One was Thiba Point. This was located at the top of the hill, near the bungalow of King Thiba. The view was lovely. A vast expanse of greenery spread out below. One could see the long-winding river that embraced the sea and its deep waters, the limitless rolling expanse of the Arabian Sea, the Pawas Hill standing in the midst of the sea on the left and, on the right, the historic fort of King Shivaji, with a sky-high *sthambha* or pillar at one end and the Ambabai temple at the other. When the rays of the setting sun suffused everything with a deep saffron hue, the scene left one mesmerized, spellbound! Lovers, of course, did not forget each other, since love is supposed to be supreme, after all!

The other point was Phanshi. This was the antithesis of the first one. There was a small rivulet in Phanshi. A girdle of huge mango and phanas trees and the thickets of berries on the river bank provided daring pairs of lovers with a convenient cover, where they could sit in each other's arms, hidden from the world. I used the word *daring* because the boys who roamed there were known to be vagabonds. A lot of them would play cards there. Often lovers would break up after a quarrel there, and the cardplayers would end up beating each other up. That's why in Ratnagiri "Let it go to Phanshi" was a popular expression, meaning something like "Let it go to hell." It is still in use.

When I was young, I had been to Phanshi many times with baskets for Mother's customers. But I did not dare to go to Phanshi with Harishchandra. For us it had to be the Thiba Point. Of course, my brother was a big problem. But I was all right in my studies; at least I had not failed after my fourth class. I used to win prizes in sports, drawing, and other competitions. That would somewhat blunt the edge of my family's anger at me.

On a couple of occasions, however, I behaved in a way that placed me in the ranks of people like Sawant and his mehuni. Our tenth-class examination was over and a get-together of students was on. We presented a program called Maharashtra Darshan in which I played a farm laborer, flinging stones at birds to ward them off. I was supposed to wear a green sari and a traditional blouse for this program. We did not have any such sari in our house. So I borrowed it from a friend and changed in school. We were the first to perform. After the program, I changed into other clothes, folding the sari neatly and wrapping it in a piece of paper to return to my friend's mother, and walked to her house. Suddenly, I heard someone calling from behind, so I turned. It was Harishchandra.

"You? Did you come to see our program?" I was quite surprised.

"Yes."

"How did you like it?"

"You looked lovely."

Like Kakodkar's heroine, I was thrilled. "Let's go home." I invited him.

"Not home. Let's go and sit somewhere."

"But ... I have to return this sari to my friend!" A feeble protest from me!

"Never mind. Do it later. Come on. Let's go for a short while." He insisted.

So we went and sat on the rocks right in front of the school gate, behind the Government Guest House. We could see the gate from where we sat. But since it was getting darker, nobody could see us. We went on chatting away about the same old things over and over again ... both of us narrating them with energy and enthusiasm as if they were completely new. While we were chatting like this, the program was over and students left in groups for their homes. We sat quietly in the cool of the evening. Then suddenly Harishchandra glanced at his watch and exclaimed, "Oh my, nine thirty! Mohan must have waited for me and had his food by now. Now our hotel will be closed. No food tonight! Must go hungry!" This last sentence awakened the maternal instinct in me. I said, "You wait here. Let me go and get you something to eat from home."

In spite of his repeated remonstrations, I left the sari with him and ran home. Everybody at home had eaten and was preparing to go to bed. Mother thought I had just returned from the program, so I would eat and go to bed too.

I looked for the leftovers. A dish had some rice and the other had a lot of fish curry. Probably it was meant to serve for tomorrow as well. I took a container, filled it with rice and poured some fish curry on it. Then I took a jar of water, put it in a bag with the container and sprinted off to the hillock where we had been sitting. Poor Harishchandra had got tired of waiting. He was about to leave when I got there. When I placed the container in front of him, he said he had tears in his eyes! We fed each other the rice and curry. It was twelve o'clock by the time we finished eating.

Meanwhile, when my family found that I was not at home there was a commotion. Everybody went out in search of me. My brother had twice passed the school gate. But we had not noticed him! The guest house watchman tried banging his stick against the road. But, since we did not come within his jurisdiction, he had given up trying to oust us from the place.

Finally I got up, worried about what would happen at home. We repeatedly swore to meet each other soon and then pushed off. He offered to take me home. But I knew that if my family saw him they would beat him up. So I declined his offer. He was aware of this as well.

I remember how it was when I got home. When I entered the court-yard, I saw all my family members pacing up and down the verandah, frantic with worry. They looked like a bunch of wild tigers to me. I was sure they were going to pounce on me so I braced myself for the attack and stepped onto the verandah. I was carrying the green sari in one hand. The paper in which it was wrapped had dropped off somewhere. In the other hand I carried the container. My face still had the stale makeup on. I had forgotten to remove it after the performance. My forehead was smeared with kumkum. When they saw me like that, distraught, instead of pouncing on me, they got terribly worried. They all thought that some ghost had possessed me. My sister, who was right at the door, suddenly moved four steps behind.

"So, where were you?" Aaye tried to make her voice stern.

What could I say? Without saying a single word, I dropped the sari and the bag in a corner, got into bed and hid my face beneath the covers.

"Don't ask her anything now. Let's ask her tomorrow morning." I heard my sister's timid whisper. When they opened the bag they discov-ered the container of rice and fish curry and water jar. This convinced them that a ghost had indeed possessed me and it had forced me to get food from the house. For a long time they kept whispering. Finally they went to bed and the whispering grew quiet. But the light was switched on, and I could see from under the covers that Aaye was sitting near my bed, sick with worry. My heart burned with repentance. Finally I dozed off sometime in the early hours of the morning.

In the morning, I could sense every eye observing me minutely. Aaye asked me quietly, "So do you remember what happened at night? And whose sari is this? Did someone give it to you? Did you eat last night? And whom did you take the food for?" She was asking me so many questions. But I never opened my mouth. I just sat there near the stove without saying a word!

"Thank God!" she exclaimed. "Thank God the ghost did not crumble you up. The god of this place has saved you! It's the spirit of the ancestors that's protected you!" She folded her hands and began to pray, facing the east. I felt like bursting into tears. The mystery of the sari was unraveled the next day when I returned the sari to the friend from whom I had bor-rowed it. She had come home to take it back. But the mystery of the rice and fish curry container remained a secret forever. I mean it has remained a secret so far. I did not have the courage to explain it. And it is only now that I am revealing it through my writing.

After this the love fever came down and I turned to studies once again. But, just like malaria, the fever of love too stays dormant for a while and again begins to rear its head from time to time and make the afflicted one shiver. One day I went to the market for something and on my way back looked in the direction of Harishchandra's room, since it was by the roadside. I saw two policemen and some people standing in front of his door. I was suddenly frightened. I went in and found some more policemen inside. They were taking Harishchandra's statement. He was there, standing in the room, saying something, wiping his tears intermittently. My heart started beating fast.

"What's happened? Hein, what's happened?" I enquired.

"Our dear Mohan is gone … " he said and started sobbing again.

"Gone? Where? Why? How?" I was completely bewildered.

Harishchandra did not answer. He was talking to the police.

"Yesterday was Thursday. He was fasting. He had eaten nothing during the day. He had planned to go to a place called Chinchakhari, famous for its Datta temple, where he would end his fast. Since it was Datta Jayanti, many people were going to visit the temple. He would go by a small boat, as usual. But nobody imagined that it would be only two or three."

The police were recording his statement. I found what he said rather confusing. There were a couple of women standing at the door. Finally I went to them and asked what had happened. That's when I came to know the whole story. Mohan and a couple of his colleagues went to Rajiwada after work. They planned to take a boat to Chinchakhari. But that day there was a great rush of disciples. Had they waited any longer, they would have been late reaching the temple. So someone suggested that they take the newly constructed road in the creek to reach Chinchakhari. They were told that many people walked down the road. Immediately three or four friends set off on foot, and Mohan was among them.

It was evening by the time they left. It was a full moon night, and they could see the road. But they never realized that the water level was gradually rising. By the time they noticed, it was too late. The road had disappeared underwater, and they were surrounded by rising waves. The four friends were terrified. Two of them could swim. They somehow began swimming. A friend got stuck in the mud. Mohan went to give him a helping hand, but he too got stuck. Both disappeared in the mud. The two swimmers somehow managed to reach Chinchakhari and raised an alarm. The police were informed. By this time it was early morning. The police had taken a boat, looked through the creek for their bodies, and, finally, when they were certain that they could not be rescued alive, had come to Harishchandra to take his statement.

Was he an alcoholic? Did he have any other addictions? Did he drink? When did you see him last? Who stays at his home? What were his relations with his folks? How was his relationship with you? So many questions!

Finally the questions were over and Harishchandra set off with the police toward Chinchakhari, weeping copiously. Forgetting why I had come to the market, I went with him to Chinchakhari. The police continued to look for the bodies. We sat under a tree, completely nonplussed. I could see Mohan's face in front of my eyes. He did not speak to me much when I called on them. But he used to tease Harishchandra a lot. His parents and brother lived at Rajapur. They were sent a message. The people who were milling around kept saying that the other person who had accompanied him was the only son of his parents, born after five daughters, and they were all feeling sorry for him. I sat by Harishchandra's side till late in the afternoon. I knew that I was there because I was worried more for him than for Mohan. I also knew that Aaye must be waiting for me at home, terribly worried. The police were uncertain about how long it would take to find Mohan's body. Finally I had to leave Harishchandra. By the time I reached home, it was evening.

This time my elder brother gave me a couple of resounding blows and Aaye abused me soundly. I, however, sat near the stove. Not a single sound escaped my lips. But I felt like crying bitterly.

Now Aaye began to urge Bhai in every letter to look for a good boy for Manjula. He brought a couple of prospective bridegrooms. He sent one of them to our house to interview Tai. His name was L. K. Tambe. He was a dark young man, with a hefty physique, a B.A., L.L.B. from Mumbai. Tai wanted her husband to be a lawyer who would later climb to the position of a judge. That was her dream. L.K. fitted this agenda to a T. But he wanted to marry a girl who would work and support him, since he wanted to devote his life to social work without doing a job himself. So she rejected him.

In reality, words like *lawyer, judge* were far beyond the widest scope of our community's imagination. But Tai had a friend called Manda Rege. Her father was a lawyer. Tai used to visit their house quite frequently. She must have got this idea from there. I too would be sent to Mandatai's house with seedlings and flowers from our garden. But whereas I came back only with admiration for her mother, who used to pat me affectionately and press a piece of very tasty coconut *burfi* in my hand, Tai returned with ambitious dreams. Tai was quite a practical and ambitious person, like our father. Aaye used to say, "This daughter of mine will count even the feathers of a flying bird. But look at you. You will find it difficult to count the feathers of even a dead bird!"

Later, I repeated this sentence to my husband impulsively, out of my love for Tai. He repeated the same sentence, but he replaced the word feathers with an unspeakable word and threw it at me quite often. Anyway, that's that.

Tai was a good-looking girl, with sharp features. She was dark skinned, thin, and not very tall. Two teeth protruded from her lips. She was more like Baba. I was an exact replica of my mother.

Tai was the first Dalit girl to have passed the matriculation examination in what is known today as the Ratnagiri district. She had all the assets required for getting a good husband: good education, a job, and a well-placed educated family. Yet she could not get a good proposal.

Finally, my brother made her give up her job and took her to Mumbai with the hope that since it was a place teeming with plenty of eligible bachelors, she would be able to find somebody to suit her own taste. In those days there were jobs aplenty. Once one registered his or her name in the employment exchange, one received at least three or four calls. People would offer jobs to anybody anywhere, out of "pity or sympathy for the poor," without references from influential persons. After going to Mumbai, Tai got a job in a few days. And soon afterward, a relative arrived from Mumbai with a sensational piece of news.

The news was about my sister. It was the first day of the month. She had received her salary that day. After office she was waiting with her friend and her brother at the bus stop at Victoria Terminus to catch a bus to Cotton Green where she was staying. It was the peak hour when all offices closed and it was extremely crowded. Twice they tried to board the bus, but in vain. Finally they managed to get into a double-decker bus. My sister got a place to sit near the back door at the next stop. The conductor came from the front, selling tickets. Her friend's brother put his hand into his pocket to take out his wallet and discovered that somebody had picked his pocket. He shouted, "Conductor, please stop the bus. Someone has picked my pocket. Just now! Please don't let anyone get down." The conductor stopped the bus and stood in the door blocking it. Now the thief, who was standing near the door, was trapped. So, pretending to be a gentleman, he said, "Here is your wallet! You had dropped it here." The brother took the wallet from the thief. He and the other passengers in the bus began to rough him up. There was complete chaos for some time. My sister was watching the scene completely stunned, when someone's fist accidentally landed on her face and two of her front teeth fell out. Her sari got drenched in blood. Now people turned their attention from the thief to my sister. They took her to a dispensary nearby and after applying first aid, sent her home. "They will fix her mouth with a couple of false teeth in a few days," the relative told us.

The news bulletin was over. It left us equally stunned for quite some time. Then suddenly Aaye began to cry. "Suppose she had been hit in the eye or nose!" The very idea made her weep harder. I thought, however, that this was glad news, indeed! Now my beautiful sister had got rid of her protruding teeth that marred her beauty. The impediment to her marriage had been removed! At the same time, I also wondered how much of this story was fact and how much fiction! But I must admit that soon after this her marriage was fixed.

When Tai went to high school, she picked up all the mannerisms of her Brahmin friends. First she started to call mother *Aai* (the standard form) instead of *Aaye* (which was used in the dialect).[2] Then she made us change the informal way in which we used to call our sister-in-law, with the singular verb form. She made us use the plural verb form instead, like the Brahmins.

She was obsessed by brahminic forms of behavior and language! She had a Brahmin friend, Prabha. Just because Prabha's mother addressed her husband by the honorific *Apan,* she also began to call her husband by that pronoun. But, in the process, she forgot the simple rule that if you treat another person with the respect that he does not really deserve you automatically devalue yourself. And she had to pay heavily for it; but that is another story.

After Tai got a job, she had an enclosed stone latrine built for us in our own backyard. Until then we had to go to the bank of a stream far away from our backyard to attend to nature's call. The place was thickly populated with mango, cashew, and other huge trees. A small path led toward the hills through them. We had to sit there hiding ourselves, taking care not to be seen by the men who passed by. Even we, the children, had heard that men attacked women there. A lot of ghost stories were in circulation. It was said that the ghosts shook the branches and grass to produce different noises and that they whistled and shouted too. According to one of my cousins, once she suddenly saw a huge foot right in front of her. Leaving her tin pot behind, she just ran for her life. My mother often wondered who it could have been, a ghost or a sexual pervert. We used to be quite scared to go there alone. We had to take someone along. If we had to go alone, we sat there holding onto the tin pot tightly. But then, in place of the pot, we imagined a big foot, and the very idea was scary enough to make us constipated.

I had a keen desire for new clothes. But the only new clothes I would ever get were school uniforms, which Aai had to buy. I had never worn chappals till I was in the ninth class. Once a boy called Gangaram Kamble stayed with us for a year. When he went back to his own village, he left his tattered old canvas shoes behind. Shahu used those shoes for a whole year after that. In such a situation, who would care for my poor feet? So when Tai bought a lovely silk skirt and a blouse and high-heeled brown sandals for me, I felt like the proverbial woman who set fire to her own house because that gave her a chance to flaunt her new gold bangles and impress those who would admire them. I too wanted to set fire to all the baskets Aai kept in the courtyard for sale so that I could dance around the fire, flaunting my new clothes and sandals. Tai was such a loving sister! Often I failed to understand the expressions in her eyes. I still recollect an incident.

Those were the days of the Shimga festival. It was the custom for the children of the poor to impersonate a mythological demon called Shanka-sur and go begging for alms. They would cover their heads with black cloth on which they drew eyes and noses and go visiting people, asking for alms. The children would dance, singing songs like

> Come on, you can't say no,
> Without money we won't go!
> The mother of the fox eats coals for food,
> For a dhabu paisa, in the attic she looks.

They would jump high in the air, shout, and beg for alms. Sometimes, a group of khele artists from distant villages would come to our door and dance to the beats of the *mridunga* in the blazing sun. Rivulets of sweat would run down their bodies, glistening in the sun, and the sweaty smell would assault our nostrils when we gave them some coins.

At night a group of people from the Bhangi community in Ratnagiri would arrive in the fields. Some would be heavily made up to look like women—eyes lined with kohl and lips painted red. They would be dressed in brocaded long skirts and short blouses and wore elaborate wigs and flowers like dancers in the films. Some would wear stylish trousers and shirts with colorful kerchiefs tied around their necks, while some would be in shirts and dhotis and wore brocaded caps on their heads. They danced to the tunes of beautiful songs from fresh Hindi films and captured the audiences' admiration with their rhythmic movements. This group was called Rombat. They would first dance in the courtyards of rich people. Toward the early hours of dawn, they came to our neighborhood, a little jaded and tired. The moment we heard the sounds of their drums and harmonium, we rushed out of our houses. The fragrance of their scents and attar lingered long after they left. Sometimes Shahu and I followed these people to other people's doors where they performed.

Sometimes some patients from the leprosy hospital in Ratnagiri tried to imitate the Bhangi people in order to make a little money. Once some lepers came to our field dressed in colorful saris, heavily made up, carrying petromax lamps to perform. The moment they arrived, a stink, like that of rotting fish, assaulted our nostrils. While I was rushing forward to see them, my mother pulled me back. One of them was carrying a harmonium, hung with a string around his neck. His fingers had rotted, but he played on the harmonium with whatever was left of them. A couple of them had just two holes where the nose ought to have been. Yet they had applied layers of makeup on their wasted faces. They sang, throwing their necks back. All wore canvas shoes, into which they stuffed their feet. Their swollen blackish legs looked so pathetic with those shoes on. They began to sing an erotic song in which a woman invites her lover to come and sit with her on a bed of flowers. After they had sung a couple of stanzas and danced a little, Aai nearly drove them out, "All right, all right, that's enough! Now go and dance at someone else's door." She gave them a couple of coins and they departed, the anklets they wore making a musical sound. Tai's eyes filled up with tears. In a voice almost choked with tears, she said, "Poor things! All joy is over for them! Yet they are trying to give joy to others!"

So when this sensitive sister of mine left for Mumbai, I should have felt sad. But I was actually happy. It meant one watchman less! She kept a close watch on me! In any case, she was going for a good cause.

Before going to Mumbai she went to Phansawale to meet Govindada-da, Thoralibai (we now used the Marathi word *bai*, giving up the dialect one, *bay*), the sisters-in-law and their children. She was the one among us who loved the village the most. She swam in the river, but I don't remember ever seeing her play. For that matter, neither did my brother Shahu. He sometimes played *gilli danda* with Shantaram in the paddy field, but that was very rare! All my siblings had somehow given up their childhood too soon and became adults at a young age! Who knows whether they had grown up prematurely or if it were I who remained a child, even as a grown-up!

Finally Tai received the proposal she was waiting for. The man was a graduate and doing his L.L.B. He was very industrious. Since he had passed his matriculation examination, he had been doing small jobs to support his family and cope with the expenses of his college education. He used to sit in front of the post office or the ration shop and help people fill in forms for a small fee. He had also involved himself in so-cial work, such as collecting funds for people affected by the floods, the movement advocating a ban on cow slaughter, the Samyukta Maharash-tra movement for a separate state for the Marathi-speaking people, the election campaign of candidates of the Scheduled Caste party, and so on. But he was not like the earlier candidate Tambe. He did not want to get trapped in social work. He wanted to practice as a lawyer and later become a judge. He fitted Tai's dream perfectly. He also liked Tai. They approved of each other.

After this first meeting, however, a series of other meetings had to be arranged to obtain the seal of approval from the community and the Caste Panchayat. Poor Bhai had to do a lot of running around. First he had to organize a meeting of the community to inform them that Tai had received a proposal. In the second of these our future brother-in-law's family had to propose to the girl in front of the community. A third was held to inform the community that the groom approved of the bride, and a fourth (this time both the bride's and groom's extended families had to be present) to decide on the date of the marriage. A final meeting was held among the officeholders of the local Panchayat to allow Tai and our future brother-in-law to apply for membership in the Bauddha Jana Panchayat and seek their permission to fill in forms and sign them at the time of the wedding.

Poor Bhai would get so exhausted running around! He had to go to each office bearer's house to invite him for the meetings, and he could do so only after attending office. People of the village now living in the city were located in diametrically opposite directions! One was at Bhendi Bazar, another at Tardeo, besides Vikroli and Andheri. None of our people had gone beyond Andheri. Most of them were employed in diverse workplaces. Some of them worked in mills, some were sweepers, and some did private jobs. Their schedules would never match. And if one got invited while the other did not, this would invariably lead to misunderstandings.

"Why would you invite me? I am no sahib! Just a small man! The rich enjoy sweets, the poor get kicks. So why should he invite me?" The Panchayat members would never come on time. When Bhai somehow managed to bring them together for the meeting, they would go on and on about trivial things.

The same questions asked earlier, in the first meeting, would be repeated endlessly. "So, tell us, how did you manage to come into our farm?" "I came to know that there was a nice flower in your farm." If the girl were uneducated, the word *flower* would be replaced by *animal*. Then they would ask for the "biodata" of both: name, village, address, and so on. Then the most important questions, "Had you seen him/her before?" This had to be answered in the negative even if they had known each other.

Once these hurdles were over, the most important item on the agenda would be *basta*: the wedding attire. People from both sides created a lot of problems, especially at this time. Finally, they gathered together at some cloth shop in Mazgaon in the Mahatarpakhadi area. Tai did not come to buy her marriage sari. Instead, she sent me with Bhai. She had asked me to buy a pink nine-yard sari for her.

In the end, some fifteen or twenty women from both families entered the shop for the basta. Men stood outside on the street. When we started to look at saris with interest, they sent a message, "Buy the white marriage sari first." They pulled all the strings as we shopped! The shopkeeper showed us a couple of white nylon saris, which were quite transparent. He appeared to be quite well informed about our Buddhist-style marriages! "You buy this," he said. "How long will the bride be required to wear this sari? Only for a short time!" The women selected a better sari from among the ones shown to us and sent it out for the men's approval. When everybody, including the bridegroom, approved it, the sari came back to us. I remembered the old times when the bride's sari went around among the marriage guests for their approval. When the assistant brought out a bunch of *shalu* saris, that is, heavily brocaded silk saris, I said, "Tai wants a nine-yard sari." The women were surprised. They began to ask Bhai, "Really? Is the bride going to wear a nine-yard sari?" When he nodded in affirmation, their faces glowed. "This girl may be educated, but she still believes in the old ways. She is a simple girl, not like these city-bred ones!" I could read their minds. My respect for Tai increased by leaps and bounds. She really had been able to count the feathers of a flying bird! She had also specified the color so as not to make it difficult for the women and the shopkeeper. A pink shalu was duly selected, sent outside for the men's approval, and finally this leg of shopping was over. Then we went to shop for the groom.

Tai's marriage took place in a hall with much fanfare. A band played. This was around 1964 or 1965. The custom of serving ice cream to the wedding guests had just started among the neo-Buddhists around this time. Women learned to sing songs without using the names of gods and goddesses around the same time. The women were eager to sing songs at Tai's wedding. So they sat at one side of the hall and, egging each other on, began to sing.

The Sarcar [government] has fixed at Bykhulla a new iron rail
On which it has started running the fire-train.
The bride Manju sits in a compartment at the back,
And bridegroom Jairam sits in a compartment at the front.
What are you doing, Manju in the compartment at the back?
"I embroider my sari with a golden thread in the compartment at
    the back."
What are you doing, Jairam in the compartment at the front?
"I embroider my cap with a golden thread in the compartment at
    the front."

Tai went to stay with her in-laws after the wedding. They must have been shocked by her brahminic conduct. She used honorifics while addressing her young brothers-and-sisters-in-law and her husband, in Prabha's mother's style! But this effort toward endearing herself to her in-laws was a complete waste, as they took her to be a dumb girl of subhuman intellect.

Tai's house was a one-room "apartment" in a block that consisted of such apartments in a chawl. In that small space lived her parents-in-law, three schoolgoing brothers-in-law and two sisters-in-law. There was only one common toilet for all the families living in the chawl. Tai tried hard to cope with the problems: space, crowding, people, heaps of dirt, spit-covered walls, hoards of flies hovering all over, and the rats and mice. But soon she was at her wits' end. Besides, she had a morning job. She had to get up at the crack of dawn, make chapatis and vegetables for all the people in the house, and reach her office in time to sign the register. She returned to a house in which soiled clothes and dirty utensils would be kept so that she might wash them. Once she had cleaned them, she had to cook the evening dinner! Her mother-in-law had a rule that food should be ready before evening, though it could be eaten any time. She got angry all too easily—when Tai was late in doing something, when she took help from her sisters-in-law, when she did not like what Tai did. Any of these would make her get mad at Tai. She thought that work in the office was nothing but just sitting in a chair and relaxing. She complained, "How much more work will I do?" The outbursts invariably ended in a threat to commit suicide under the train. Sometimes she really pretended to walk out of the house for that express purpose. That's when Tai's father-in-law and husband vented their fury on Tai. Poor Tai poured her heart out to us when she came on a visit, and my brother would say, "Here she comes with her tales of woe!"

I used to feel so angry about Tai's imitating the Brahmin Godbole family! Using honorifics before the names of husband and in-laws, indeed! Our uneducated illiterate village women were much better! They never addressed their husbands so! It was always the singular "you"! I think Tai's use of honorifics created a distance between herself and her husband, which was never there in a husband-wife relationship in our community.

I went to Tai's place a couple of times to meet her. I would always find her busy, working at the stove or cleaning the pots and pans or washing clothes. I would sit on a stool, watching her in-laws and listening to them. Tai's sister-in-law was in the seventh standard then. She would take pity on Tai and offer to help, "Vayani, listen to me. You talk to your sister, let me do this."

Tai would answer, "Even your saying so is a great help. But no, you go and finish your homework! Listen to me and do as I say." The dialogue moved around: "You listen to me," and "No, you listen to me!" The younger brothers and sisters kept running around, constantly flitting in and out the door. The younger sister-in-law would listen to this dialogue and report it to her mother, relaxing on a cot outside, "Aaye, did you hear what Susha said to Vayani? She is telling her not to work." Then Susheela, the helpful sister-in-law, had to explain, "Aaye, I was sitting idle, that's why I offered to help." Their Marathi was very influenced by Hindi. The verbs were formed on the lines of Hindi suffixes. I found it very funny. Later on, of course, their Marathi became more anglicized.

English had been advantageous to our community in many ways. People from the previous generations used to have names either like Kacharya (meaning dirt), Dhondya (stone), Dagadya (stone), Bhikya (begger), or they were given the names of gods. Then names began to be written with English initials, like R. L. Tambe, K. D. Kadam, G. B. Kamble, and so on. Our Nathuram Sakharam Kamble changed his name to N.S. after Nathuram's terrible deed. Everybody called him by his initials, N. S. My sister changed her husband's name from the caste name Kamble to a caste-neutral place name Dabholkar to indicate his town Dabhol rather than his Mahar caste. That would help his lawyer's business more, she thought. Even I was going to change my name from Pawar to Bhirwandekar, but, since Pawar is a surname among the Marathas as well, the plan did not materialize.

Coming back to Tai's mother-in-law, she would always be angry about something. On top of it, when she heard her daughter offering to help Tai, her anger would know no bounds! She would shout at her daughter, "Hey, why do you want to work? Are you her maidservant?" Tai's father-in-law and husband watched all this mutely, without uttering a single word in her favor. They neither protested nor came to Tai's rescue. Anyway, Tai herself never uttered a single word in retaliation.

One day I just dropped in on her. I had to climb three staircases, each of which had some girls and women, brushing their teeth with masheri. They could not visit the toilet early in the morning because of the long queue as they had to reach their offices in time. So they queued up in front of the toilet after returning from work. Their entire timetable had gone haywire. They had to perform these morning chores in the afternoon or evening, and brushing their teeth with masheri while waiting in the queue was a part of their everyday routine. I thought one such girl wanted to tell me something, but she was unable to open her mouth for speaking, as it was full of spit. She just managed a smile at me.

I had to pass by the toilets from which a terrible stench assailed my nostrils. So I pinched my nose hard, walked on, and stood in front of Tai's door. The door was ajar, but there was darkness inside. My eyes took some time to adjust to the dark inside, but Tai saw me from inside. She asked me to come in. For a few minutes I just stood at the door, then saw that something was going on inside. Tai's father-in-law was sitting on the cot, his legs hanging from the bed. Tai and her mother-in-law sat on the floor, leaning against the wall. Lying on the mother-in-law's lap was a small baby wrapped in a thin cover. She had given birth to it at the time of Tai's wedding. I sat near Tai and inquired, "What's wrong?" "The baby has fever," she said. "Since when?" "For quite some time now," she replied. Then she asked if everybody at home was well. But even before Tai had finished asking her a question, Tai's mother-in-law burst into tears. Tai's father-in-law tried to console her, and Tai too began to weep. The baby boy woke up and started a weak whimper, flailing his tiny arms and legs. The thin cover on his body slipped down. I bent down to look at him. His entire body was covered with tiny black pimples. His face and forehead was swollen.

"Is this chicken pox?" I asked. The mother-in-law's tears became still more copious. Then I decided to leave. Tai came to see me off at the staircase. "It is not chicken pox," she said, "it is smallpox." I reported this to Bhai, and when my mother came to know, she dispatched Bhai to Tai's place to fetch her home. But Tai refused to go. "How can I leave my in-laws when they are suffering so much?" We were speechless. Tai took leave for a month and nursed the baby back to health. This was the last epidemic of this dreaded disease. The famous slogan in the campaign against smallpox, "Inform the government of a smallpox case and get a reward of one lakh rupees," came later, though no case was reported. Smallpox had disappeared by that time. Anyway, Tai's selfless service, however, did not amount to much. Her harassment continued. Finally, when it reached beyond the limits of endurance, Tai left her in-law's house and started living independently.

Our visits to our village became less frequent as we grew up. Only when the school or office was closed on account of some holiday could we see the women returning to the village, while they stopped at the well in our small farm to drink water. Among them would be some of our own classmates. But now they were married and carried the burden of their homes on their shoulders. The tradition continued through them. Some worked as stone quarry workers; some had married sweepers and worked in Mumbai somewhere as scavengers. They got suffocated in their eight-by-ten-foot one-room flats where two or three families stayed together. The room would be divided into two or three sections with partitions of hanging saris or covers, one section for each family. Men would sleep on footpaths or somewhere outside in the ground in dry months. But in the rains they all had to cram themselves into the small room. Bhikiakka used to tell us, "We sleep with our legs raised against the wall." This would intrigue me no end. How could they sleep with their feet raised against the wall at ninety degrees? Don't their legs ache? We used to ask her; then she would laugh and answer, "Of course, they ache! When they do, we pull them close to our stomachs and turn on the side. Later we have to stretch them against the wall, in the same position."

Who knows how they managed to do this particular yogic asana! And yet, when many women returned to the village for the planting season, they would be pregnant. Many of them put on a little weight; their cheeks were chubby. They wore new saris and flaunted new bangles, necklaces, earrings, and imitation jewellery, which would be far more fashionable than the jewellery sold by the Gosawi women in the Ratnagiri market. When a woman wearing such things followed her husband with a sack of onions, potatoes, or dry fish and chillies on her head, people would turn back to watch her closely.

If this woman had a civil tongue and a generous hand, women would speak to her with admiration, "Good, now you look so much better. You used to look so tired when you were here," they would tell her. On the other hand, if she was a woman with a caustic tongue and gave herself airs, they hated her. "See how the whore is all decked up! She can't even move her neck, she's so swollen!" Then they would ask each other, "Why has she swollen so much?" And some said this was the *randki suj*—widow swelling!

I had heard this word first from my mother. Aai used to say, "I am a widow but I have never got randki suj!"

When I asked Bhikiakka the meaning of this word, she was taken aback. Instead of answering me, she examined her own arms and asked me a question, "Who has got randki suj? Who says so?"

"No, no! I'm asking this because that's what the village women say about the chakarmani women!"

Akka laughed when she heard this. "You know, for some women, when their husbands die, it is a release from oppression. Then they look a little better, fresh, so people say they have got the randki suj." Then she grew grave and said, "But, let me tell you, I have always been like this, somewhat plump, even before my husband died."

The chakarmani from Mumbai came with a lot of pomp but would invariably ask people for money when returning because he would have squandered all his money away on liquor. I remember one such man who had come to Aai completely drunk. In spite of knowing what a miser my mother was, he refused to budge from our small farm. He kept repeating, "I'll send your money by a money order the moment I reach Mumbai. But please lend me some now!"

Aai lost her temper, "You say you don't have any money now! Then how come you have money to drink?" But he went on and on. "I need to drink because the work I do is strenuous, filthy. When I drink, the work is no more work and filth is not filth." Nobody was interested in listening to such wisdom from a drunkard. People took loans from moneylenders, Pathans or Makadwale, at a heavy recurring interest, to buy things like food, liquor, or treat illnesses. The loans accumulated to such an extent that paying back became impossible. The moneylenders would bash them up. The drunkards would often absent themselves from work, thus giving a full stop to the job and finally to life!

The village people would somehow manage to survive on whatever their tiny farms produced, and a couple of mango trees bore fruit throughout the year. The women in our house like Vithavahini and Parvativahini worked to earn a little money for their families. Their children would neither go to school nor have anyone to guide them. They were like dry leaves fallen off the trees, carried all around by the wind.

Shantaram, my cousin Babi's son, was one such. He attended school intermittently, for a few years, and then dropped out and became a vaga-bond. He whiled his time away in the company of other similar boys, play-ing *viti dandu* with them in paddy fields. He used to steal the cashew nuts and mangoes, coconuts and areca nuts from people's farms at night, cut their grass, and let his animals loose to graze in their fields. He would sell the grass and get drunk on that money. His bundles of grass sometimes contained frogs and even poisonous snakes tied with the stolen grass. Nothing was safe from him. He would steal anything, sell it in the market, and drink on the money thus earned. His logic was "All these were our lands." He would say, "These people, well, their ancestors duped us. They snatched all our land, and now we have nothing. So what grows on these lands actually belongs to us. What's wrong with taking it?" People in the village, of course, would abuse him and complain to his father, following which Govindadada, his uncle, would scold him. Both behaved as if they were sworn enemies.

One day, the women from the village came to my mother with a special bulletin. "Mastarni, do you know Shantaram was going to axe everybody in the house last night!" they said. My mother exclaimed, "You whores!" This was her way of expressing surprise! If she were talking to a woman, it would be "whore"; if it were a man, it would be "You slave!" Anyway, she said, "What are you saying?"

"Let my tongue fall off if I lie," the reporter said and continued with her story. "You know, Shantaram wanted his father's bull for bullfighting. But the old man declined, as he wanted the bull in the field. So Shantaram grew angry and was so furious that he cut up his stick and blanket into tiny pieces using an axe." The reporter left after telling this, but Aai sat stunned for a long time.

Shantaram had loved a girl. But, apparently, she belonged to another caste, and he could not marry her. That was the reason for his frustration, which made him so reckless. In those days, he also used to participate in the *jalsas*, performances that were held by the Ambedkarite movement. But, whereas the other boys sang political songs, he would sing those of frustrated love and broken hearts. Later he got married. Though her name was Pramila, we called her "Shantaram's wife." Because of her use-less husband, she too had to slog to earn her livelihood, along with her mother-in-law, selling grass bundles and other things in the market. Shan-taram did not get along well with her and would often beat her.

Once she came and stood in front of my mother—her forehead covered with blood. Shantaram, for some silly reason, had bashed her head with a big stone. She lay unconscious in a pool of blood for a long time. No one demanded an explanation from him nor came forward to help her. People felt that he was her master and had the right to do anything to her. While she lay unconscious, her master, her savior, was shamelessly making a public announcement, "I have killed a sheep in our field. Anybody interested in getting the blood?"

There were several such women around who suffered at the hands of their heartless husbands. When the torture crossed the limits of their endurance, they came to my mother to confide in her, to give vent to their anger. One such woman, I remember, came to us from the village Pali.

"The son of a bitch beats me up without any rhyme or reason. May his face burn!" She started cursing him. Then she saw her husband coming by and, terrified, asked Mother to hide her. We made her climb the ladder to the loft and hide there. We hid the ladder as well.

The husband arrived with a stick in his hand, his eyes spitting fire. "Where's that whore?" Without asking my mother's permission, he pushed his way into our house. This infuriated her. She shouted, "You bastard, whose house do you think you are in? Get out, get out first!" But he was dead drunk. He searched for his wife everywhere in the house, even looking under the small wooden bench. He asked us, the children, all kinds of questions in order to find out about his wife. When he could not find her, he went up to Aai and, repeatedly touching her feet, apologized again and again. He called Aai Akka! He was a cousin of our first mother, our father's first wife. He kept making flimsy excuses for beating up his wife. By this time the anger had subsided.

"You idiot, you drunkard! What reasons you give!" Aai shouted, "Get up and get out! Go, leave this instant." But he wouldn't stop. "My wife quarrels with my mother. She tells her to get out. She doesn't even wash her sari. She steals food from the house."

His wife, listening from the loft above, started shouting, forgetting that she was hiding from him. Then, without waiting for the ladder, she stepped on the plank in the wall and jumped down. Standing in front of her husband, sitting like a spent force now, she fired at him. "What are you saying? I steal food? What do I steal? Your mother locks up all the food. Even on festival days, when she makes vadas, she counts them before going for a piss and makes sure their number is the same when she comes back. What is there for me to steal? Why should I wash her sari?"

He got up and walked out, his head hanging low, but this was not because he agreed with her but because the effect of the alcohol had worn off.

After he had left, Aai would try to make his wife understand, "Where will his mother go now? Treat her well. You know, every stove will have a *bhanosa!*" Aai always used a saying while speaking to such women, "A woman must eat in the shadow of her thigh," meaning that a woman may eat as much as she wants, without letting anybody know.

A husband from the Pangri village was extremely suspicious of his wife. He would even question her after she returned from attending to nature's call. He would constantly keep a watch on her, beat her, and harass her. This was harassment for him as well.

It was not only husbands or family members who beat up women. If a woman was suspected to have erred, she was brought before the Panchayat for justice and punishment. She was publicly judged, and her other relatives would beat her up as well.

I must have been in the ninth or tenth standard then. One day some women from the village came reporting that a widow was found to be pregnant. The whole village knew who the man was. The village ordered her to abort the baby. She did not listen to them. So she was judged before nine villages and punished in keeping with their verdict. She was made to stand leaning forward, and women kicked her from behind till the child was aborted. The villagers felt this was a valiant act of bravery. They felt proud that they had protected the villages' honor! In another incident, when an eight-month-pregnant woman openly accused her husband of having illicit relations with another woman, the villagers gave her the same punishment. Women, mad with excitement, kicked her till the baby died inside her, and the woman died in pain in a week's time. Why should this so-called honor, this murderer of humanity, this tool of self-destruction, be so deeply rooted in women's blood? Why?

When I was in the ninth standard, we had a teacher called Vasantrao Deshpande who decided to stage a one-act play called *Kalalavya Kandyachi Kahani* (The tale of the onion that poisoned people's minds) for the interschool one-act play competitions. The story is simple. A princess once found an onion among the fruits. Out of curiosity, she started peeling it, which made her eyes water. The tears simply would not stop. The king made a public announcement that the man who made her laugh would receive half his kingdom. So many people came and gave it a try and finally the princess did laugh. The subject was amusing enough for children.

At that time I was quite a hefty girl. My elder sister, who was thin as a straw, used to say, "Don't stand next to me! You will break my bones if you accidentally fall on me!" The teacher thought that I looked funny enough for the role of the king. I had no stage fright, as I regularly participated in many programs. The teacher also knew that fellow students found my mimicry of other teachers quite entertaining. For the role of the king's cook, he chose a girl who was the daughter of our English teacher, Nene, who did not like this and insisted that his daughter be made the king, which Deshpande did not accept. We did lots of rehearsals and performed well in competitions but did not win any prize, but I got at least one for my performance. For quite a long time, the water seller named Aagashe, near Lata Talkies, and some people would call out, when they saw me passing by, "So your royal highness, how are you?" People remembered my role for a long time.

But the impact of the play was not limited only to this. I was asked to speak in a low-pitched loud voice while doing the role of the king for comic effect. So my voice would get hoarse. Then I would chew herbal medicines like *kankol* and *khadi sakhar*. This story had sort of a subplot. Deshpande, our teacher, had fallen in love with a doctor in the town called Tara Lubri. Madam used to come to the rehearsals occasionally. She had a very distinctive personality. She looked like a beautiful sculpture carved out of marble by an accomplished artist. She would be gracefully dressed in a white nine-yard sari and a well-fitting blouse that covered her back and bosom well and yet managed to highlight her figure. The pleats of her tightly draped sari fell gracefully over her feet, bobbing up and down when she walked. She always walked straight with her head held high. One end of her pallav would be tightly wound around her waist, and sometimes she would just wind it around the little finger of her left hand. She wore a small wristwatch and a small white purse swung from her wrist. Her hair was tied in a neat bun at the nape of her neck. She looked so beautiful that even children like us were very impressed by her. Besides, she was our teacher's friend! Since she was a doctor, she often sprayed some medicine inside my throat, and she carried this spray to the rehearsals. And it proved very effective too, because my voice would lose the hoarseness. This must have happened at least seven or eight times. I had to use the spray even on the day of our performance in the competitions. Later on I realized that my voice had gone permanently hoarse. I suspected that this was because of the spray, and doctors confirmed it. Even today I am assailed by the feeling that my voice is not sweet like that of other women. I have to consciously fight against it.

Tai left her job in Ratnagiri and went to Mumbai. But much before that Harishchandra gave up his job in the mamlatdar office following a bitter experience having to do with caste prejudice. As a part of his job, he had gone to inspect a place in a taluka, accompanied by a peon from the office. After the inspection was over, the *talathi* in the village insisted that Harishchandra should dine at his place that night. Harishchandra tried his best to fend him off. But the talathi would not listen. Finally, he accepted the invitation. He sent his peon ahead to see where the house was located. The first duty that the peon performed was to tell the talathi about Harishchandra's caste. When Harishchandra arrived at the talathi's house at night, he was given a very lukewarm welcome. After some time, the talathi came with food served on a plantain leaf and said, "Come Bhausahib, sit and eat."

Harishchandra was somewhat surprised. "Sit? Where? And where is our peon?" he asked. The verandah, where he was served, was covered with dirt and filth. Shoes and chappals lay strewn all around. Goat droppings could be seen nearby.

"Oh, he will come later," the talathi answered summarily. "You sit down here; otherwise you'll be late!"

Harishchandra glanced inside the house. He saw the peon sitting there, eating his meal. He felt as if someone had thrown acid on his face, the acid of humiliation! The verandah, the filth, the chappals, the goat droppings … and the talathi deeply entrenched in caste ideology! He turned his back that very instant and vowed never to go to a village. He resigned from his job, though I do not know whether he was aware of what Dr. Babasaheb Ambedkar had said: "Leave the village," he had told his followers. "The village will never help you progress. Go to the city!"

Harishchandra was born at a time when Dr. Babasaheb Ambedkar went on a whirlwind tour of the Konkan region. Local leaders like Kalsulkar,

Arulekar, Kirloskar, Hadkar, and Hindalekar had organized a huge public meeting for him. In his speech, Babasaheb appealed to the people to give up their traditional caste-specific duties of *mharki*,[3] and that is what people did. Harishchandra's father vowed never to do such duties again. He had spoken of this so many times. This probably was at the root of his sense of self-respect.

After some days, Harishchandra got a job in the post office at Ratnagiri. Since the post office was right next to Gogate College, he also enrolled in the college. But he could not continue his studies beyond the intermediate level because he would often be transferred. However, he studied the area surrounding the college quite well. It was because of him that we came to know that the lawyer Thakur residing in the bungalow near the post office was the father-in-law of the famous Marathi writer P. L. Deshpande. We never saw Thakur in person, but the bungalow, which was so far quite inconspicuous, suddenly became very noticeable.

In those days, post offices would be a dime a dozen. There was one right in front of our house. Harishchandra had worked there as well. I do not know how much he worked in the post office, but I certainly discovered that I had plenty of work there. My brother predicted that I was going to fail in the matriculation examinations, and Aai became more abusive than ever.

Luckily for me, Harishchandra was transferred to Alibaug and I could concentrate on my studies. I was not worried about any subject other than mathematics and English. Since all I would get in math was a big zero, I gave it up. But English was a compulsory subject. The only positive thing was that we were allowed to pass in that subject later. However, there was no escape from my brother. He imposed English on me.

I was not only scared of English I also hated it. Besides, the English teacher was Nene, the one whose daughter was given the cook's role in the play. We had had a passing acquaintance with English because it was introduced to us in the eighth standard. So I had not progressed much beyond the alphabet. But he would always target me in class by asking me about tenses, idioms, phrases, and spellings, especially the more difficult ones. When I could not answer, he would speak in an extremely satirical way. "This is English, the milk of a tigress; it is not easy, like acting in plays." He would humiliate me in front of the whole class, and the other students laughed at me. So to me the period for English lessons was like facing a tiger. Naturally I would skip the class. And, because I skipped classes, Nene would not allow me to sit in the next class. I could not speak about this at home. Aai was illiterate, and my brother sided with Nene. The inevitable result was that I started regressing in English. If I went to my brother for some readymade answers, he would begin from abc. I would invariably fail in English. But I was good in drawing and would be pushed into the next standard with grace marks.

During my last year, when I was going to appear for my matriculation examinations, there was an incident that would have seriously interfered with my studies, but fortunately I woke up in time and escaped the consequences. A young man called Barve came to our house. He was an acquaintance of our Khedaskarbhau from some village near Rajapur. Since Khedaskarbhau was a tenant in our house, and since he thought that our house was more educated than the others, he sent this young man to us. He used to stay in someone else's house in Ratnagiri and was newly employed in a local office. It was evident from his appearance and surname that he was a Brahmin. He was a soft-spoken and fair-complexioned young man, with a slim build and sensitive eyes. His hair was always combed and parted neatly. When he went to Vasantivahini, she asked him to sit on the bench on our verandah. I was around. So he began chatting with me. He told me about himself, "My father is a priest, and I have a stepmother and a brother. We have a little land." Because of this reference to the stepmother, I became a little compassionate toward him and a little expansive. Then he said, "It's so nice in a village. The people there are more affectionate. I yearn for someone of my own in a city."

I took it casually because I thought he was a simple soul and therefore did not read any other deeper meaning into his words. He came again in the holidays and told me that he had read novelists like Phadke or Khandekar, the two well-known romantic writers at that time. He had also read B. R. Tambe, the romantic poet. He went on to say that he had become a member of a library and asked me if I would like him to get me some of the works by these writers. I avoided him by telling him that I had not even read my textbooks yet. I had had an earlier experience to reflect on. So I simply was unable to respond to him. When he came, I would ask him to sit on the bench on the verandah. Sometimes Aai would be busy weaving her baskets. She had customers. Besides my family members, neighbors and children from their families would be constantly moving in and out of the house. I felt quite secure that people on the street could see us, and we talked openly. One day Barve said, "Now one thing is done! I have a job. The next thing is marriage, and I want to have an intercaste marriage." Saying this, he gazed at me with emotional eyes.

I was completely bowled over. I was not sure whether this was some sort of a signal to me. But I did not want to risk anything. I changed the topic and started talking about other things like how much I had to study and so on. But I did not say, "Why do you come to see me? Don't come here from now on." So this one-way traffic continued at full speed. And why not? I had not prohibited him. I was unconsciously encouraging him by making girlish exclamations like, "Oh, really? How very clever of you" and so on, which probably sent the adrenalin racing through his blood. So one day he came to see me with a face that showed that he had resolved to say something significant. He sat in his usual place on the bench on the verandah. After some small talk, he said, "I like the poet Tambe, but I don't think I like his poem 'It Is Indeed in Death That the World Lives!'"

Now my knowledge of Tambe was virtually nil. I had heard Tai singing his poem, "You are asking me for nectar, friend, but all pots of nectar are lying empty." I had liked it very much. But beyond that I did not know anything about him. So I asked him, "Why? Why didn't you like this poem?" He answered, "Well it is really in love that the world lives, doesn't it?" The word *love* carried an extra emphasis in this question, and his voice had become infinitely tender. While he was gazing at me thus, someone passed between us and I got the message! I moved my eyes away from the back of the person who had passed between us. Had I said "Yes" to his question, I would have seen the world end in my own death! The body language of the person who had passed had made it amply clear to me! So I ignored him completely and applied brakes to his superfast car. He took the hint and stopped visiting.

Some six months passed. He came one day, bubbling with joy and enthusiasm. Happily he announced that he was getting married. He said, "She works in the same office as mine." I deliberately asked him about her caste. He answered, "Bhandari! She is a Bhandari! But nobody from their family goes fishing, mind you!" Then he laughed—a pure, genuine, *satwik* laugh!

I felt a pang deep down. "Here goes my chance of an intercaste marriage!" I said to myself. That is probably why he lingered in my mind for a very long time. Since he lived in Ratnagiri, I came across his wife once. She was an ordinary-looking girl, just like me. They had three daughters. It was obvious that he cared a lot for his wife and daughters. Well, what's the point of crying over spilt milk?

Neena Varde, the wife of the nephew of the famous Marathi writer P. L. Deshpande and the sister-in-law of Satish Dubhashi, the well-known Marathi actor, had been my classmate since the tenth standard. Her mother worked as the MRO in the Civil Hospital in Ratnagiri and her father was a retired military officer. They lived in the huge quarters provided for doctors. I would go to Neena for help with my studies. I realized what a great difference there was between them and us. It was in their house that I enjoyed very tasty dishes such as *varanbhat,* rice with spices and a lot of ghee, spicy mutton curry, fish, and delicacies like shellfish bhajis.

"Hey, why don't you bring the sweet dishes that your mother cooks for you?" Neena and her brothers and sisters always asked me. I used to treat it as a joke. Now once it so happened that my sister-in-law was admitted to the hospital for delivery. I was taking her lunch to her. Since I needed a book from Neena, I went to her house first. When Sheela, her sister, saw the tiffin box in my hand, she snatched it from my hand and opened it. Her face fell when she saw the coarse grain rice, with a little dal and vegetable on it. Without saying a word, she closed the lid. After that none of them ever asked me to bring them a sweet dish.

We did not have the custom of serving a different kind of food to women who had just given birth. For the first two days, she would be given rice with a little coconut milk mixed with a bit of molasses and pepper. After that she ate the same food as everybody else. My vahini liked fish. Her father used to bring a variety of big fish for her, like *gejar, shingata, modawasa,* and *towari,* both cooked and raw. Vahini would simply devour them. She could eat just fish without any bhakri or rice. Aai used to frown at this. "What monstrous eating, this!" She would exclaim. But Vahini never suffered for eating fish.

The relationship between my mother and sister-in-law was quite traditional, riddled with the usual tension and strife. But my vahini never allowed any of that tension to affect us. She would work in the house without expecting any help from us. That helped us immensely to pursue our studies. I can never forget this debt to her.

It was in my last year at school that I realized for the first time what it meant to study! I was good in all subjects except English. Teachers like Deshpande for Marathi, Limaye for Sanskrit, and Sohoni for geography taught us very well, without any prejudices. Sohoni Sir was a short plump man. He would always be in white trousers and a white shirt, which he would tuck in. He would roll a handkerchief around his left hand and thrust it in his pocket. He drew a perfect circle on the board and I felt he was drawing his own picture. That is probably why the earth's round shape must have fixed itself in our heads. There was a teacher called Mahadik from the training school when I was in the primary school. He prepared a beautiful mud model of India on which he marked the states of India, mountains, major rivers and directions so well that the map was imprinted on my mind. The only subject that petrified me was English. I sat on a branch of the cashew tree behind our house and tried learning the answers of possible questions by heart. But untimely love, like untimely rain, would at times ruin things. I felt like writing nice long letters to Harishchandra even while I was studying and I did write them in a very ornate language. That is why my essay writing must have improved.

I was not sure till the last day that I would appear for the examination. But, at the eleventh hour, Harishchandra's maternal uncle sent me some model answer scripts from Mumbai. These and a writing pad with blotting paper beneath, which my brother bought for me for the examination, gave me a lot of moral support. When I handed in the last paper, I felt light as a feather.

We had a teacher called B. B. Thakur Desai who taught us English in the eleventh standard. He used to offer private tuitions at his home. But he was a strict disciplinarian and known to be a terror. So I did not choose his private coaching class. I went to another teacher called Godbole instead. He was a sweet man, like his name, which means "one who speaks sweetly." Besides he taught us in a relaxed way, sitting in an armchair in his courtyard. In between, he read the newspaper and also gave instructions to the people in the house. His teaching finally helped me reach the required 35 percent in English and thus my boat finally arrived at the harbor of success.

After my matriculation examinations, I was no longer worried about studies or what to do next. I decided that I would go home, sleep, and then look for a job. That's all! Neena Varde planned to go to a movie that night with her parents. She had already decided what to do with her life after the examinations. She told us about all her plans. First she would go to Mumbai, then to the USA! Every day a car, owned by one family friend or another came to drop her at the examination hall and pick her up later. So Neena went to Mumbai. That was the last time we were together. Later on, when she returned from America, I did take leave from the office and went to see her. But somehow old friendships were lost in the company of new ones.

After the examinations, there was one more interlude! This was getting to be like the rehearsals of a play. The same house, the same people, the same dialogues, and the same roles too! Our neighbor Vasantivahini was from Kolhapur. She had a younger brother called Ramnath. Once he and two other siblings came to stay with her. Ramnath was a dark, tall, and thin chap, with sunken hollow cheeks. He had a sharp nose and would comb his hair in such a way that it stood like a nice balloon. He had dressed carefully, like a bridegroom, because he had come to stay at his sister's place. Had his sister had a grown-up daughter, I am sure he would have married her. (Such marriages were allowed in their community.) He used to work as a doorkeeper in a theater in Kolhapur, maybe the Liberty Theater. But he was neither intelligent nor crafty enough to quote the dialogues at the right place in the conversations. He was a quiet, reticent, simple soul.

He had come to stay, but their place was quite tiny so they spent most of the time on our verandah. It was the same verandah, the same bench kept at right angles to the road, the same me sitting on the bench, swinging my legs … the same casual chatting. "How very smart! You're a doorkeeper, hun? So you must get to see lots of movies!" His face bloomed with happiness when I said this. His small brothers stared at his face as if they were seeing him smile for the first time! Suddenly Vasantivahini came out and said, "Vimal, take all of them out after lunch and show them the sea. These people don't believe me when I tell them that the sea is a big thing." Vahini would always use masculine forms of verbs for herself, a typical Kolhapuri style!

Ramnath said snootily, "Bah! How big can the sea here be? Maybe twice, three times more than our Rankala!" Rankala was a big lake in Kolhapur.

Vasantivahini tried to explain to him, "Hey, Rankala is a lake, but this is the sea. Go and see it. And only then will you understand!" I had not seen this Rankala anyway, but heard about it. Jadhav Guruji, with whose family Akka used to stay in Partavane for her schooling, had lost his son there. He had traveled to Kolhapur on his school trip and got drowned in Rankala after getting stuck in the lotus creepers there. I had some idea from the discussion how big Rankala was. So I welcomed it as a challenge. I took these guests to the Bhagawati temple at the top of the ancient fort built by Shivaji Maharaj. The deep blue waters of the Arabian Sea spread out in front of us from the fort up to the horizon. After seeing the sea, one comes to believe that three-fourths of the earth is really covered with water! The sight of the huge expanse strikes you dumb!

The guests from Kolhapur were speechless! Ramnath was staring at the sea with big round eyes. I clapped my hands loudly and said, "So, what have you got to say now? Remember the geography lessons?" His eyes looked into mine as if they were trying to find the reflection of the Rankala of his feelings there! I was immediately on my guard.

When we returned from the sea, however, he created a big problem for me! After dinner Vasantivahini called out and said to me, "Vimal, come here, I want to talk to you." Then she went and sat down on a rock at some distance. Before going out, when I casually peeped inside her house I saw Ramnath lying on his bed, but he was merely staring at the ceiling with unblinking eyes as if he were waiting for something. The younger children were sleeping. I went and parked myself near Vasantivahini. She watched my face in the faint light of the street lamp and said, "How do you like our Ramnath?"

Young women immediately get the implied meanings of such questions. I was no exception. Yet I asked deliberately, "What do you mean?"

"I mean, he likes you. Do you like him? He wants to get married, so he asked me to ask you. That is why ... I ask." Even in this situation I could not help noticing her use of masculine verb forms. It made me feel so odd! It was as if Ramnath himself was proposing to me through her mouth. I was surprised. I had known Harishchandra for the last four years, since the time he had come to stay in her house as a guest. She knew we loved each other. And yet she was asking me this question! So I said, "Didn't you tell him about Harishchandra?"

"I did. But he says, he doesn't mind. You too think about it. So? What should I tell him?" A sister was proposing on behalf of her brother so hopefully! Oh, look at the kind of liberal men I was coming across! I got up and returned to my house without saying a word!

I wondered, was it what Ramnath had wanted or was it Vasantivahini's imagination? Be that as it may, I had learned my lesson. Boys will simply interpret anything that girls say to suit their interests. I became serious. My heart was completely captured by Harishchandra. His smile, his loving gaze, his speech ... everything made my heart flutter even in my dreams. At that time, he used to wear a cotton bud dipped in *majmua,* a popular scent, in his ears. The fragrance lingered around me even when he was not there. Even today this scent breathes new life into the memories of those days. But those boys probably gave me a cold!

In those days, the famous Marathi stage actor Shantabai Jog came to stay in Ratnagiri. Her husband was transferred to the local state transport office. Although she had come to a small place, the actor in her would not allow her to sit quietly. Besides Ratnagiri was a place teeming with theater lovers. Any theater company from Mumbai would come to Ratnagiri first before embarking on the tour of Maharashtra. There were many theater groups.

Our Marathi teacher, Vasantrao Deshpande, was an amateur theater artist. He performed the main role of Dada in the play *Vedyacha Ghar Unhat.* People liked him so much that he founded a group called Natraj Sewa Mandal. Many people like Baban Bane, Suresh Gandhi, Shanu Mestri, Bhau Shetye, and Bapu Pandit became its members. In those days women artists were difficult to get; they had to be hired from Mumbai. So they forced my friend Sumati Vaidya and me to be members of the group. Maybe they believed in our histrionic abilities!

I had participated in many programs in school. I had presented fishermen's songs on the stage, with real fish in a basket, and won prizes. When I was in the sixth standard, I had written a play, *Shrikrishna's Pendya,* and directed it myself. Our teachers wanted the students to write and present a program for the Dasara festival. I had kept the role of Pendya for myself; a silly girl called Hemalata Potnis was given the role of Krishna. I assigned the roles of milkmaids to my stout friends like Sushila Dhumak, Kamal Chavan, and Sunanda Bhosale. They were not too keen at first. But when I assured them that all they had to do was walk in a circle on the stage, saying, "Come on, let's go, we are late," and beat up Pendya, who came to stop them, they gladly agreed. They acted their roles quite realistically and beat me to a pulp as a reward. I won a prize for this role, most probably because I had valiantly endured their beating without crying. After that the play *Kalalavya Kandyachi Kahani* ruined my English, since the teacher ignored me. Yet my itch for theater had not subsided!

After hesitating for some time, I finally became a member of the club. Shantabai suggested that a theater workshop be organized for the members. Accordingly, the first theater workshop was organized in a classroom of the girls' school under the guidance of experts like Nandu Khote and Chinchwadkar. We were given our first lessons in acting: how to use the voice for expressing different emotions, which action was required or not required at a particular moment in the play, how body language can be used, how to shed tears at a moment's notice. We were taught all these techniques. Later on, of course, my life exposed me to such a variety of colorful experiences that I did not have to use any technique to bring tears to my eyes. These came quite naturally!

Many plays were presented under the direction of Shantabai Jog such as *Kabuliwala*, *Kaunteya*, and *Sunder Mi Honar*.[4] The performances helped us collect money for the Soldiers' Fund. I always used to get supporting roles because of my stout figure.

When people gathered for rehearsals, Sumati and I would go to call on Shantabai, who lived in Shirkewadi, a neighborhood near our house. Her mother looked exactly like her, though a little older. She had the same face, same hair, and same slim figure! She would be in a nine-yard sari. She would invite us in and go into the house to call her daughter. Shantabai's young, four-year-old son, Sanjay, a chubby, beautiful child with lovely blue eyes, would stand in the door with his arms akimbo and shout at us, "Go away; my mother will not come with you!" He made us laugh so much!

Ratnagiri had only one drapery shop. They claimed it was the only one. Because of this shop, Ratnagiri's people could satisfy their artistic desires. Lots of items required for the traditional khele would be available there to rent—mythological costumes, crowns, maces, swords, and so on. But it did not carry brocade saris and blouses. So we had to go gallivanting all over the town looking for these. Somebody from a rich family would assure Deshpande that they would lend their clothes. Usually, Sumati and I would have to go to people like Dr. Tara Lubri, the advocate Parulekar, Shirke, and Suresh Gandhi to borrow saris. These people were so rich that we would be scared even to go to them. Besides, often the saris we got made us feel like beggars asking for old clothes on an eclipse day! And we could not complain to the teacher about this. He would scold us and come up with new addresses!

In one of the performances of *Kaunteya*, the top of the mace flew off, leaving just the handle in the actor's hand. Barring this humorous incident, the rest of the five or six performances were quite good. Shantabai was in Kunti's role and Vasantrao Deshpande played Karna. The rest of the roles were average. I don't know how much the workshops and the plays helped me on the stage. But the acting skills I gained certainly came in quite handy when I was going out with Harishchandra and still wanted to project the image of a babe in the woods!

Six

After Tai got married, marrying me off became an issue of utmost importance on Bhai's agenda. No one at home approved of Harishchandra. That, of course, had no effect on me. They knew that I was having an affair with him and that I lied about it through my teeth. They were absolutely convinced that I would bring disgrace to the family's good name one day. Besides, in our community, more boys were getting educated than girls, and some of them had very good jobs as well. So my family believed that I could easily get a much better match than Harishchandra.

I enrolled myself in a college. At the same time, I also did a few jobs: nothing permanent—these were temporary jobs; I worked in leave vacancies, that is, I filled in for people who were away. Both my office and college were at a stone's throw from my house. But it was difficult to attend morning college, get home, change clothes, wear a sari, and go to the office carrying a tiffin box. So I used to carry my lunch to the college and go to the office straight from there.

At that time, I possessed only one sari and two or three skirts. I usually wore a skirt to the office. Why not, I reasoned. Didn't working girls in Pune and Mumbai wear skirts? So why couldn't I? People, of course, did not say anything to my face, but they considered me a very "fast" girl!

After a few days, I got a job in the state transport office, and Bhai came with a proposal from a prospective bridegroom. This young man was working in a private office in Mumbai, in those days an excellent qualification for an eligible bachelor. A government job, on the other hand, was less impressive. Everybody was impressed with this proposal, but I marched out of the house without a word. The young man understood and went back. As the family had done with Tai, I too was packed off to Mumbai, where they hoped that somehow they would be able to fix my marriage. While in Mumbai, I did several temporary jobs at many places like the civil court, the election office, the Glaxo Laboratory, and so on.

Meanwhile, Harishchandra's visits to Mumbai became more frequent. One day he arrived at Bhai's house with his baba, kaka, mama, and mami and made a formal proposal of marriage. My vahini was completely in favor of our marriage and, by this time, the opposition of the others in the family had considerably weakened too. As a last resort, however, Bhai sat me down and gave a long lecture on there being more educated boys around to choose from, but I remained quiet and firm, so finally he had to give in.

Once Bhai gave his consent, he put forth some conditions to which Harishchandra readily agreed. Finally, our marriage was approved. The conditions were: "The marriage will take place at your village Bhiraunde; the expenditure of the marriage will be shared equally by both parties; we will not buy any clothes or a gold ring for the groom; we will not insist on your buying anything for the bride; our own traveling expenses to and from Bhiraunde will be borne by us!" Since the marriage was going to take place at Bhiraunde in his own house, Harishchandra was not going to demand money for the pandal or lunch expenses in any case, nor would he have to bear the expenses for our travel. So the arrangement was convenient for both sides.

At that time, I was working as a packer in the Glaxo Laboratory. Had I been a graduate, I would have been appointed as a clerk. When I applied for leave, I was told that they did not allow girls to continue after marriage. So I had to leave the job although the pay was good.

Bhai did not have to arrange meetings of our community, as he had to do at the time of Tai's marriage. First, my marriage was imposed on my family; it was against their wishes. Second, Harishchandra's family in Bhiraunde was not a member of the Bauddha Jana Panchayat. So the Panchayat could not harass them by demanding that they became members or by asking them to pay the membership fee right from the time of birth or compelling them to buy gifts for the members! Harishchandra said, "In the past, there used to be a "Mahal" or group of six villages, Kankavlli, Soundal, Kudal, Rajapur, Karveer and Salas. When people from these villages attended a marriage, they had to be honored with gifts. The bride's or groom's parents had to wash their feet. If they did not get the honor due to them, they would march off in a huff. Then the family would have to pay a fine. But now after the conversion, nothing of the sort happens." Bhai put the same argument in front of the Panchayat who gave their consent in just one meeting.

There was hardly any shopping as such to be done. My family was not going to buy anything for Harishchandra; on his part, Harishchandra was going to buy some saris for me. Accordingly, from our side only I accompanied his maternal uncle and aunt on this errand. They bought one whitish brocade sari and a white marriage sari for me; I bought a sari for which Bhai had given me some money, and a couple of blouse pieces. That was all. At that time we did not think on the lines of matching petticoats with saris! Any petticoat would do for any sari.

A few marriage invitations were printed on thin paper, just as a formality. The Neo-Buddhist *Namo Buddhaya* had replaced the traditional invocation of the family deity on the top of the invitation! But the traditional *Chiranjeev* and *Soubhagyakankshini*, respectively, before the groom and the bride, were retained. They still are. Usually a bride would not distribute her marriage invitations in person. Since I did not have an option, I had to do it myself. In the end I took my young niece Saroj along. I stood at the gate while she went in and passed along the invitation. When I gave the invitation to my friends, they would ask me in surprise, "Hey, your surname is Pawar and your husband's surname is Pawar too! How can that be? Is that allowed? Doesn't it mean that your family and his come from the same ancestors?" Then I piped up with my well-rehearsed answer, "Now we are Buddhists! Now nobody looks at the *kula*![1] We have discarded our caste-specific surnames now and taken on new names. This is a caste-neutral name."

Who knows when we had taken these surnames! On some papers in Baba's trunk, his name was written as *Arjun Chimaji Mahar* and on some others, about land, his name appeared as *Powar.* Baba had struck down the *Po* there and corrected it as *Pa.* The reason was that *Powar* was a surname among the cobbler caste. So he had never liked being called Powar. Sometimes, Aai used to call him by that name just to tease him. Then he would get really angry!

None of my friends attended my wedding. Sunanda's hero got married the same year, so she boycotted my marriage as well. Finally, only a handful of guests, thirteen or fourteen in all, including Govindadada, a couple of villagers, Mama, my cousins Bhai, Aai, and Vahini, boarded the morning bus and reached Bhiraunde.

I looked at the village, which was going to be mine soon. I liked what I saw very much. It was a beautiful view, with the blue Sahyadri mountain ranges on the horizon, dense greenery at the foot of the hills, houses with saffron-tiled roofs peeping out from the trees, square pieces of green farms all around, as if moving along with us. A yellow path led us onto a square where four paths went off in different directions. Tall sky-scraping teak trees grew all around this place, through which a tiny road disappeared in the direction of the hills, another led to a well, and yet another danced its way to the river. There was a school nearby, and a flour mill run by a Christian man called Bastadkar; and then there was the khot's wadi. Harishchandra had described all this to me so graphically that it was almost printed on my memory. The scene unfolded before me exactly as he had described. I had already met the people in his family, on some occasion or other. So there was no quickening of the pulse and thumping of the heart!

When women and children in the village got wind of our arrival, they crowded around to see me. "Who is this girl Harishchandra is bent on marrying?" they seemed to be wondering. But I must have disappointed them! A pandal had been erected in the space between two houses. The ground was polished with cow dung. Confetti hung from above. So this probably was the "marriage hall"! Harishchandra was standing right there. Dressed in a white pajama and *kurta,* with his hair combed well, he looked so prim and proper. His face broke into a welcoming smile when he saw us, and my heart skipped a few beats! He came forward courteously and took us to the place where we would be staying. I noticed a gold ring on his finger. He must have bought it with his own money! What could the poor man do? After a year I somehow forced Aai to buy a ring and some clothes for him. But she should have done it at the time of the wedding! What's the point of doing something if not at the right time? On top of this, Aai said, "Ha! The blind man wants to celebrate the festival after it is over!"

While we sipped water given to us by Harishchandra's people, the women kept whispering, "The bride is a bit fat! But her hair is nice." Long hair appeared to be a symbol of beauty here. I had used some additional hair switches to bolster my own hair and tied my hair into a stylish bun like Sharmila Tagore did in films. So I could not untie my hair in front of them. I just patted a few stray hairs into place.

Harishchandra was constantly on the move, giving instructions to various people, talking to them, casting furtive glances at me all along. And then my sasu—mother-in-law—arrived on the scene; she wore a beautiful nine-yard sari that fell gracefully at her feet. She had a huge pearl-studded *nuth* on her nose that looked majestic. A set of new green bangles covered her wrists, a necklace with some five or six strings of black beads, and a big vermillion bindi adorned her forehead. Her face glowed with happiness and broke into a lovely smile on seeing us. She looked stunningly beautiful. I noticed that these people did not seem to have the custom of women covering their heads with the sari pallav.

My sasu came forward and embraced Aai and all the other women who had come with us as a mark of welcome. She looked gloriously happy. She came, with Harishchandra behind her, to invite us for lunch. Once again he informed us that meals were "arranged" in their house. He used the word *arrangements* often, trying to put across the idea that everything was well organized and absolutely under control.

We stepped out, following them. Our women arranged the pallavs on their heads properly. Children followed us in a procession. My sasu climbed up the stairs of a tall, one-storied house to what looked like the verandah of a school. The house, jam-packed with people, almost shook like an overcrowded bus. In front of us was a square-shaped huge hall, decorated with confetti. This is where the men, including my brothers, sat down to lunch.

There was another verandah to the right of this room. My mother-in-law cut her way out of this crowd, warding people off with her hands. "Give way, give way ..." she kept muttering, "The bride is going to stay right here. Then you can look at her to your heart's content, but let us pass now." We walked on till we came to a small staircase with only three or four stairs. We climbed up and turned left to reach a room that appeared to be part of another floor. The room up here was crowded once again, this time with women. These must be close relatives of the family, I surmised. There was a sweet looking, fair young woman sitting against the wall, nursing her child. She was my elder *jaau,* the wife of Harishchandra's older brother.

Suddenly a tall, slim girl came forward and, taking my hands in hers, broke into a happy smile. She too was a sister-in-law, another jaau, Mai, and was called Vimal before her marriage, but the in-laws changed her name to Jayashree afterward. The elder jaau was called Janaki. Now I was worrying whether they would call me Janabai. But I had already decided on the new name and told Harishchandra that he had to give me that one. Mai was hurrying to and fro. There was a room on the right, also packed with women. A fifteen- or sixteen-year-old girl quietly stood at the door. She was my one and only nanand, my husband's only sister, Shalini. She appeared to be so aloof and quiet, completely unaffected by the commotion around.

The women in our family looked around and appeared to be quite impressed with what they saw. I could hear snatches of their conversations, "Looks like they have plenty of land!" "Did you see those huge cane containers?" "Oh look at the cropped paddy against the wall! Almost touching the roof!" "Good, good! Our Vimal is lucky indeed. Such nice people!" As they spoke, leaf plates were put before us and piping hot lunch was served. Rice, hot green peas cooked with a lot of spices, round wadas like puries without holes in them, and a vegetable made with tender grapefruit buds comprised the lunch. At home, we would make wadas with holes in them, so our women began cracking jokes, "Hey, don't you have holes! Look at the wadas!" Then they guffawed loudly.

While the women from my *maher,* my natal family, were speaking and laughing so, the women from my husband's family were laughing for a completely different reason. They were whispering, laughing at us. I was straining to listen to their words. One said, "Where did they find this bride from, the Bele Mahars? Didn't they get any from the Pan Mahars?" This was talk about the two subcastes among Mahars in Sindhudurga district: Bele Mahar and Pan Mahar. Nobody really had an idea about how they had evolved. But Shankar was the god of the

Mahars. People who worshipped this god with bel leaves were called the Bele Mahars, and those who offered any other leaves were called the Pan Mahars. The Bele Mahars were supposed to be more advanced, compared to the Pan Mahars who were backward. There would be no intermarriages between these communities. Harishchandra was a Pan Mahar. Now, though in Ratnagiri there were no such subcastes among us, these women had branded me as a Bele Mahar and criticized me! I could not hide my smile.

After lunch, I began to prepare for the wedding. I could not risk doing my hair again. So I simply combed it superficially and began to apply the special powder that I'd bought for the wedding. Women and children around were watching me closely. When I began to apply the powder to my face with a puff, some young girls hungrily eyed the powder. For one moment I considered handing over the powder to them. But no! I called them forward one by one and began to make them up. This went on for quite some time. The makeup man in me had awakened! Finally Aai poked me in the ribs and said, "That's enough!" Startled, I looked around. The women around were, indeed, laughing at me, trying to hide their amusement behind their pallavs.

Dressed in a white sari and a white blouse, I entered the pandal. I found Harishchandra already seated at the table on which were placed photographs of Ambedkar and the Buddha. He was in the same clothes, except for a cap on his head. It made him appear a little silly, but his bright, shining eyes made up for it, giving him a handsome look. I felt a pang in my heart that Bhai had bought neither a ring nor clothes for him. I had worn one of Bhai's rings, with a white stone in it. But when we were getting out of the house to go to the bus station in the morning, Tai reminded me that it was Bhai's ring and made me remove it from my finger. I was quite upset by this.

First we got engaged in front of the photographs of Ambedkar and the Buddha; the marriage rites were performed immediately afterward. I was made to look down all the while. Finally I got bored and raised my head like Harishchandra. I found the women who had laughed at me while I was applying powder laughing again.

Then both of us took oaths: to be loyal to each other, to do all the household chores without any complaint, to give gifts to the wife and to keep her under the thumb, and so on. Harishchandra got many gifts; I, however, got only a bowl and a jar! That was all my people had given me!

In earlier times, they would make the bride sit in front of the tulsi plant,[2] wrap the sari pallav around her head, and give her a new name. However, all that had changed now. Somebody in the pandal said, "So give the bride a name ... what is it?" My sasu said, "Taramati! Harishchandra and Taramati! Like the famous couple from the *Puranas*, the old Hindu myths."

But I did not like that name. Harishchandra looked at me. When he noticed the frown on my face, he said, "Urmila! That is a good name!"

I had liked this name for a long time. Urmila is a character from the *Ramayana*. She is Lakshman's wife, always marginalized. But in spite of being sidetracked, she is a great woman. She fascinated me, and I had fascinated my husband! So why would he listen to his mother? He said, "I have given her the name Urmila!" "Hurmila? What does it mean?" my sasu was quite irritated. But when people clapped and showed their appreciation of the name, she had no alternative but to nod in agreement. She smiled sweetly and backed out. My naming ceremony had gone off just as I had wanted it.

Keshav, Harishchandra's brother, brought his camera to take photographs of the wedding. Harishchandra kept frantically signaling at him to click his camera. But the poor man had exhausted the entire roll of film taking pictures of trees, people, and even bullocks, which appeared to have changed so much in his absence! So he would not budge from his place. It was evening now. The next day my brother-in-law did take a few snaps of ours under the burning sun with the departing guests, but he was not at all sure whether they would actually work. Amazingly, a couple of photographs did come out well, a proof for posterity that we had begun the journey of life together.

The day after my wedding, all my relatives from my mother's side left for Ratnagiri without leaving any woman behind to keep me company, as was the custom.

Maybe they thought, "She has done a 'love marriage'! Now why would she need anybody as a support since she knows her husband and all his people so well?" In any case, my people allowed us to be married as if they were doing a great favor to my husband! On the third day of our marriage, my husband and I went to my mother's place for a visit, as custom demanded. We took the morning bus and reached home around lunchtime. My mother had decided not to perform any of the rituals associated with sending a young bride off to her parents'-in-law in an elaborate way. My sister Manjulatai had come to stay with her for the birth of her first child. She suffered from an infection in her breast that gave her a very high temperature and great pain. The entire house was worried sick because they suspected it was cancer. Therefore no one was bothered enough to note that the brand new *jawai*, the son-in-law, was coming home for the first time. At least Aai had neither time nor inclination to give him any thought.

After we reached home, Aai picked up a bag and went off to the market. I thought to myself, "All right; maybe it is a bit late in the day, but better late than never! She will at least buy some chicken, mutton, or fish!" However, all Mother bought was around two kilos of cheap shellfish called *muley*. She boiled some of these, took out the flesh, and fried it in a pan with some onions, salt, and chilli powder and served us. The rest were put in a bag and handed over to me as a gift for my mother-in-law, since she liked shellfish.

Now to deliver the gift to my sasu, we would have to return immediately after lunch. In fact, that is precisely what Aai wanted. She did not want us to stay. I was really of two minds about the stupid gift. Should I reject it, as it was really a silly thing to give as a gift? On the other hand, should I accept it because she had at least *given* something to my sasu, however cheap and silly? Finally, the false pride for my *maher* won, and I picked up the bag to follow my husband, who had already marched out of the house and stood on the street.

He grimaced when he noticed the bag in my hand. Aai however, kept on shouting instructions from behind, "After getting down from the bus, go straight home. Don't you loiter around!" So she was more worried about the bloody fish reaching home safely rather than about her daughter and son-in-law dropping dead after so much travel in a day! We would reach home only around midnight! However, she was hardly concerned about us! "Don't you forget the bag … !" was her constant refrain!

"What a mother! Damn … never even asked us to stay the night!" My husband went on grumbling angrily! "I could at least have booked the tickets for the bus!" He went on complaining, as we waited for a very long time to catch a bus. He was a very systematic man. He never traveled without reserving tickets first. He hated traveling by bus, standing, and waiting endlessly for someone to get down! Finally, the bus arrived and we were able to get seats, though in the very last row!

Fuming, he sat down and began to stare out of the bus, completely ignoring me. I tied the mouth of the bag carefully with a string, kept it under my feet and sat down, deliberately pushing into him. Maybe this will bring his mood back, I hoped! The bumpy ride gave me good support! Every time the bus passed through a deep ditch, we bounced high, till our heads almost banged against the roof of the bus. The rocking bus made us bump into each other too. Every time I bounced, I clutched my husband tight. Finally, he caught on and reciprocated. Initially, every time the bus gave a jolt, the shellfish bag rolled away and I tried to hold it back. However, once my husband caught hold of me, the bag lay forgotten.

After we got down at Kankavli, he suggested that we stay in a hotel rather than go home. The catching game in the bus had a delayed effect! "The house is packed with guests. So let's eat something here in a hotel nearby and celebrate our honeymoon in a lodge somewhere!" His eyes sparkled as he spoke, and his face looked so sweet! I liked the idea of eating in a hotel. However, I had never stayed in a lodge before.

"And what about these shellfish?" I showed him the bag in my hand.

"Aw, they'll keep alive for a day or two," he assured me. "Come on." I picked up the bag and followed him out of the bus stand. First we ate puri bhaji in the canteen at the bus stand. By the time we finished, it was ten o'clock at night.

In those days, there were only two or three lodges in Kankawali. My husband turned to the one that we could afford. It was more like a two-storied country house with a tiled roof than a lodge! We crossed the front courtyard, polished with cow dung, and climbed the steps to enter the lodge. A man was sitting at the counter. He first looked at me from head to toe in the yellow light of the faint bulb. After my husband had signed me as his wife in the register, the man at the counter handed the key over to him; but before doing so, once again he cast a searching look at me to ensure that I really was a wife! All I could see of him, however, was his snub nose.

Once we opened the lock and entered the room, I kept the bag of the shellfish under the bed. Now the fish were making a *khut khut* noise inside the shells and the water was draining out too. The bag started leaking. I felt quite embarrassed. I sat down awkwardly on the bed. My husband, however, had started examining the walls, doors, and windows for any possible apertures made for peeping toms, like a detective.

After his examination was complete, he came to the cot and suddenly threw his arms around me.

"The light ... the light ... " I somehow managed to mutter, getting up from the bed.

"Never mind!" My husband's hands were groping all over my body.

The tiny room with its peeling walls, the single iron bed with its creaking iron strips, the smelly, moldy mattress with hard lumps of cotton, the dirty, stained old bedspread, the flat hard pillow smelling like a naphthalene bag ... the sharp yellow strip of light from the bulb piercing the eye ... the constant fear of falling off the iron bed and the shellfish bag making funny noises under it! I was completely thrown out of gear! What was I doing? I could sense nothing except my husband's terrible disappointment.

"So frigid!" He said in the morning. That was the certificate I had earned from my husband after our first night! Yet he smiled to himself. Maybe he did expect me to be "frigid" on the first night! A sign of my being a virgin! Had I taken any initiative, he would have suspected my virginity! I was not at all frigid! I understood every move very well. However, these were being done to me against my wishes.

Next morning, we left the hotel. Before leaving the room, when I bent down to gather the shellfish bag, I found that all the water had drained out of the shells on the clay floor, giving out a horrible stench. I picked up the bag as if it were a dead rat and brought it out. The lodge owner, with his swollen eyes and bulbous nose, peered suspiciously at the bag in my hand. I felt so embarrassed! I was worried that he might even ask me to polish the room with dung! By the time my husband finished the formalities like handing over the key and settling the bill, I had crossed the courtyard and reached the street.

I am dead sure that the manager must have looked under the bed and concluded that I had had an abortion in the room! He must have blamed himself for letting me go without making me clean up the mess!

The moment my husband joined me on the street, he snatched the bag of shellfish and threw it into the nearby gutter. I tried to protest, "Hey, what are you doing? The bag would have been useful."

He pinched my arm hard and exploded, "Ugh ... what a house! And what a mother-in-law! Miser of the first order! What a gift she bestows on her son-in-law! A bag of shellfish! To hell with your mother and your family!"

My poor arm received yet another pinch! My husband's frustration for the miserable night had found yet another expression! He kept complaining about my mother. Every husband abuses his wife's mother when he is upset with her, doesn't he? My husband was no exception. For the rest of his life, the shellfish bag provided him a stick to beat me with.

When we reached my sasar's house, I found my sasu sitting outside in the verandah, cutting a big jackfruit and taking out the raw buds that were inside. She arranged them neatly on a clean cloth. The buds looked fresh and beautiful, like white champak flowers. The very sight of them made me feel hungry. By the time she had collected them for cooking, I had devoured some ten to twelve buds.

"Hey, don't eat them raw. Your stomach will ache." My sasu tried to warn me.

"Oh, let her, Mother!" taunted my husband. "She is city-bred! Probably never even saw these before. Besides, she has a penny-pincher for a mother!"

I simply ignored the insults and ate the buds to my heart's content.

In the evening, my husband wanted to take me around. He wanted to show his wife everything in his village: the trees, the hills, the river, his farm, his school, and the places where he had played as a child. I wore a nice brocade shalu to flaunt my being a new bride, and went out with him. It was summer and farmers were burning the land as a preparation for the next planting season. The farms were barren, as were most of the trees; the grass and shrubs had a parched dry look. Yet I was looking at everything with very appreciative eyes. We walked along the embankments between various fields, chattering sweet nothings into each other's ears. People watched us with curiosity and affection and called out to us kindly. "Hey Hari, what does your wife say? Does she like our village?" "So, girl, do you like this place?" "Your farm is on the other side, you know! Can you work in the fields? Can you plant paddy? Does your mother have any land?" This went on for a while—people asking me questions, my husband showing me things, and then, suddenly, there was a sharp pain in my stomach! I somehow tried to ignore it and answered the questions with a smile on my face, but the pain persisted. My stomach started making funny noises, like the shellfish bag. I had probably eaten too many jackfruit buds! I tried to ignore the noises. But finally I could pretend no more. I gave up and told my husband, "Let's go home." I turned back without even waiting for his reaction and hurried home.

He reached home much later than me. My elder sister-in-law asked him, "So Anna, did you have a nice long walk?"

He answered, "Oh, I wanted to show her so many things! But she just turned back in the middle of our walk!"

My sasu said, "What could she do, poor thing?" and immediately went on to quote a proverb, "The marriage is about to take place and the bride wants to shit!" Everybody laughed, but I felt horribly embarrassed.

In the evening, my sasu served dinner to all and then sent almost everybody to sleep in the verandah outside. My sasra, the two elder and younger dirs, a few guests—all went to sleep outside. My sasu, her daughter, my jaaus, with the two children of my elder jaau (the younger of the two kids was born at the time of my wedding) were going to sleep in the inner room. My jaau Mai had turned the middle room into our bridal chamber. My husband's face glowed, but I felt a little embarrassed. However, I entered the room as if it was nothing special. My husband followed behind. The moment he came in, he bolted the door. All the people were awake outside. The wooden door had big crevices. I blew the light out in spite of my husband's protest. Light had no place in the embrace.

I got up in the morning and was horrified to discover that I was bleeding. My periods were regular. So I was quite confused as to how this had happened. I got up and came to the back door where I found Mai cleaning pots near the big stove. I told her what had happened with gestures and begged her for some cloth. She laughed, got up, and washed her hands. Then she went inside and broadcast the news all over the house.

My sasu said, "Oh, she has got her period? All right, tell her to sit at the back door. Here we have to observe the custom of sitting isolated." Then she turned to me, "I too was a girl from Mumbai. But here I have to behave like a village woman. That is the custom here. So you too behave like that ... " Gradually the news spread all over the wadi; Mai got me some old cloth ... and then the bleeding stopped!

I asked my husband, who was loitering behind me in the verandah, "*Aho,* how did this happen?"[3] He gave me a sharp tap on the head and said, "You idiot, don't you understand? Let's go in; I'll tell Aai. The first time is always like this." But he was not really scolding me; he was laughing. He had yet another proof of my virginity! Of course, this may not happen with all women.

I stopped him from telling his mother. "No," I said, "Now the whole village knows about it. No point in saying anything otherwise." He became visibly upset and stormed out in a huff, stamping his feet. I told this to Mai when we went to the well to wash clothes. She laughed and said, "Now, you must sit outside for three days!"

I spent the next three days at the back door. My husband grew more and more impatient. He constantly made signs to me. It was very difficult to ignore him. On the fourth day, according to custom, I washed my hair and had a bath. Then I polished the outer room and verandah with cow dung and entered the house. Only seven or eight days after this, my menstrual course began. This time it was real! Now this was a problem. I took Mai at some distance from the house and confided in her. Again she burst out in laughter, and said, "Well, just keep quiet about it and stay inside. Avoid going to the well and to the *nirvasha's padavi.*" *Nirvasha* had a special meaning. Among our ancestors, one man had died without a son. On festival days, some food used to be kept in this verandah as an offering to appease his spirit. It was believed that he would be angry if the offering was not made. Now who knows why the dead man got angry while his wife didn't! The dead man's wife had also died without a son, but the food was kept only for the dead man, not for her.

In the meantime, I freely roamed around everywhere except the well and the verandah of the childless one. When our eyes met, Mai and I would break into peals of laughter. My sasu asked us why we were laughing. But in answer we would laugh again. She thought we were laughing at her.

During those days, washing the pads was a great problem. I had to hide them. When I went to wash, Mai would accompany me and draw water from the well. Again my sasu asked, "Haven't you washed clothes just now? What are you washing again? And why are both of you going at the same time?" She would watch me like a policeman.

Her keen eye reminded me of a watchman at the Glaxo Laboratory where I had worked. One day the Gurkha watchman at the gate stopped my friend on our way out after work. Her purse contained a packet of pads, which he asked her to show him. She was scared and very embarrassed. Her reluctance and embarrassment increased his suspicion. We also found it very difficult to explain this to the Gurkha. She began to cry and started saying in Hindi, "The flow is too heavy ... so I need more." But he was simply unable to understand. Finally, a couple of senior girls intervened and rescued her. I was scared lest I was asked to show my sanitary towels.

I had polished the outer room with cow dung only eight days back. So there was no need to do it once again. But Mai had the idea of "vital" pollution firmly entrenched in her head. So, for her sake, I polished the whole house, with her help, of course! My sasu felt happy too! She had got a suun who kept the house clean and worked hard. The day my periods began, my husband picked up his bed from our room in the middle and was about to sleep with the others outside. "Aho,[3] please don't go!" I tried to reason with him. "If you go out, everyone will get to know about my periods. They will be angry with me as I am freely moving around." But he refused to listen to me. I went outside too and slept beside my sasu.

One night my sasu and sasra had an argument that ended in his bashing her up. He had passed sixty, and she was more than fifty. Everybody felt very bad about this. They had married sons, their wives, and children living in the house. But could anybody stop a fight between a husband and a wife?

In the morning, I glanced at the stove. My sasu sat in front of the chulha, applying hot compress to her aching shoulder with a hot pipe. She drew on a bidi heavily in between. I went to the well with Mai without saying a word. She too kept quiet. Then suddenly she exploded, "He thrashed her at night!"

Usually, Mai spoke to me in standard Marathi. She had switched over to the Malavani dialect now. "Now, if anybody asks, do you know what she will tell them? She'll say she slipped on the stairs or had been to the toilet where she slipped and fell and hurt her shoulder!"

I peeped into the house to see where she was after I returned from the well. She was still sitting in front of the stove, drawing heavily on the bidi in her hand, staring at the burning wood in the stove.

I bathed, washed my hair, and started moving around in the house. My husband kept following me, trying to touch me all the time. I drew him into an alcove and asked, "How long does a man have this desire?" "Till his death!" came the reply, like a slap in the face.

Three or four days passed like this. My mother-in-law continued being mute. Except for a few perfunctory words she did not speak to anybody. She didn't move from her place before the stove. She sat there and cooked for the whole house. There were many utensils, huge in size, to meet the requirements of a growing, large household. The clay pot for warming the bathwater, grinding stone, stones for husking paddy, pounding pot and pestle … everything was huge in size. We could not manage the grinding stone by ourselves; we needed help. Her reasoning was simple: "I have a large family, I need to grind spices and garlic for cooking; so I need a big grinding stone and pestle!" But nobody except her dared use it. An outsider would have found the old woman grinding laboriously and her young daughters-in-law watching. After she finished grinding, she would return to the stove. In the meanwhile, my elder sister-in-law gave her child a prebath massage and then went on to bathe it. We, the two younger daughters-in-law, washed the clothes, pots, and pans, swept, got firewood from outside for the stove, and generally tidied up the house.

The wedding guests had departed long ago. My younger brother-in-law went to Kankavali for his matriculation examinations. The elder dirs, both teachers, went to their respective schools in the morning and re-turned only in the evening. My nanand went to school. My sasra left for his building and construction work. My husband too was planning to leave me behind for a few days and join his office in Chiplun. I was quite upset. I'm not sure whether it was because of his decision or the unnatu-ral quiet in the house, but it did not feel good. He said, "Come along if you want to. I have rented a small room there." But that would not have looked right. Besides, except for my sasu being unusually quiet, everyone was so nice! That made leaving so difficult!

Finally, one morning, she ended her silence. She was sitting in front of the stove as usual, mixing rice flour to make ghavan for breakfast. Mai and I were on our way to the farm with tins of water for our morning ablutions. It was so funny! We had to hurry and arrive early before the herds arrived to graze. If we were late, we would find cows and buffaloes watching us. Then we had to throw stones to drive them away. They moved a little further and again turned to watch us. When we sat down, keeping an eye on them, another herd arrived behind us. Again we had to get up and run away from them. I would often remember our going to the stream in Ratnagiri for morning ablutions and becoming petrified by the imaginary foot of a ghost—it made me laugh.

We came home and were washing our feet with water drawn from the huge waist-high clay drum in the backyard when a woman began to call out loudly from the front, "Hey, Shantaram's mother … Deu's mother…

what are you doing? O Shantaram's mother ... where are you? O Deu's mother" The woman was using the names of both the sons so as to please both. Using the name of only one son would have upset the other. I had noticed that this happened only when both the sons were present. If one were absent, his name would be dropped. Quite a calculated move, this! I thought.

The woman kept on calling, but not a word came out of my sasu! She was busy cooking, mixing flour.

I crossed over to the front door and found a dark woman with sunken cheeks, uncombed hair, wearing a tattered sari and a blouse in no better condition, sitting on the steps. She was trying to peep inside from where she was sitting.

Mai said, "She has come to ask for something. You clean the pots; I'll fetch water from the well." She departed with two small pitchers and a large one too. The woman began to ask me, "Why, girl, where is your sasu? Why doesn't she give a reply?"

I was able to place her now. At my wedding, she had patted my face, broken her knuckles at my ears and wished me well, undoubtedly with a hope that I would come in handy for some help in the future. But I kept mum, as if engrossed in the pots and pans I was cleaning. Again she started calling out loudly, "O Shantaram's mother! O Deu's mother!" Suddenly my sasu sitting at the stove got up and came out, shouting at her, "What's happened? Why are you shouting as if you're dying?"

The woman's voice sank to a whisper against this tirade. "Oh, it's been two days since I've been trying to visit your house. But you had so many guests, how could I? Anyway, I have come to ask for some dry chillies." My mother-in-law said frostily, "Ha! A good time you've chosen to ask for dry chillies! So early in the morning! As if you cooked without chillies for two days! Don't tell me you didn't cook at all!"

"No, no! It was like this, you see! I had a little ground chutney saved in the salt bowl. I survived on that. But now there is simply nothing! There is no man in my house whom I can send to the shop! And who else can give me some! Is there anyone else but you in this entire locality? Lend me a bit; I'll return yours, when I buy some."

My sasu pretended to be angry at this. "Ha! A fat lot you've returned! Last time you borrowed onions and tea leaves! Did you ever return that?" Going back to her stove, she said, "How come you only find me to borrow whatever you want?" Now her voice had become soft with pleasure.

She wrapped some dry chillies in a piece of paper and gave them to the old woman, who happily got up, saying, "So nice of you to give me this! Now I can cook breakfast for my son." As she was going down the stairs, my mother-in-law called out and said, "Send your suun after a while; I'll give her some rice water." Then she stood straight and said in a loud voice, "There is everything in my house! I have built this whole edifice myself! Though I was a city-bred girl from Mumbai, I worked with my sasu till my bones creaked." This probably was her way of warning us, her daughters-in-law. "When I came in this house, there was nothing! It is because of me that you have everything now." Her voice gradually lost its edge and became normal and free. She began to move around as usual.

Then she came to where I was cleaning the pots. She took in the whole scene at a glance and warned me, "Mind, don't you spill too much water here; it will become very muddy and somebody might slip and fall!" Then she peeped into the water pot. "My, this is almost empty! Now when will they fill it up and when will people bathe?" Then she brought out some burning coals, lit the stove underneath the pot, pushed some sticks into it, and went out to check whether the pens were cleaned or not yet. Now the responsible housewife in her had taken over.

One day my sasu told me why she did not like seeing water spilt near the stove. Something horrifying had happened once. She was pregnant, in the ninth month. She had filled up a pitcher of water and went to pour it into the one kept atop the burning stove. Suddenly she had slipped, fallen on her stomach, and started bleeding horribly. People put her into a palanquin and carried her to a village called Kanedi from where she was put on a bus to Kankavli and from there on another bus to Mumbai. Her husband and two young children accompanied her. On reaching Mumbai, they went to her father's place in Bhoiwada. From there she was taken to the K.E.M. Hospital, where the doctors operated on her. The baby had died inside. My mother-in-law, however, survived this. She returned home without the baby.

A couple of days after this, Harishchandra got ready to catch the early morning bus to Chiplun. Sasu had gotten up early. She had kept chicken on the stove to cook on low heat all night. She had also prepared some ghavans. She had packed the pancakes and the chicken in a tiffin box and kept it ready for him. But Harishchandra refused to carry it. When he was about to step out, she held it out to him once more. He snarled at her, "Didn't I tell you I won't carry anything? Remember what happened last time?"

But her mother's heart would not take a "no." She held it before me and said, "Go, give it to your husband." I did not know what to do. Harishchandra kept repeating endlessly what had happened before. He was appearing for his matriculation exam at the time. His mother had neatly packed some ghavans and a little fried chicken in a plantain leaf. In Ratnagiri there were three Brahmin lanes: upper, middle, and lower. His hostel was in the middle lane. In the bus somebody told him that, since the hostel was in the Brahmin lane, nonvegetarian food was not allowed there. So Harishchandra gave away the lunch packed for him to a coolie at the bus stand. When his mother and the boys in the hostel came to know of it, they were very angry because it was ages since they had seen even the feather of a hen, and here he had given away the tasty chicken dish to a coolie. Since then, he had decided not to carry any food from home. Even as he was getting inside the bus, Harishchandra kept repeating the same story over and over until the bus was out of sight. His poor mother grieved over it for a long time.

Harishchandra, now a responsible husband, had to leave his wife in the village and go away for the first time. I should have felt sad. But I felt nothing of the kind; because I never felt I had come to a strange place when I came to live with my parents-in-law. His family was so nice, and I had come to know them quite well. All my five dirs were affectionate. There was no harassment whatsoever! On the contrary, even my sasra addressed me affectionately, in the plural form rather than singular! He would even tease me, "So, Hari is off! When are you planning to leave?" And I would answer in the same vein, "No way, I am not going anywhere, I am going to stay right here!" like a daughter in playful banter with her father! His affection for me was quite evident!

My sasra was a military man. People addressed him as Sarkar (governor)! He and Gopalbuwa, the grandfather of Sanjay Pawar, the well-known Marathi playwright, were "community judges." Cases from all over the five villages in their jurisdiction came to them for judgment, and they dispensed justice. Naturally, these two were highly respected in the village.

When my husband was on his way to his place of work, I was reminded of a distant cousin of mine whose husband worked on a trawler.

His first wife did not have any children. So he had married another woman—my cousin. He would come home once every three years. How the two wives pampered him! At the end of his leave, when it was time for him to go, both wives competed with each other to demonstrate their love. If one bathed him, the other wiped him dry; if one helped him put his shirt on, the other came forward with his trousers; if one fed him rice, the other put a piece of bhakri in his mouth. They would even go to the port to see him off. There they would burst into tears when he got into the small boat that carried him to his ship. Thus there would be constant competition between the two to show who loved him better. How we used to laugh at them! But today I realize that they wept because they wanted to be able to smile. It was a desperate attempt to ensure marital security.

I was sure about being secure. My husband loved me. Yet a sentence Aai once said had made a deep impression on my mind. "If the husband calls you a whore, the whole world is ready to sleep with you." So I was absolutely sure that I wanted to have good relations with my husband. At any cost!

I was able to learn the ways of my sasar since I was staying with them. Our customs were quite similar; only people's attitudes were different. I would always compare Aai with Sasu. The first thing I noticed about Sasu was her generosity. Whatever she made was always in large quantities; so much so that it would often go waste. One thing was strange though. Like Aai, she used to tell the same story to her daughter and grandchild—the one about the boy who ate his bhakri by just touching it to the vegetable pot, pretending he was eating well.

In my mother's house, only a few pieces of firewood stood near the stove; once those were used up, Aai would buy some more from the women selling firewood. Here, however, it was completely different. The childless one's verandah was stacked to the roof with firewood (they would cut, chop, and dry a whole tree for fuel) and a great heap of dung cakes with paddy chaff, which my mother-in-law made for fuel. So, whether something was cooking or not, the stove would be burning for a long time! No one bothered to pull out the wood and sprinkle water on it to put it out.

The same applied to food. A huge potful of rice was cooked in the evening. Naturally, a lot would be left over. Next, it would be mixed with other leftovers and water and given to the animals in the pen. My heart would bleed at this sight! "What a waste! We could have warmed and eaten it in the morning!" I would say!

"Bah! Who will eat stale rice in the morning?" My sasu would ask me, "And it is not a waste! Our bulls are eating it, aren't they?" She would ask me. Then she would go on repeating to me how she had created all this prosperity from naught! "I am a city-bred girl, the daughter of a 'Mumbaiwala'! and yet have managed to achieve this feat!" was her constant refrain. Her parents were mill workers in Mumbai. Her father had promised to give his daughter to his sister's only son. He had kept his word, and at the tender age of eleven my sasu was married to her husband and came to live in Bhiraunde. Her life was a valiant struggle with poverty, and the present prosperity was a result of her labor.

She was not very sure of me, because I was educated, and worried how I would cope with her family, people, and their customs. After Harishchandra left, she told me quite a few things to initiate me into their ways of life. Two points were always highlighted. One: "Always address your dirs with respect, in the plural. Never call them using the singular form, even though they are younger than you!" But I noticed that she had not included her daughter in this category! A man always has greatness thrust upon him, whereas a woman has to achieve it!

The second point was about the books of Bhiraunde. I said, "Oh, by books of Bhiraunde, you mean their habit of repeating themselves, don't you?" She answered with a smile, "Well, there is that, of course! But what I am telling you is quite different. You know their flag flies high everywhere!"

"Flag? What flag?" I asked.

"I'll tell you! They used to have important books in the village, like the *Ramayana* and the *Mahabharata,* brought by certain people long, long ago from Kashi! In the month of Shravan it was the custom to read these books in the temple. First, these books would be worshipped. People from many villages around ours used to borrow these books to read in their temples. So they carried these books ceremoniously in a procession to their villages. When these were read, they would be brought back in the same way, in a procession, with a band playing. People would ask respectfully, "What procession is this?" And they would get the answer, "Oh, those books from Bhiraunde!" So you can see that the village is famous for books!" Then she would conclude in a sharp tone, "The village flag has always flown high, and that is how it should be, understand?"

My sasu said all this as if she was personally responsible for keeping the village flag flying high! And I too nodded vigorously, as if the job were a cakewalk.

I liked my sasu very much. She was a very nice, affectionate, and enthusiastic person and loved to chat with people. She was very fond of wearing flowers in her hair. Like my mother, she was also very keen on weaving aaydans, and her fingers too flew over the baskets.

Harishchandra used to say, "Our mother is a very simple soul. A simpleton really! She does not understand anything." But this was not right. She was simple all right; but she was by no means a simpleton! While speaking to another, she realized the importance of place, time, and the person concerned. In front of my jaau, she told stories about her husband's childhood. "My Shantaram has been very kindhearted right since his childhood! When I served him meals, he used to take the food outside and feed the dogs first! Once a bullock in the cow pen had a terrible stomachache; it kept mooing the whole night. Shantaram sat in the pen near the sick bull through the night." My jaau would blush with pleasure when she heard her husband being praised for his kindheartedness.

She would tell stories of how her second son had toiled in the fields right from his childhood and how he had always been a great support to his parents. His wife, Mai, would smile happily at this.

The stories about my husband were different! This would be about his obstinate nature. "This husband of yours loved to eat molasses!" she would tell me. "Here I am at the grinding stone or working in the fields, and he comes from behind and pesters me for molasses, clinging to my back, punching me with his small fist, demanding molasses." Then she would say proudly, "I had to give him a big piece of molasses! He would not let me go otherwise! But one thing I must admit, he was very good in his studies!"

I too grinned from ear to ear when I heard this story! He had demanded a different kind of molasses from me and got it too! All stories, however, used to end in the constant refrain that she was the city-bred daughter of a Mumbaiwala! "I gave birth to eleven children ... how I suffered! But did a single sound ever escape out of me? No way!"

These stories, however, went a long way to cementing the bonds of love between her sons and their wives. They're really endeared our sasu to us. There was one more reason, however, why we felt that she was very close to us. She never allowed any backbiting. She never encouraged us when we complained about each other. Instead, she would effectively silence the person who complained. One day, my eldest jaau was terribly upset. She had refused to eat in spite of our repeated entreaties and quarreled with everybody who asked why she was so upset. I casually said to my sasu, "Why does she behave like this? What a nuisance she is to everybody!" My sasu said witheringly, in a clear and ringing tone, "That is none of your concern. Keep quiet and mind your own business." In the Malavan region, the eldest son and his wife were held in great respect. Maybe that was why my eldest jaau received the largest share of my sasu's praise. In fact, my sasu was even a little scared of her!

The people from Malavan are famous for their sharp and caustic tongues. It's very difficult to get a straight answer from them! This is how they receive a guest: "Hmmm! So! You have come, have you? Well, now that you have come, sit down if you want. Here is a paan to chew if you want. And there is rice water, if you want to eat. And if you want to leave, fine; there lies the path, under the peepul tree!" Who would dare stay after this!

Later on I wrote a one-act play on this entitled *Now That You Have Come, Guest, Sit Down If You Want!*

I was often exposed to the lashes of that sharp and caustic tongue. Suppose someone casually inquired, just for the sake of small talk, if one had had one's meals. The answer would never be a simple yes or no. It would be, "Hmmm! I am waiting for an invitation from you to lunch!" The Konkani husband who will give a straight answer to his wife is yet to be born.

People were very fond of quarrels too. Truly, they would invite quarrels on themselves. Once, after we had all gone to bed, my eldest jaau got angry about something. She started fighting with her husband. Suddenly we heard some dogs barking. So my sasu casually said, "Whose stupid dogs are barking at this time of the night?" That was enough! My jaau turned her guns from her husband to Sasu. "Right," she exploded, "Calling me a dog, are you? That is why I am barking ... You dare call me a dog? Is this how you treat me?" When my sasu tried to reason with her, she twisted her words deliberately, and there was yet another explosion. Finally, my sasu gave up and kept quiet, and there was peace in the house.

One day, the family decided to boil paddy. Huge tin containers were filled with water and boiled. The paddy was put into the boiling water, strained into huge cane baskets, and finally spread to dry in the verandah. After it had dried for seven or eight days in the shade, the grains were packed in huge cane containers. The boiling of paddy went on for quite a few days. My younger brother-in-law was adept at such farming techniques. He taught me a great deal about how careful one had to be while boiling paddy, and the varieties of rice, their tastes, color, and so on. The watery stock of *ukadya* rice was tasty, but the *aatu* made from *suray* rice, a thick gruel cooked with plenty of water, was more to my taste. It was a complete food for infants in the village. They only knew mother's milk and not any other kind.

In a few days, I felt completely at home. In the evenings, when the sun went down, I enjoyed going for long walks on the winding path in the hills. Often, I enjoyed just standing under the jackfruit tree in our backyard, looking at the path and the hills. Women walking on the same path on their way to fetch water would halt in their tracks and watch me with interest. A sprawling, sloping patch of a marblelike stone lay nearby. My sasu brought all the dung from the pen to this patch. After every four days, she mixed some rice husk in the dung to pat huge dung cakes for fuel. When she showed me her handiwork, I could sense why she was so proud of herself. She was a city-bred woman, but had taken to village life so well! She still made dung cakes and helped her family.

My jaau had given birth to a baby at that time. She would give herself hot compresses, especially around the waist, using the heat of the dung cakes in the stove. My mother-in-law would say often, "The family can be strong only if the woman's waist is strong." Even her bathwater used to be almost scalding hot; one could not put one's finger into it. It would be the same for the baby too. First the baby was given a massage fit for a wrestler, then a bath with the scalding hot water, after which it was made to inhale the smoke of burning fennel. This made the poor baby go red hot with heat, and it howled until its voice cracked.

One obligatory ritual while bathing the baby was to clean its ears with mouthfuls of water rinses, which were considered a very healthy thing. The woman bathing the baby spat out the betel leaf she was chewing, filled her mouth with water and then squirted it into the baby's ears. This ritual was commonly found everywhere. All the women in my mother's village considered it necessary, and those at my in-law's place were no exception. This custom must have ruined so many ears! But they were not in the least aware of it.

There was yet another strange ritual, performed after the baby's bath with the express intention of averting the evil eye. After the bath was over, the woman bathing the baby would lift the baby up from her legs, collect the water dripping in her palm and, after moving it around the baby's body, throw it away. Then she would take the dirt sticking to her left toe and press it hard on the baby's forehead. Sometimes, the dirty water or the mud would trickle down into the baby's eyes. Trying to avert the evil eye would thus hurt the baby's own eyes. When the baby's nose was blocked because of a cold, they poured coconut oil into its nostrils, thus openly inviting the prospect of pneumonia. The oil would enter the baby's lungs and prepare the ground for diseases like bronchitis and asthma. My own asthma and the flowing nostrils of my brother's children are some obvious cases in point. There were many children suffering like this at both my mother's and my in-law's places.

My sasu was known in the village as a vaidya. She dispensed herbal medicines made from leaves or roots of medicinal plants. Many people would come to her for treatment. If the medicine had to be taken mixed with milk, it was easier to get a woman's breast milk rather than a cow's or buffalo's. If a young child of around five years were found to be crying all the time and not eating enough, my sasu would give him the following treatment. She would fill up a copper pitcher with fresh water from the well; pour a lot of coconut oil in the water, and keep the pitcher in the sun for a long time. Then she would pour the water on a plate and hold the child upside down on it. Some oil would stick to his head. Next she would hold the child upright and apply the oil dripping from its head to the whole body. The child would get a hot water bath only in the evening. Until then it would roam around—dust sticking all over the oily body, looking like a piglet on a dung heap!

When I lived at my parents-in-law's place, it was high summer. Most of the wells in the Konkan go dry toward the end of March. Our well did too. At such times, our women went to the well of the Maratha caste to fetch water. One day, when Mai started to go out with the water pitcher on her head, I too picked up a pitcher and began following her. My sasu stopped me and said, "Don't go there. It won't be nice." I countered, "Why not?" My sasu replied, "Just listen to me and do what I say." I thought she was telling me not to go because I was a new bride. I followed Mai to the well. When I reached the well, I saw our women standing with empty pitchers, begging the Maratha women, "Sister, please give us some water, please, oh, please." I retraced my steps with the pitcher empty in my hand.

One day we had to husk the rice on the *ghirat:* the special wooden mill, like the grinding stone, for husking grains. After lunch, Mai asked me, "Will you help me?" I was very glad to help, of course. While Mai got a basketful of rice from the cane container, I took down the two parts of the wheel-like wooden mill and was pleasantly surprised to find beautiful designs carved on the insides. The mill had such beautiful intricate art inside, and I hadn't even noticed it. Our father-in-law had carved that design long ago. The wheel looked like a carving on display in an art exhibition. How many such pieces of art lay hidden in the daily toil? Mai put the wheels on top of one another and then poured some grains through the big hole of the top wheel. We began to grind slowly. It moved far more easily than the grinding stone. The rice grains separated easily from the husk and fell out from the space between the wheels.

Once a sizable quantity of dehusked rice grains was produced, Mai gathered them in a winnow and, with rhythmic back and forth movements, discarded the husk, retaining the grains inside the winnow. But the smaller, almost powderlike husk would not separate from the rice grains. Then she would tilt the winnow to one side, hold one corner with her left hand, and rhythmically move it back and forth, tapping on the winnow with the fingers of her right hand all the while. The heavy rice grains remained at the bottom of the winnow while the light powdery husk kept falling down from the tilted end. The sweet *tipur, tipur* noise of her fingers, tapping rhythmically against the winnow, made my eyes drowsy with sleep.

One day, while we were working like this, my brother Shahu suddenly arrived at the door. "Come in, come in," my elder brother-in-law went ahead to welcome him, "How come you have come so suddenly, without any letter or message?" he asked. "Well, I have come to take my sister home, as the custom demands," my brother replied while climbing up the stairs. Then his eyes fell on the ghirat, the husk, the basketful of rice, and me sitting in front of the ghirat, covered in the husk, dirty, with my uncombed hair. He stared at me as if I were a prisoner, doing hard labor in a prison in the Andaman Islands. I, however, did not realize this then. On seeing my brother, I simply jumped up with delight and threw my arms around him, tears of joy running down my face. He, on the other hand, mistook my joy for anguish!

My in-laws killed a hen that day and treated my brother to a delightful meal. My father-in-law could have taken offense at his having come without prior notice in my husband's absence, taking them for granted, but did nothing of the kind. He did not make it a prestige issue. In fact, none of them did. On the contrary, they urged him repeatedly to extend his stay. However, he was in a hurry. The next day, I returned with my brother to my mother's house. My sasu gave me a bagful of rice grains as a gift for my mother. I remembered with shame the bagful of shellfish that my mother had sent her as a gift!

Mai felt sad when I left. We had grown to be real friends. I was going to return in a week's time after a stay at my mother's. There was no reason for me to cry, but my eyes were brimming with tears at the thought of going away from them, my people, whom I had really come to love. I hadn't shed a single tear when my husband left!

The moment we arrived at my mother' place, Shahu said to my mother, "See? It was exactly as I had predicted! She has to work so hard there! Imagine, she was husking grains when I reached her house!"

I said, "Hey, nobody forced me to do it; I myself offered to help because I wanted to." Nobody said anything about this, but I could distinctly hear the unspoken words: "Now reap as you have sown!"

Urmila Pawar's
mother

Urmila Pawar
in 1962, in class 10

Urmila with her husband,
parents-in-law, and brother-
in-law, February 10, 1967

Urmila as an actor
in the Marathi play
Bandu Natak Karto, 1970

From the left: Govindadada; slightly behind him with the white cap, Urmila's father-in-law; slightly in front of him with black cap, Harishchandra's mama or maternal uncle; behind him, Manjulatai's husband; next to him, Shantiakka's husband; *in front,* Vahini, holding Meena, her husband, Bhai, standing next to her, holding the younger daughter, Sanhya. *Center:* the bridegroom, Harishchandra, with the bride, Urmila, in white. From the right: Harishchandra's mami or maternal aunt is in front of Urmila; Saroj, Urmila's niece, stands next to her; behind her is Urmila's mother-in-law; next to her is Urmila's mother; next to her is Vahini's mother; then, in white, Bhikiakka, and at the end of the row, at the extreme right, Kerubaya.

Interviewing a participant in the Ambedkarite movement
for her book, coauthored with Meenakshi Moon, *Aamhihi
Itihaas Ghadwala: Ambedkari Chalvalitil Streeyancha
Sahabhag* (Sugava Prakashan, 1980)

Front: Harishchandra,
Manini, and Urmila;
back: Malakiva and
Mandar; 1983

Receiving the Priyadarshini Award, 2004

Receiving the Padmashri Vikhepatil Puruskar, 2005

Receiving the Maharashtra Foundation Award, 2006

On her sixtieth birthday; *from left:* Manini and her husband, Nitin; Urmila, Malavika with Moksah

From left: Malavika with Druv; Urmila, Moksha, and Ravi

Manini with daughter Maitree, 2008

Seven

After a few days I arrived in Ratnagiri. Harishchandra was still working in Chiplun. I wrote to him saying I had come and then registered my name in the employment exchange office. He came in a couple of days, and I shifted from my mother's house to his room in Ratnagiri, which he had retained. The room and all his possessions lying there were covered in thick layers of dust. I set myself the task of cleaning everything, and, while I cleaned the room, Harishchandra went out and bought essential provisions like lentils, rice, vegetables, and so on. We stayed in this room for a couple of days. It was quite close by my mother's house. Funnily, I had got so used to our clandestine meetings that it took me quite some time to believe that we were actually living together! After some days, we took a bus to his village, gathered some more things, went to Chiplun, and set up our home in his room there, which was as tiny as a rabbit hole. Though the room was tiny, our love was great! We lived there like a royal couple.

In Chiplun our landlady was an illiterate widow, a Kunbi, a member of a non-Dalit peasant caste. She was bringing up her four children by working as a maidservant. Once Harishchandra left for his office, the elder daughter would come to chat with me. She often ate her meals with me as well. One day she wanted to attend a wedding and came to borrow a sari from me. She pleaded with me, promising that she would use the sari very carefully and return it immediately after the wedding. I had no problem lending her my sari. I lit the stove to make tea for us first, opened my tin trunk, and brought out my wedding saris. When she looked at the white sari, she asked me whose sari it was. I said, "Mine, of course. We wear a white sari at our weddings." The moment the words were out of my mouth, the girl was dumbstruck. Till then she had spoken to me so ingratiatingly; now she suddenly lost her voice. Picking up my brocade sari, she walked off.

"Wait! Where are you going? The tea will be ready in a minute!" I said. But she said cryptically, "No, Mother has made some!" and walked off. After that, she never came to our room, though, of course, she took a whole month to return my sari, all soiled and stained. When I grumbled about it, her mother said, "Look for another room!" Nothing made sense! But why do I say so? Of course, everything made sense! It was about caste!

Harishchandra was transferred once again from Chiplun to Ratnagiri. And we came back to the same room in the marketplace. We painted the room, made it more habitable. But when the landlady, Malathibai Ajgaonkar, saw this, she summoned me through one of her servants to her room. Her thin, dark, emaciated-looking servant with hollow cheeks came to my door and rudely called out, "Hey you, come on, you are wanted!" He was always rude. Even when he came to collect the room rent, he would bark, "Hey, you, Powar, give the rent immediately!" It was as if he wanted us to leave the room. He had probably guessed that Harishchandra did not like being called Powar and therefore made it a point to use that name.

I asked Harishchandra, "Why do you think she has sent for me?" He said, "Well, you are a new bride; maybe she is going to perform *oti!* My experience with the previous landlady was quite fresh in my mind so I was quite skeptical. Yet I thought that, since this landlady was educated, she was really being civil and wanted to get introduced properly. So I changed into a better sari and went to visit her. A glance from the threshold revealed a big hall with a sofa set, some expensive furniture, tables, and cupboards. The flowerpot on the table had lovely roses in it … the atmosphere was quite pleasant. Then suddenly a lizard caught my eye; creeping out from under a table and up the wall where it sat stuck to the surface! It was so incongruous!

Then the landlady came out. She had a fair round face and a tiny kum-kum mark on her forehead! She wore a white nine-yard sari, the pallav draped around both shoulders. She had tied her hair into a plait, arranged like a bun at the back of her head with a flower worn in the typical Malavani style, erect, as if rising straight from the head. I had seen her many times before, passing our door, checking to see if everything was clean. Since she was a member of the municipal council, I had surmised that she was making sure that the surroundings were properly cleaned.

She pointed her finger at a chair kept near the door, signaling that I sit there, and then fixed her eyes on the lizard on the wall. "Look," she began, "our rooms are basically for bachelors. But many people get married and do not move out. But I want to make one thing very clear to you." Here she removed her eye from the lizard and fixed it on me instead. Coldly, she said, "You may not know it, but the spirit of our ancient ancestor guards this place. It moves everywhere and cannot stand any dirt. Otherwise it gets extremely wrathful. Many people have experienced this. I am telling this to you for your own good. Go find a room elsewhere!"

My earlier landlady was a maidservant and this landlady was a municipal councillor. Yet the maid and the honorable councillor were united on one point: caste. Defenseless, I got up, and returned to our room. When I reported this to Harishchandra, he gave me a disconsolate smile by way of answer!

The room was in the basement. There was a high window near the ceiling by the side of the road. Before our marriage, I used to stealthily peep into the room from the road to see what Harishchandra was doing. Now people passing on the road, pretending to talk to someone from the "malaria" office above us, peeped into ours to see what we were doing. Finally, I hung a curtain there. However, I found the darkness that I had loved so dearly before quite suffocating now. There was a gutter in front of the door in which the water used for washing malaria slides flowed continuously. The strong smell gave me severe headaches. But the room was centrally situated; the market, office, dispensary, and bus stand were close by. So we did not want to leave the room. Besides, most of the house owners had caste prejudice in their blood! So we were forced to live in the same room for quite some time.

Upper-caste families occupied the rooms above. Gradually, I began to learn their smart ways, clean habits, and the variety of dishes they made. My sister-in-law, Shalini, also came to live with us. She had enrolled herself in the tenth standard in the girls' school in Ratnagiri.

Mohan Methar from Vengurla lived in a room nearby with his wife, Neela. She loved me like her sister. She was addicted to two things: tobacco and cleanliness! I picked up both. I was consciously trying to remember everything that my mother had taught me and behaved accordingly. For instance, I never used any provisions from the shop unless I had thoroughly cleaned them in a winnow for the obvious reason that they contained mice droppings. Or I never picked up any plate or lid to use as a cover for any dish unless I was sure that nothing like a lizard was sticking under it. I never brought clothes hanging out to dry inside the house without thoroughly brushing them first, because there might be a snake or scorpion hiding inside these. I remember a girl in my school who was traveling on a bus. A scorpion had somehow got inside her blouse and stung her in many places. Yet she had not uttered a single sound because of her so-called modesty. When she got down from the bus, she simply fainted and collapsed in a heap!

Neelavahini's cleanliness could be sensed even with one's eyes closed. She used to clean her brass pots for such a long time that when she had washed them and left them out to dry in the sun they sparkled like gold. The clothes she brought for washing looked as if they were already washed; yet she would apply a lot of soap and rinse them so hard in the tin bucket that I would worry that either the bucket was going to crack or the clothes would tear. They had a small bathroom in their tiny one-room house. Even the bathroom would be so clean that one could have sat down on the tiles to dine. The small space outside her house too would be swept sparkling clean, washed and decorated with a rangoli. Her own sari and blouse would be spotless, without a speck of dust. She was a smallish woman, with a light complexion that had the glow of wheat, had wide lips, and her laughter was like a roar. She would laugh so loudly that people often turned back to frown at her, their faces clearly reflecting their displeasure. It did not become a woman to laugh so loudly! She had magic in her fingers even as a cook. She taught me how to cook tasty dishes in an economical way. In the beginning, I made mistakes. However, my friends like Hema Kadrekar and some others from the office above patiently ate whatever I cooked. They never made me feel bad, even when my culinary experiments went horribly wrong, and I valued their affection!

I was able to give up the habit of chewing tobacco only after getting the job. The reason was simple; it was difficult to spit in the office. Though I had been a confirmed spitter as a child, now I was an educated adult and found it difficult to do so.

After enrolling my name in the employment exchange, I received two appointment letters from two offices at the same time, making it difficult for me to choose. Harishchandra said, "Close your eyes and put your finger on any name. Then go and join that office." I followed his advice and reported for the job.

When I got my first salary, I could not believe that all that money was mine; that I could spend it the way I liked. Before my marriage, I used to hand over my salary to my mother. Now I started handing it over to my husband. If this is not like deliberately offering your head for the butcher's knife, what else is it?

Just when life had become a little easier, a telegram arrived and delivered a terrible blow. My eldest brother, Bhai, had died in an accident. I was terribly worried, not only for Vahini, my brother's wife, and her children who were in Ratnagiri at that time, but also for my mother. She collapsed on hearing the news. The image of Bhai's face constantly floated before my eyes. Slim, tall, with large expressive eyes, he was a man of simple habits who never possessed more than two pairs of trousers and shirts. There was no fancy furniture in his house, nor did he have any bad habits like alcohol or tobacco. He would send us money every month after getting his salary. Basically a shy and introverted person, he loved to paint and play the flute. These were the ways he could express himself, his ways of articulation. Many of his pictures depicted a winding path, melting away into the distance. Two of his paintings are still hung on the walls of Vahini's house. She had to resort to stitching clothes to earn her livelihood and raise her children.

About a year after this, I found myself pregnant. But, unlike the heroines in Hindi movies, I did not feel any ecstatic euphoria when I gave this news to Harishchandra. But he was absolutely thrilled. One day he got me a book to read with something like *Before and After Childbirth* as a title. It was a guide of sorts for baby care. When our neighbor, Mohan Methar, saw the book, he heartily laughed at us. "Mr. Pawar," he said, "If a man reads a book on swimming and jumps into water, will the bookish knowledge save him from drowning? He has to learn swimming by doing it. You don't need a book to learn that!"

"Maybe you are right," Harishchandra answered, "maybe the man will drown. But reading a book certainly helps him to get an idea about the whole business. There is a possibility that he will be able to save himself." The debate went on and on. And then Aai burst out, "To hell with the book! All I want is safety for the two lives." I understood what she meant when I went into the labor room. In truth, they should have hung a big board with "Torture Room" instead of "Labor Room" written on it! How could women keep returning to the room again and again after the first ordeal of labor pains, I wondered. They say public memory is always short. Such women must have inspired the saying! But I too was no exception because even I paid two more visits to the labor room!

My labor pains started in the wee hours of dawn. They began with a tiny spark of pain and the intensity kept on increasing. Aai had told me what to do when the labor pains started. She would often peep in through our window just to see that everything was all right. When the pains became acute, Harishchandra lit the stove and heated water for my bath and made tea for me. By the time I finished my bath and had tea, the pains became sharper. By this time, it was day. Harishchandra took me to the civil hospital nearby. While a nurse examined me and asked me to sit on a bench, he rushed to fetch my mother. When she arrived, I was virtually beside myself with the pains. She kept muttering, "It must be a son; yes, look at the pains ... coming like a snake hissing." I couldn't care less whether it was a son or a daughter; I just wanted the ordeal to be over. Finally after a shattering explosion of terrible pain, which virtually tore me apart, came the release. Mother was proved right! It *was* a son. Harishchandra and I felt deliriously happy. When I was brought out of the labor room with the baby, my vahini, Mami, and a neighbor looked at me as if I had won a great battle. The nurse told Harishchandra that I had three to four stitches. He did not have to make a public announcement of this; but he declared this loudly to my mother standing nearby, "Vimal has had three stitches." I felt so embarrassed! But then I saw male relatives of the other new mothers asking about the number of stitches quite casually and being supplied the information with equal ease, without in any way feeling ashamed of the area that was stitched up!

Since it was my first delivery, custom demanded that I went to my mother's place for recuperation, and, after spending three or four days in the hospital, Aai took us home. There was a man called Sawant from Bhiraunde, an acquaintance, who passed by our house on his way to the mental hospital where he worked. He shouted from the road to ask my mother, "Hey you, Powar woman, your daughter has delivered, right? What is it?"

Aai replied, "She had a son." The man seemed repelled! Walking away in a huff, he spat out abuses, "The bastards! They always have sons!" My mother shouted back, "Why, does that give you a stomach ache?" But he never waited to hear her reply. He knew that my mother-in-law also had six or seven sons. The fact that they were all educated and employed hurt him like a thorn in the flesh. After that, he always passed our house using the other side of the road, hiding his face. But Aai remembered his words, even after twenty-two years.

While reading the book *Before and After Childbirth*, I realized one thing: the writer hesitated in using any sexual terms. "Once the umbilical cord is cut, the baby which has come out becomes free" (out of what?). "Sometimes the baby gets in a horizontal position inside" (where exactly inside?). "Sometimes one arm or leg comes out" (out of what?). Then there would be a bit of advice thrown in: "Feed the child with as much water as milk right from birth." I was horrified that our women in villages never fed the baby anything except breast milk. Now I realize that they were quite right.

In those days, it was believed that a baby should not be breast-fed, as that spoils the form of the woman. Anyway, I never had much milk in me. It is said that when a mother nurses her baby she gets more milk. But mine was a strange case. I never had much milk; besides, I found nursing the baby a very painful task; it was as if ants were biting me. Many people recommended various remedies, medicines and diets. Some friends advised me to eat ladus made of either fenugreek seeds or haliv seeds. Special diets for the new mother were unheard of. Finally, a neighbor, Gokhalevahini, told Harshchandra how to make them, and he, in turn, passed the recipe on to my mother. He also bought the fenugreek seeds for her. She ground the seeds, mixing molasses in the powder in the right proportion. Everything was done according to the recipe, but somehow nobody could eat the ladus. They were so bitter! Finally, it was Harishchandra, the father of the baby rather than the mother, who finished them off.

Aaye made soup with a particular fish that I took with rice to get more milk. My sasu brought some medicinal herbs. I drank the juice of these herbs every morning and evening. The doctor also prescribed many medicines, which I dutifully took. But all attempts failed. I had to feed the baby with the bottle. Not that I minded it, as breast-feeding the baby was so painful. Besides, I had only one and a half months' maternity leave before and after the delivery. This meant that the baby had to be weaned sooner.

Aaye gave me many lessons in postnatal care. The first was to apply a hot compress, else the body makes farting noises or the uterus comes out. I had seen this happen to illiterate village women. So I would sit over a stove of burning coals with a blanket around me till tears ran down my eyes. I bathed in scalding water like my jaau. Another lesson was to tie one's abdomen well so as to not let it sag. This second measure would literally peel the skin off my body. I would tie a whole nine-yard sari around my abdomen so tightly with the help of a strong woman that I was simply unable to eat anything. The sari had to be kept on for at least three hours.

I would also sit with my back against the burning stove at night for some time. Village women would light a few pieces of coal and slept against the heat. Aai used to say, "You educated girls are so fragile! How much noise you make if the body gets a little torn! Look at the village women. They take pads of cloth soaked in salt water and take hot compresses by using heated pieces of earthen pots!"

Aai bathed my baby, giving him a good oil massage first. After the bath was over, she would rinse water in her mouth and spit it in his ears. Once I told Aai not to do this. She said, "All the filth in your body has entered his ears. Shouldn't I clean them?" "No, you mustn't." I replied. "All right, then," she said in resignation, "Do as you wish! You are educated! I'm only an ignorant woman!" She also used to take out the soil sticking on her left toe and apply it to his forehead after the bath. Once I saw the dirt trickling into his eyes with the bathwater and could not bear the sight. Finally, I started bathing the baby myself.

Women had their own ideas about male and female bodies. While massaging baby girls, women squeezed their tiny palms in their fists so as to make them small; but they would press the palms of baby boys with their thumbs so as to make them broad. They would also pull their fingers to make them long. Girls' buttocks would be pressed downward so as to press them inside, whereas, when it came to boys, the massage was exactly in the opposite direction so that they would stick out. More pressure was applied to the girls' sides and pelvic bones; their noses also would be pinched upward to make them straight. Boys' noses were never touched. Babies would scream hoarse during the massage and sleep like logs after the hot water bath. Many working-class women gave opium to their babies to make them sleep longer. My elder sister, Akka, harbored the suspicion that she was given opium as a baby and that was why she felt she was not bright enough.

Once Aai made some spicy chicken curry and Harishchandra got brandy. I remembered how we had made liquor from cashew pods, rinsed Govindadada's bottles, and drank the water. I drank the brandy, but was worried nonetheless: suppose I became drunk; suppose I could not hold the baby! But Harishchandra said, "Go ahead and drink. Nothing will happen."

On the twelfth day, my sasu came for the naming ceremony from our village to my mother's house. My nanand Shalini and Harishchandra were in our room. Two days before the ceremony, I was sitting with the baby on my lap. Because my son did not sleep well at night and cried a lot, my brother Shahu kept teasing me. He had found an almanac in the house with the help of which he pretended to read his future. "Just bear with his crying for a few more days. It is Rahu that is troubling your son. Once that is over, he will sleep and allow you to sleep well too!" We laughed heartily over this.

One night I was trying to put the baby to sleep. Suddenly, the bed began to shake violently. Pots and pans on the plank in the wall beat against each other. For some time, I thought my sasu, who was sleeping on the floor near the cot, had unwittingly kicked the cot in her sleep. But then I realized what it was. "Earthquake, earthquake!" I shouted loudly. By this time my mother and mother-in-law were wide awake and Shahu, who was sleeping out on the verandah, came in shouting, "Come out, come out; this is the earthquake!" But we remained sitting inside. We had no idea what an earthquake could do. We could hear the commotion outside. The floor went on shaking for a couple of minutes. Then all grew quiet. After some time Harishchandra came on his bicycle, scared to death. But he was so relieved to find us safe and sound.

The next day we read about the earthquake in the Koyna region. The dam was safe, but the surrounding area was completely devastated. Newspapers were full of news about the earthquake. Shahu said, "See? Your son was born and the earthquake came. Your son is going to be a great man. He will give us great shocks!" The naming ceremony was performed shortly after this. We named him Mandar. Like the mythical mountain, he was the pinnacle of our dreams, our hopes.

At that time I did not know what "great shocks" my son had in store for us. But in the next few days my nanand did give us a great shock! My sasu had left for her village immediately after the naming ceremony, as she was worried about what havoc the earthquake had caused in the village. I had planned to stay with my mother for a couple of weeks and return to our room afterward.

One day Harishchandra came to visit us at Aai's place. We had had our lunch and sat chatting casually. It was around two-thirty in the afternoon. Suddenly Harishchandra noticed two of his acquaintances standing at the door. He went forward to greet them. They whispered something to him, and he immediately put his chappals on and hurried out with them. I surmised that there was some urgent work at the office. But why leave suddenly like this, without saying a word? I kept wondering. Aai too was quite surprised.

It was evening when Harishchandra returned to my mother's place. But he was not alone. Shalini too was with him. Her eyes were red and swollen, as if she had cried a great deal. She kept sniffing. She rushed in, threw her arms around me, and burst into tears.

"What's happened? What's happened?" Stunned, we kept asking her. Harishchandra sat on the verandah while the girl kept weeping. I made her sit down. Aai gave her some water to drink. Still, she would not speak. Finally, exasperated, Aai said to Harishchandra, "Hey, Pawar, what's wrong? Say something! How do we know what happened?"

Harishchandra burst out, "Today, this girl almost got me hanged!" He glared at his sister.

"What did you do?" Perplexed, I asked her. But she hid her face in her palms and cried even more. Both Aai and I looked at each other helplessly. Now Harishchandra told us the whole story.

"Yesterday, I scolded her because she is so weak in her studies. In fact, she is weak in all subjects. But I never imagined she would take it to heart like this! Do you know what she did? She gave me hot water for the bath as usual, tea and chapati to eat for breakfast before I went to work in the morning. Now ask her what she did after that!"

Again we were at a loss! She was such a simple soul, so quiet and unassuming. Was there an affair with some young man? But no, there was no chance of her falling in love with somebody! Then what had she done? Finally Aai asked in sheer exasperation, "She will say nothing. So why don't *you* tell us?"

What he told us shocked us to the core. The girl felt so terribly hurt because of Harishchandra's scolding that she had gone to the seashore, climbed atop the cliff under which boats laid their anchors, and flung herself down into the deep, raging waves below. Fortunately, there were some Muslim fishermen around. They saw her jumping down and immediately jumped in after her and dragged her out. Luckily, she had not swallowed much seawater and they were able to revive her soon. They asked her her brother's name, his office and home address! The whole sequence was straight out of a film.

Harishchandra ceased talking, but we were speechless with shock. Aai began to cry. Any sad events invariably reminded her of the tragic events in her own life and she broke down. Then I scolded Harishchandra. "What a dreadful temper you have, really! You do not stop after you have said something. You go on repeating yourself an infinite number of times. When will you learn to notice what this does to others? See the effect on Shalini? This is how you scold me too!" I deliberately said all this to put Shalini at ease, to show her that I was on her side. Then I drew her affectionately toward me. "Shalini," I said, "if you pay good attention to what he teaches you, you will definitely do well in your exams. It is not too late. And even if he scolds you, isn't he your own brother? Why should you take it to heart to such an extent?" One thing, of course, was true. She could not adjust to the school in Ratnagiri. Her village school was so different from this city school! Naturally, she was under a lot of pressure here. Her brother's scolding was like the proverbial straw that broke the camel's back.

Harishchandra kept telling my mother, "This girl does not speak even a word to me! I ask her a thousand questions. But she keeps quiet! It is impossible to know what she thinks. I so much want her to talk to me, even fight with me! But she does not utter a single word! One day I gave her a notebook and told her to write down the line 'I will talk to you' a thousand times! Then I went to the office, thinking that now, finally, she would talk to me. When I returned from the office in the evening, she quietly handed over the notebook to me, without saying a word. She had literally copied the sentence a thousand times! It was all over the note-book! Now tell me, when will she really speak to me?"

A girl speaks only when she is given her own space. Shalini was no exception to this. My father-in-law found a good boy with a good job and married her off. After her marriage, a few children followed and she became a completely transformed person. Now she could converse on any topic very well. She has some very good qualities. She is a stickler for cleanliness. She sits near the tap for hours together, looking for stains on clothes and pots and pans and washing them clean. She is a very good-natured woman. Though she is the only sister of my husband and his brothers, she never shows off her status, nor did she ever poison her mother's ears against her brothers' wives as a traditional sister-in-law is wont to do. So she is a great favorite with all her sisters-in-law. Her husband's uncle, B. B. Tambe Master, was like Mr. Appasaheb Patwardhan, the great philanthropist. He was a Gandhian and had devoted his life to the amelioration of problems faced by the Dalits in the region. He was a great support for many needy people. A boys' high school in Kankavli was about to close down for want of government grants. But he went from door to door, raising funds for the school, kept it going for some seven or eight more years and saved it from closing down.

Shalini looked after my baby for a year, until she got married. After she left, I had to employ quite a few girls to babysit. But none of them was able to work for long. They were mostly village girls, school dropouts re-ally, who sat at home doing nothing. Somebody or other recommended them to me, and I brought them to Ratnagiri. But the ambience of the city had a bewildering effect on these village girls and they could never get used to it. I could see that they were young, forced by circumstances to work. Even so, I would lose my temper with them. I knew in my heart that I should treat them kindly, but I ended up scolding them. When that happened, some of them would suddenly leave. The baby suffered, and so did I, because I had to work harder, both at home and in the of-fice. Then there would be problems related to taking leave and writing memos. Gradually, however, I learned from experience and grew wiser. The caretakers began staying for longer periods. But I never thought about educating them, teaching them a little from books. Why, I never even gave a thought to educating my nanand! She could have, at least, cleared matriculation! I could and should have helped her do that! But the thought never entered my head. Today I feel guilty for not having done this. But what is the use of feeling guilty now?

When our son was two, I found myself pregnant once again. I wanted another son so that I could go through the family planning operation. This was the common thing to do. Many women went through sterilization after having two sons and showed off their status! But my second child was a girl. So Harishchandra said, "Let's take one more chance." But once again it was a girl! I thought how simple and easy it was to have a baby, like saying let's have one more cup of tea!

Our children called me Aai and Harishchandra Anna. In those days, it was getting fashionable to call one's parents Mummy and Papa! But somehow we never gave up our Marathi spirit. My mother-in-law used to visit us occasionally to meet the children. When she came, she would invariably perform *tan,* a kind of magic, the traditional ritual for the children, even if they had a common cold. Finally, I found a way to help her and rescue the children from the ordeal. I got her some bamboo sticks from my mother's house. She happily sat down to weave basket after basket of various shapes and sizes. Bits and pieces of bamboo were scattered all over the house. Harishchandra would be angered by the mess and scolded her. "Why must you weave baskets at this age? Just eat, drink, and rest!" But rest was anathema to her. Indeed, weaving baskets was her only relaxation. She would proudly tell my neighbors, "You know, I am the daughter of a Mumbaiwala; but I can still weave baskets!" I found this quite amusing.

She had another hobby. The first thing she said after coming to stay with us was, "Take me to a doctor!" Her problems were quite strange: "The tap in my tummy is swollen" or "I feel like cutting off my waist" or "There is a strange twitching in my private parts" or "My feet and hands are burning badly!" She screwed the earrings in her ears so tight that there were inflammations on her earlobes. So I brought an ointment and squeezed the contents of the tube on two fingers. My logic was simple; two fingers for two ear lobes. But Sasu took the medicine on one finger, applied it on the lobes, and said, "How the educated lack in basic intelligence!" I burst out laughing because I had not realized that one finger would do for both earlobes!

By nature I could never sit idle or be complacent. They say that once you paint your face and the theater bug bites you, you can never rest easy! I was no exception. In the annual entertainment program held in our office at the time of Ganesh Utsav, many employees like Madhav Desai, Mohan Gavankar, Kadwaikar, Birje, and Bhosale staged plays. Women from Ratnagiri were a little hesitant about acting in plays. There were two women called the Hegishte sisters who could be hired to act in plays. But they were busy. So someone asked me if I would like to act. I agreed on two conditions: no late-night rehearsals and no physical contact with co-actors. I acted in several full-length plays, such as *Mala Kahi Sangaychay, Ashrunchi Zali Phule, Shantata Court Chalu Ahe*, and quite a few one-act plays, like *Bandu Natak Karto, Bandu Undir Marto, Swapna*, and so on. My role as Benare in Tendulkar's *Shanata Court Chalu Ahe* was widely acclaimed and I won the first prize for acting. Harishchandra did not object to my theater activities, as I did not come home very late. And yet I did not wish to pursue this career. In the first place, I had a terrible complex about my voice, which was hoarse, unlike other women's. It made me feel so nervous.

There was a music teacher who gave lessons in classical music. Since he lived near our office, I went to ask him if I could sing. He said, "Come to my class. I will turn you into Shobha Gurtu in a year's time!" Shobha Gurtu was a very famous singer then. Anyway, the women who came for lessons from this music teacher sang so terribly that finally our boss got mad and ordered our office to be shifted elsewhere! As a result, I gave up the idea of taking music lessons. A lucky escape indeed, both for Shobha Gurtu and the people in my office!

I staged a one-act play called *Swapna* (The Dream), by Padma Gole, with the girls in our office. I was doing the role of a rich old widow in the play. Now a widow meant a white sari, and that too a nine-yard one! By this time our Deshpande teacher and Ms. Lubri had got married and settled down in Ratnagiri. I naively thought my problem of obtaining the nine-yard sari was as good as solved. I only had to ask! I went to their house. He was sitting on the verandah all by himself. After the initial small talk, I put forth my request and his face fell. The same man who used to send us off all over Ratnagiri in search of drapery, like beggars at the time of an eclipse, said, "Well I cannot promise. Let me see! I'll ask my wife. She might give it. Come later." He was protecting the individual freedom of his wife! I just wanted to tell him, "Sir, if anyone asked my husband, he would take it off my body and give it away! He would not have said what you are saying!"

We, of course, did not think of the other option—of not making the widow wear a white sari. Once again I went to him begging for a sari. He managed to procure an old sari and did not forget to warn me to use it well. Somehow I wore it for the sake of the play. I had the sari washed and pressed in a laundry before returning it. It's a tiny incident, really, which has somehow got stuck in the sieve of memory.

Shantabai Jog was able to live in Ratnagiri for a couple of years. Later, she went back to Mumbai. She asked me affectionately to look her up in Mumbai if I were ever there and assured me that I would certainly get work there if I wanted to act in plays.

Then my brother-in-law happened to get married in Mumbai, and both Harishchandra and I went there for the wedding. Shantabai's play *Nat Samrat* was running in Shivaji Mandir, so we went to see it. The real reason was that I was keen to meet her! And it was not because I wanted to get a role, as I had a terrible complex about my harsh voice! Besides, I already had a decent job. A bird in the hand is always better than two in the bush!

Since I was not able to see her before the play, I went to meet her during the intermission. She was somewhere inside; we were told she was changing her costume. She came out after some time—reddish eyes, whitish make up ... dark kohl on the eyelids ... like the Kathakali mask. She came close and gave me a false smile, like in the play! She asked me casually, "How do you like the play?" and, without waiting for my answer, just turned her back on us and walked off! Maybe she had not recognized me! When she stood close to me, I got a faint whiff of alcohol. I thought she walked on slightly unsteady legs. But when the curtains went up after the intermission, she performed so well! We returned home happy to have seen a fabulous play.

Eight

Mumbai fascinated Harishchandra. He had lived in Mumbai as a student for two years, when he was in classes 7 and 8. He lived in Naygaon with his maternal uncle, in Chawl no. 12. In those days, Naygaon and Lalbaug were the two areas where a large number of workers from the Konkan region who came to Mumbai in search of work would stay. The work helped them survive, and the Dalit and workers' movements helped them live their life with dignity. Many political meetings took place there, and people had a chance to listen to several leaders. A makeshift stage would be made with wooden planks between two buildings for such public meetings. Harishchandra had listened to many such speeches. Once he got to hear Dr. Ambedkar speaking and was mesmerized. He told us about his impressions of Dr. Ambedkar many times! Every time he did so, I could see Dr. Ambedkar's piercing eyes reflected in the sparkle of Harishchandra's own. The memory of those golden days always made him yearn for Mumbai. It was only in Mumbai he felt our children would have a real opportunity to progress.

At Harishchandra's behest, we finally decided to move to Mumbai with the children. Our belongings would come later. We decided to put up with my sister Manjulatai in Kurla until we got our own place. She had a small two-room flat, built under the Maharashtra government's housing scheme, in which both our families, Tai's and mine, lived with our husbands, children (three each), and two ayahs or nursemaids (since both of us were working women). There would also be guests and visitors. My brother-in-law, Dabholkar, had just passed his law examination and started a lawyer's practice, but lived very simply like any ordinary worker, worrying more about our comforts than his own. He and Tai put up with us for a whole year. They looked after our children as they would have looked after their own.

In the meanwhile, I was able to obtain a room at Bandra. But because of the children's examinations, it was not possible to shift immediately. At the same time, one of my colleagues in the office offered to get the electricity connections of our flat done and asked for the keys. I consulted my husband and only when he agreed did I hand over the keys to my colleague. After a few days, we decided to visit our flat to check how far the work had progressed. When we entered the flat, I got my first shock! Nothing had been done. Our luggage was due to arrive from Ratnagiri at any time, and the flat was not even ready! There was another shock in store for me, which made me blow my fuse!

My colleague had sublet my room on the sly to an architect, from whom he had taken a lot of money as advance payment. So we had to go and see the architect. We showed him our agreement papers. He coolly told us that he would not vacate the room unless he got his money back! Then he locked the room right in front of our eyes and walked off to visit his wife's parents in Shivaji Park.

Even today I get gooseflesh when I recollect how we walked around Shivaji Park in search of the architect, holding hands so as not to get lost in the crowd, how everybody else, including Tai and her husband, squarely blamed us, how my lawyer brother-in-law made a fantastic plan to get our room back, and how we were abused because of our caste.

He asked us to request the architect to let us have the key just to put our luggage, which had arrived from Ratnagiri, on the loft inside the room. We were to assure him that he could keep his things in the room and remove them only after he had got his money back from the man. We took our luggage with us, and the architect himself supervised the process of putting our things into the loft. In any case, what we had was so little! Just a tin cot, pots and pans bundled in two sacks, a table, and a chair! Harishchandra and I were stupefied to find that some ten or twelve relatives had been brought along to help us. After we had placed the luggage in the loft, I began to thank my relatives, "Thank you very much for coming. Now let us move out." But I was astonished to find my brother-in-law rolling his eyes at me. Then he turned to the architect and quietly told him, "Look here, we are standing in our own room with our own luggage. We also have the papers to prove that this place belongs to us. So now you get out with your things!"

A big drama followed this pronouncement! Many rich and powerful relatives of the architect came and shouted at us. Finally when they realized that it was their own mistake, they began to abuse us! "These are low-caste people! So what else can you expect from them? Look at their things! A tin cot and cheap pots and pans! The moment we saw their things, we knew what they were! Dirty, mean, uncivilized … !" We had to listen to all these insults, though it was not our fault, while the people in the building enjoyed watching the whole scene.

Once I talked about this experience and other similar ones in a health camp. The activists in the Ambedkar movement realized that here was a woman who could speak in public programs. Eventually I received an invitation to speak at the Ambedkar birth centenary celebrations organized by them.

Both Harishchandra and I had read Dr. Babasaheb Ambedkar's *Buddha and His Dhamma* and Dhananjay Keer's biography of Dr. Ambedkar when we were in Ratnagiri.[1] I had no stage fright because of my participation in school programs and theater. I had heard the speeches of leaders like Nathuram Kamble, Bandya Chavekar, and Haribhau Aayre in Ratnagiri. So I prepared a small speech and went to the centenary celebrations. Until this time, I considered our local leaders as great and modeled my speech on theirs. But when I listened to the impressive speakers at this program, I was afraid even to open my mouth. The import of Dr. Ambedkar's words "Leave the villages and go to the cities" dawned on me afresh. I was getting an entirely new perspective here.

After the program, we went to visit the memorial of Dr. Babasaheb Ambedkar at the Chaitya Bhumi and later browsed through the many bookshops on the beach, which had stood their ground braving the wind and the waves. In the crowds here, we came to know people like Usha and Vilas Wagh and many other Dalit writers. I first saw Usha Wagh when she was asleep in a bookstall, under the shade of a banner. I felt a great respect for her when I came to know that Usha, a high-caste girl, had married Vilas Wagh, a low-caste man, and never made him sever his links with his community. On the contrary, she quit her job and devoted her entire life to the project of bringing the works of Phule, Ambedkar, and Marx to Dalit homes.

In the crowds here, I met a young man named Ramesh Haralkar and his friends. He started visiting us regularly. A man with a very handsome face (he would have made the best Shivaji on stage), piercing eyes, thick beard, and moustache and a slender build, he had an impressive personality! We realized that he was the leader of the scavengers. He had a wealth of information and told us so many things, for instance, that a huge number of people who worked as scavengers were from the Konkan region, their comparative ratio with the workers from other regions, their addiction to alcohol, the reasons for their untimely deaths, the percentage of women scavengers, P.T. women workers, their sexual exploitation ... He talked about so many things! He would trace each issue to its root. We were used to seeing people from our own and surrounding villages working as scavengers in Mumbai. But it was Haralkar who actually opened our eyes to their real condition. He sketched before us the picture of their lives in Mumbai with almost surgical precision. After listening to him, we felt as if we had an overdose of the *beebhatsa rasa*.[2] Haralkar once told us one of his own experiences, "When I was a scavenger myself, I was cleaning in a narrow corridor between two buildings, collecting the slush crawling with maggots from the drains in a basket. Suddenly, some woman upstairs threw a used sanitary napkin down. It dashed against my face and then fell down into the drain ... my sweat trickled into my mouth ... there was a funny taste on my tongue ... as something else trickled into my mouth along with the sweat!"

Once day after I had joined the Mumbai office, my name appeared in the list of people selected for training. The work that I did warranted no training, because all I did was copying: transferring everything from one piece of paper to another! What was there to learn in this? But it was decided by the powers that be that I had to be sent for training! Yours not to question why! The training, however, proved to be a blessing in disguise because I got plenty of time for writing stories and publishing them. There was hardly any encouragement as such from the home front, nor was there a tradition in the family of pursuing an activity such as this. So it must have been the good remarks I received in the school for my essays that encouraged me to pick up the pen and write! Whatever it may be! I felt a terrible restlessness growing inside me, which refused to let me sit quiet. My own experiences, those of my friends and other women, that of living in the village, caste discrimination, being a woman built up a pressure inside me!

Every morning, after the training sessions, I sat and wrote stories. Once, when I was busy writing, a friend of mine called Raut told me about a writer called Dattaram Baraskar whom he knew. He suggested that I should show my stories to him and take his guidance. He also introduced me to him. Baraskar worked at the daily *Nava Kal*. When I went to see him, he was sitting in a small cubicle at the *Nava Kal* office. While discussing story writing with me, he suddenly said, "Decide your destination first; Churchgate or VT!" I was at a loss to know what my "destination" had to do with my story writing. Then I realized his import. "Decide how you want to end the story! Then take your story straight toward that end, without any procrastination." Ah ha, this is so good, I said to myself! So far what I had done was to pour all the complications in my mind about events, characters, and situations directly on paper, but had not been able to tie them up neatly, in a proper packet. Now I was clear in my mind. I had to decide how my story was going to end and proceed in that direction.

Once, while talking about his own stories, Baraskar said, "Two or three stories of mine have appeared in *Satyakatha*." I had no idea that *Satyakatha* was a prestigious Marathi literary journal. I thought it was a magazine where stories of thefts, murders, of people being duped, and so on appeared. But he was clearly very proud of this. He added, "Only those who are published in *Satyakatha* are great writers!" "Oh ho, so that is how things work!" I thought. "This *Satyakatha* seems to be quite a prestigious affair!"

My stories were mostly published in the Diwali issues of a couple of very ordinary, "see-and-throw away" magazines. The magazines were quite silly, really. But my joy knew no bounds. I proudly showed my stories in print to my friends in the office. "We cannot write even a few sentences; but look at her! How much she has written! It is even printed!" Their wonderment was a reward in itself!

I began to write. I would write anywhere: sitting in the office, traveling in the bus or train, waiting at the bus stop, even standing in a queue. I scribbled furiously. Sometimes there were interesting reactions. Once I had bought the ticket and began to write, the person sitting next to me would try to see what I was writing. Men would feel I was making a pass at them and lean more to my side. That would disturb me. But my terrible handwriting and the speed of the vehicle would make it impossible for them to decipher anything. Then they would straighten up, and my writing would proceed without any further hitch. Sometimes I forgot to get off at my stop and went further on. Then I had to get down and trudge all the way backward on foot. Sometimes I had to pay a fine to the ticket collector. At night, after I had satisfied everybody else's needs and mine as well, I would sit down to write without any disturbance. I used to sit in the kitchen, so as not to disturb the others, and write stealthily. Sometimes my eyes would droop, heavy with sleep, and I found myself dozing off. Then I would start, shake the sleep out of my eyes, and scold myself severely, "Hey, lazy bones, wake up, wake up! How dare you sleep! Come on, write!"

Sometimes Mr. Pawar got up either to drink water or to go to the bathroom. He would be angry to see me sitting like an owl in the kitchen. "Have you gone mad?" he scolded. "What if you fall ill? Come on. Go to bed." He would switch the light off. But I would switch it on again. "I will go to the doctor if I fall ill, I promise. You go to bed." I told him. Sometimes I got severe headaches. Of course, I never asked him to press my head. How can a wife ask her husband to do such things! I also avoided asking him to do such things. Not because I wanted to save him that bother, but because if I asked for something, he would demand something else! Many a time, I would write in the dark. I would keep a pen and papers near the pillow and write whatever came to my mind, even in the dark. I did not want to forget and forego. Thus I continued to write.

One day, Vaman Howal, the famous short story writer in Marathi, called on me. He had spent a long time trying to locate my house. He said, "I came because I know you write stories. We are organizing a *sahitya sammelana* at Vikroli.[3] I have come to invite you to read your story." This was something quite new to me. Sometimes I would borrow material from my stories and use them in my speeches. But telling a whole story to an audience? How do you do it? How can you recite a whole story verbatim? Then Howal said, "You are going to tell your own story. So what's so difficult about it? Come on, tell me the plot of one of your stories! Let's see how you do it."

So I told him the plot of my story "Shalya," about a woman called Jyoti who gives birth to five daughters in a row. When she gets pregnant for the sixth time, she is afraid that she will give birth to yet another girl and will be tortured by her husband and sasu. In the hospital, she gives birth to a girl and another young woman produces a baby boy. She confides in the nurse and exchanges the babies. Everybody at home is delighted that finally Jyoti has produced a boy, but Jyoti comes to find out that the other woman is an unwed mother and the baby daughter has no chance of survival; it will somehow be killed. The guilt of pushing her daughter into the jaws of death hounds her till the end.

After listening to the story, Howal suggested, "Why don't you change the third-person narration of the story to first-person? Use 'I' instead of Jyoti. That will make it more effective!"

When we were getting ready to go to Vikroli, Harishchandra said, "Let us take our son along." I understood why he was saying that. I was going to narrate that I had only daughters; but people must know that in reality I did have a son. My son grumbled, but finally went along, and, doubtless, he was quite bored that evening.

That was my first program. After that, I read my stories many times, especially in the Asmitadarsha Sahitya Sammelanas organized by Gangadhar Pantavne. Often, writers like Howal, Yashwant Kharat, and Bhimsen Dethe would tell their own stories. People appreciated my stories in the literary conferences organized by the Dalits and in one that focused on Konkan and Marathi literature: Dalit Sahitya Sammelana and the Konkan Marathi Sahitya Sammelana. They were turned into radio plays and broadcast, some presented on television as well. My elder sister, Akka, was so moved by all this that she said to me, with tears in her eyes, "You should have been the eldest child of our father. He always wanted his daughters to achieve something! You would have fulfilled his dream in his lifetime had you been born earlier." I knew, of course, that, had I been born in Akka's place, I too would have become another Shantiakka!

The literary conference at Vikroli gave me an inkling of what a writer's lot can be. At that time, Padmashri Daya Pawar's autobiography *Baluta* was published and had become the topic of intense debates. Some readers were moved by it, but some were incensed. In the literary conference there was a panel discussion on the form of autobiography. Many writers were present onstage, including Daya Pawar, Bhausaheb Adsul, Appa Ranpise, and I. Everybody had good words to say about *Baluta,* but Adsul said, "In this book Daya Pawar has torn to shreds the dignity of our mothers and sisters! Had Babasaheb Ambedkar been alive today, he would have banned this book!" Many people were speechless at this outburst, but some nodded their heads in agreement! I had not read *Baluta* then, but kept feeling that Adsul had not really understood Babasaheb! What the writer writes about is social reality and not his or her individual life! Why don't people understand this?

One day a man came to visit me in my office. He was tall, dressed in modern clothes, wore a neatly trimmed moustache and beard, and looked quite different from the usual visitors. He pointed to the chair nearby and politely asked my permission to sit down. That was another unusual thing!

"Please have a seat," I replied.

"I am Vilas Kelaskar," he said. "I had come once with Vijay Bhingarde to your office near the Victoria Terminus. I did not know then that you were a writer. But afterward Vijay told me that you have published your stories." I realized he worked in the same office but in another section. I was a senior officer, and he was younger than me. So I thought there was no need to address him by using the plural form, as is the custom in Marathi.

I was quite pleased to know that my writing was being noticed. "Nothing much! I scribble something that gets printed; that's all!" I said modestly. But he said, "How can you say that? Many people write, but their writings are not printed!" "Why, do you write too?" I asked him. I thought he would say no, but he said, "Yes. I do. Stories and poems!" He was speaking without any airs.

"Oh ho, that's so nice!" I said. "You must write, you know. Don't worry about publishing. I know a couple of people who will accept your writing for publication." The sole basis for this substantial promise, of course, was my acquaintance with Baraskar. Then I casually asked him, "Have you published any stories so far?"

"Well," he replied, "Nothing much, except some three or four stories in *Satyakatha!*" He was still very modest, but I collapsed! Baraskar had already impressed upon me the prestige of *Satyakatha* in the literary world. For a minute I thought he was pulling my leg. A writer published by *Satyakatha*? In this concrete jungle? "Why don't you bring your stories to show me when you come next time?" I asked him, without saying anything further.

When he came to see me next, he brought a file of his stories along. He had no degree in literature, yet had given a new dimension to the Mardhekarian form—a more formalistic kind of literary approach in Marathi in the 1950s and 1960s, of which Balkrishna Sitaram Mardhekar was the major proponent—in his story "Once there was one … " The theme of the story went like this. There is a hidden form in every stone, waiting to be discovered; you have to break the outer layers first. He reorganized this statement in his story, as if to say, "If even the broken chips are organized well, a new form is created. Second, if the form that the artist has in his mind is lost, the stone itself creates a new form out of itself." It was a fantastic story. I also thought that, although they appeared to hang in a vacuum of fantasy, his stories were firmly rooted in reality. To me he looked like a small sapling of a peepul tree, growing out of the walls of a dilapidated house. Its pinkish velvety leaves swaying in the wind looked as if they belonged to a fantasyland, but were actually firmly rooted in the walls of that house. I felt a great respect for him.

When I spoke about my method of writing stories, by deciding my destination first, he said, "No. Art cannot be so formally restrictive; so predetermined. Our minds are full of many events and incidents that have neither beginning nor end, but aimlessly wander through our heads. We can choose any one of them and begin the story. The beginning chooses its own path. All that we can do is follow the story. Just as many pieces of iron get attracted to the magnet, many events and incidents attach themselves to the beginning, and the story takes us toward the end. We should never drag a story to its end." He spoke at length. It was as if I were sitting in an M.A. class of literary criticism. The debates and discussions with Kelaskar gave me new perspectives with which to view writing.

Once the Konkan Marathi Sahitya Sammelana was taking place in Sahitya Sangha in Mumbai. I was present as a member, and Vilas Kelaskar had come too. Here I met a friend of mine who had been abroad for some time and had just returned. She too was a short story writer, so I introduced her to Kelaskar. In a short while we were no longer acquaintances;

we had become friends. The three of us started furiously writing stories, though I was still a novice, really!

He came to my office one day and said, "We both have written good stories. If you have written something recently, bring it along. Let us go for an outing one day and read the stories to each other in the company of nature."

I liked this idea very much, so I called my friend and asked her if she was willing to come. She was quite ready. So we went to the Aare milk colony and climbed atop a hill where they have nice little cottages and rest houses for tourists. The plan was to sit together, read the stories, discuss them, and return. It was a beautiful place. With the cool breeze blowing continuously, the greenery around, the open skies, the clean air, it was difficult to believe we were in Mumbai. We congratulated Kelaskar on his choice of the place. After a little debate about who was going to read first, the readings began. First my friend read her story; then he read his. Both stories were very good. I did not read mine because it was not well organized. I was quiet for a while. Then I realized that if one had something concrete to tell one could say it anywhere. The venue, whether it was in nature or a crowded room in the office, made no difference. I was, in fact, upset for another reason: the way he showered praise on her story.

"Great! You write beautifully. You have lived abroad, but it has not affected the excellent grasp you have on the language. How is it so civilized, so cultured, so rooted? There are no traces of the other language! How did you manage this? It is a marvel, really!" He went on and on. But the word *cultured* pricked me like a thorn. What exactly did he mean? Which culture were they talking about? Whose dominance were they praising? Patriarchy? Caste system? Class? What was it? And why was *our* writing termed uncivilized, uncultured? How? These questions raged in my mind. I did not even participate in the discussion. Of course, the points could be discussed and debated. But there were two of them, whereas I was alone! Besides, I myself was a little shaky about whether I was right in feeling so hurt by that word. So I chose to keep quiet. For me the literary picnic had gone sour. We returned from the trip, but I could not forget the words and the deep hurt that had been inflicted on me. Finally, when he came to meet me in the office, I literally fought with him.

He said, "You will never understand it. You need an IQ for that!" This added fuel to my fire. His ideas about IQ were ridiculous. I knew these upper-caste people so well! He had a great loathing for the poor, the beggars. "They do not want to use their brains! Every man is happy in his own situation. But you unnecessarily force your ideas of happiness upon them and pity them." He used to say with contempt. He also believed that one has to be born with a high IQ. He would cite the names of all big scientists in support of his argument. I angrily retorted, "IQ is a big myth. IQ depends on the opportunities a human being gets for his or her development."

Then he exploded, "Suppose you were given the same opportunities that these scientists got, would you be a Newton, an Einstein, a Jayant Narlikar?" I was so angry; I wanted to crack a coconut on his head.

Gradually, quite a few people in my office came to know that I was a writer. Some of them were officers with literary sensibilities as well. I told them I was myself. Usually, nobody in the typical bureaucratic setup would have taken serious note of such creative enterprise. But one day Mrs. Tambe, the wife of one of our senior officers, Mr. S. R. Tambe, came to our office to invite me for a program. She was looking for me. She was a writer herself and also taught in a college. "Where is the writer, Urmila Pawar? I want to meet her!" she kept on saying, and my colleagues raised their eyebrows in astonishment! I felt so proud!

One day Tambe Saheb came to inspect our office. He sent a message with a peon, through our immediate boss, that if anyone had any suggestions or complaints to make they could go and see him. Incidentally, he was the only officer who was interested in the workers. The rest would always intimidate and threaten anybody who wanted to say anything to them. "How dare you come to me with this complaint? Go and pay more attention to your own work!" they would say. So when Mr. Tambe sent out a word like that, all of us were impressed! In the same appreciative mood, I went to his office to present him with a copy of my recently published book, *Mauritius: A Journey*. Had anybody else been there in his place, I would have got a memo for having done something sacrilegious. Not only did he accept my book graciously, he also said that he was very proud of me! Actually, I thought he was being a little extravagant in his praise, but it had a terrific impact on my colleagues. They almost fainted with shock!

This incident, however, also added fuel to the fire of resentment some people had already started feeling about me. They resented the reservation policy and my caste, because of which I got the promotion. In truth, my promotion hardly meant anything to me. There would be a meager raise in my salary, some fifty or sixty rupees. But I had achieved some power, and that was precisely what irked people. I had taken this job in 1966. During the ten years after that, that is, up to 1976, it was rare to hear people say, "Oh these low castes! No less than the sons-in-law of the government!" or "They are such a pampered lot!" or they would refer to low castes as "the arrogant," "the bigheaded!" But in 1970 the roster system was introduced in government jobs, and it became mandatory to appoint Dalit and tribal candidates. The resentment against the Dalits and other reserved category people began to rise. This was the period during which such expressions began to be increasingly used against the Dalits! This was also around the time I had become the branch manager. Sitting in my chair at work would make me very happy. Up until that day I would have to ask my boss for his permission; now I would be the one to grant permission to my juniors! Those who felt happy about it congratulated me from the bottoms of their hearts, while some others just pretended to be happy, since they very much resented my promotion! The moment a man was promoted, he immediately became a *bhausaheb* or *raosaheb*. But women remained simply *bai*, without the *saheb*, even after their promotions! Besides I was a Dalit! "Why should she expect to be addressed as baisaheb?" "Why should we ask for her permission?" some people grumbled.

These days, however, every woman, whether a housewife or a working girl, has become madam, because of the tremendous influence of English, which has reached our kitchens. Because of this verbal promotion, even a woman peon is now addressed in the plural form, with a show of outward respect. This has generated self-respect, which finds expression even in the lowest of the low.

The people from the Dalit movement, however, treated women in the same discriminatory manner, as if they were some inferior species, as they did the ones at home. Probably it was unconscious behavior. Once I was invited to a program organized by a group of Dalit activists in a printing press. They repeatedly called me on the phone and urged me to deliver a speech as a part of their program. I accepted their invitation and reached the hall in time. But there was nobody to receive me there except the man whose loudspeaker was hired. So I quietly sat down on a bench outside. For a long time nobody came, and I was bored to death. Then a huge crowd of men arrived with some member of Parliament, whom they ushered into the hall with great fanfare, with many garlands and flowers. Welcome speeches were broadcast from the loudspeaker. All the while I kept sitting on the bench. I was about to get up and leave, when somebody remembered me. I did not want to say a word; my mouth had a bitter taste. Finally, I said something about Phule and Ambedkar and left, saying I was getting late. But nobody took any notice of that either. They were all busy dancing attendance on the MP!

I always felt that since Harishchandra had to leave his education half-way, he must complete it—he should at least be a graduate, a degree holder. I also wanted him to pass the L.L.B. or other similar examinations like my sister's husband. Some of our friends, like S. R. Jadhav, Sadanand Jadhav, Hindalekar, and Ramakant Jadhav, were doing the same thing. They had jobs and simultaneously attended morning classes in Siddhartha College. Some of them registered themselves as external students. But Harishchandra was more interested in sports. He loved to play badminton, table tennis, volleyball, kabaddi. He was a member of the sports team of his office and participated in many competitions in Pune, Mumbai, and Nagpur, winning prizes as well. He was not able to continue with his sports activities later.

There was something he really loved: reading newspapers from one end to the other. He loved to read political news. He never put a book down without having read it through. He never showed off his reading, but sometimes, in discussions and debates, he would quote from the books verbatim and surprise those who were present. He was a great union man as well. He had worked as the president and secretary of the postal workers' union and village organizations. He was a good public speaker. But he lacked one thing: he was never obsessed by the will to do something! That was his weak point. I often pointed this out to him while countering his verbal attacks on me.

Harishchandra had remained in the Sane Guruji's school at Dapoli for some time. Suresh Bhat, the great Marathi poet, often called him Sane Guruji just to tease him. Other people also found him a man of simple habits. He was really a simple man, too. But when it came to his wife, he was transformed into a different being altogether. This system has a special chemistry for making husbands!

My office was quite close to Siddhartha College. So I desperately wanted to complete my education, which I had left incomplete in Ratnagiri. When I asked for Harishchandra's consent, he said, "Look, you can do what you like only after finishing your daily chores in the house. Cooking, looking after children, and all that stuff. If you think you can do this and get more education, fine!" This was actually his way of saying "No," but I took it up as a challenge.

There were two or three women in my office who came to work all the way from Pune or Nashik, cities at a considerable distance from Mumbai. There were quite a few like them outside as well. They got up early in the wee hours of dawn, cooked meals for the family, finished all the household chores, and yet managed to arrive at the office on time. They reached home very late too. Some of them would depend on their own family members to look after the children, while some employed an ayah. My younger daughter was now six or seven years old. Besides, I had an eighteen-year-old girl, a relative of ours, to look after the children. Harishchandra would need to pay a little more attention, and I was sure that he would do so. Thus I finally admitted myself to Siddhartha College to study for a B.A.

I used to get up at four o'clock in the morning, make chapatis and cook the vegetables, and then at six I would be out of the house. After college was over, I rushed to work, and after office I rushed home. When examinations drew near, I left the children in the ayah's care and rushed to the university library and sometimes to the Mumbai Marathi Grantha Sangrahalaya at Dadar. I left only when I was literally pushed out of the library by Sarita, Khanolkar, and Mungekar, the girls who worked there. At home I studied till late at night.

I fractured my leg when my B.A. examinations were very close. That was a funny story. Working women in Mumbai often adopt various shortcuts to save time, given their busy schedules. They board moving trains, jump from one train to another, and cross roads right in the teeth of the approaching vehicles. I was no exception. One day, in the Chatrapati Shivaji Terminus (it was called Victoria Terminus then), while jumping from one train to another in order to reach the platform ahead, I fell down in the space between the two. A crowd gathered. Somebody grumbled, "These women die like this and then the trains are delayed!" Somebody pulled me up. I thought I was all right. But my left leg began to swell, and I was unable to put it on the ground. It began to hurt a lot. I had to squat down!

A fisherwoman looked at my huge swollen leg and brought me a big piece of ice to apply as a cold compress. I gave a man nearby two phone numbers, one for Harishchandra's office and another for mine, and requested him to break the news on the phone. I tried giving him money, but he refused to take it. I was a little worried, unsure if he would make the call. Besides, it was the first of April. At both places they might take it as a prank played on them! I was going to suffer unnecessarily. I had to stay put where I was and wait for people to come and help me. I could not even move away because if someone really came for me and failed to find me there, it would certainly look like a prank! I sat where I was, applying the cold compress to my leg. Then I realized that the ice was melting and trickles of water flowed a long way from under my leg. Now this posed another problem! What would they think? To avoid any misunderstanding, I kept changing my place within a tiny periphery. Besides, it was peak time, and this was the terminus; every two minutes local trains poured people out like ants all around. Huge crowds flowed around me in all directions. To save myself from being trampled, I kept getting up, trying to stand on the broken leg, and then stumbling on to a different place. This went on for a long time. Finally, I saw Harishchandra jumping down from a train onto the platform and was flooded with relief.

The moment he got down, he began to declare loudly to the crowd around what a stupid woman I was. He also made a prophecy that I was going to die like this one day. Then he marched off in the direction of the stationmaster, loudly inquiring about what the railway police were doing while all of this was happening. I continued doing my "sit-ups." After a considerable time, he returned with a stretcher and two railway workers. Then I was put on the stretcher and taken off to St. George Hospital nearby. I could imagine what it must be like being carried to the cremation grounds on a bier.

The doctor put a plaster around my leg up to the knee. He also handed me a stick as a support for the other leg and sent me home. While I hobbled out to catch a taxi, I imagined what lame beggars must feel. Finally, when I entered the house, literally jumping like a frog all the way from the staircase to the door, my children were tickled to no end! They thought their mother was playing an "April fools trick" on them!

The plaster stayed on for a whole month. Then I had to go to the Sion Hospital, because it was nearer the house, for various exercises. Here the adventure of the broken leg took a new turn.

This accident had caused a break in my studies. When I was worrying about how I was going to compensate for the time lost, a brother of sorts came forward with a helping hand. He was not my real brother, of course—actually the brother of a friend. In fact, he was not even her biological brother, but an adopted one! Since he was the brother of a friend, I began to consider him a brother as well. He had crossed fifty, but was a very simple soul. He reminded me of Shantanu, my classmate in the eighth standard. Quite a harmless man!

Bhau's house (I called him Bhau, brother) was very close to the Sion Hospital. He once said to me, "You come to the hospital to receive treatment; after that you can come and sit in my house. I have many books and notes, which you can use if you like. Trust me as your own brother. Don't worry about anything; just sit and study as much as you like." I remembered my brother Bhai. I was so grateful. At home, my young children would disturb me a great deal. So Bhau's offer was a boon for me, as I could save time and study undisturbed. A few days passed like that.

Bhau had three children. They would drop in, in between. But the atmosphere was quite open. After a week, I discovered that my woman friend was a little upset. She said, "You know, his wife does not live with him. And yet you go to his house every day! What must people be saying!" I was simply aghast! How we women nurture and protect patriarchy, like a baby in the cradle! A woman's character is always on display! Always suspect! Anybody can come, gaze at us with their eyes on our flesh, drool, and lick their fingers!

Somehow I managed to complete my studies and became a graduate with second-class marks. Harishchandra felt so happy! He would tell everybody that his wife was a graduate. He even put my B.A. certificate in a frame and hung it on a wall in the house.

At that time he did not have the faintest idea that later on he would think of all the encouragement bestowed on me as a heavy rock he had dropped on his own feet. And nor did I!

Because of Harishchandra's encouragement and my newly earned confidence that I could do well academically, I enrolled myself for the M.A. course. Frankly speaking, I had a great desire for further education. It was at this particular point that Harishchandra realized that he had lost control over his wife, that I had gone too far ahead of him. In truth, studying for an M.A. was not a very pertinent thing. It was not going to fetch me any special benefits. Nor did I harbor any ambitions of teaching in a college or making a career in that line. But I still wanted to do an

M.A. Education is that nectar which once tasted makes you feel thirstier still! I was intoxicated with the study of literature, the poems and stories! Our life together, which went on smoothly until then, received a serious jolt. Harishchandra said, "Why do you want to do M.A.? Now pay more attention to the children and the house."

I retorted, "Look, I am paying enough attention to the house and the children. I take good care of their food, studies, and all the household work. Besides, I work in the office as well. My children are quite healthy. And if they ever fall ill with some minor ailment, I take leave and nurse them without sleeping a wink at night. I am looking after them very well, thank you! It is you who needs to pay more attention to the house now. Instead of going to the bar, why don't you come home early and pay some attention to their studies? That would be far better. Besides, whatever I study, I do it in my spare time! Why should you object to it?"

Harishchandra did not agree with this at all. He firmly believed that looking after the house was the sole responsibility of the woman. He kept stating his philosophy that a man has the right to behave any way he likes. This angered me and led to fights that went on and on.

Our children, all three of them, had been enrolled in the Marathi-medium municipal school. We were not at all aware of the long-term effects of this. We were happy that they passed examinations with merit, studied on their own, were well behaved, and did not have to endure the poverty and insults we had experienced in our childhood. Of course, they experienced caste discrimination, in subtle ways, though not poverty.

My younger daughter, Manini, must have been in the fifth standard then. It was her birthday and she invited her friend Kishori to share the birthday cake with us. Kishori and her brother came, ate the cake, and went home after celebrating the birthday. Kishori's brother told his mother that he had seen photographs of Ambedkar and Buddha in our house. The next day, Kishori's mother came and stood at our door. Without even stepping inside, she started abusing us. "We did not know that you belonged to this particular caste! That is why I sent my children to you. From now on, don't you give my daughter anything to eat if she comes to your house. We are Marathas. We cannot eat with you." Before I could say anything, she had left!

A semiliterate woman had insulted me, standing at my door, and at the same time created a vertical split in the mind of my young child—and hers too. I related this incident to my daughter's class teacher. She said, "Never mind! She spoke that way because that was what she felt; just forget it!" What was the difference between the two then?

After this incident, Kishori stopped coming to our house. My daughter complained to me that she did not talk to her. But, after a few days, Kishori started coming again. I thought there was a lesson for the grown-ups in this, as far as caste was concerned!

I was introduced to Hira Bansode during the second year of my B.A. course in Siddhartha College. A plump person of medium height, Hira was quite fair-skinned, with a cheerful face and a sugar-sweet voice. Her whole personality was very sweet. Had she decided to make music her career, she would certainly have been tough competition for Lata Mangeshkar! I saw her, talked to her, and fell in love with her. She used to write beautiful poems. I wrote stories. Then we started going together to literary programs. Her office was quite close by. Our meetings became so frequent that often we went to each other's office to have lunch together because there were so many things to talk about: Babasaheb, the movement, activists, organizations, literature, and so much more!

The movement for changing the name of the Marathwada University to Dr. Babasaheb Ambedkar Marathwada University was gaining ground. Mumbai reverberated with the slogans raised at processions held by activists from all over Maharashtra. We saw innumerable activists camping in the Azad Maidan, the public park in south Mumbai, with their banners. Since it was very close to our offices, we got to watch these scenes every day. We saw so many women from the villages and slums walking in the processions, carrying children in their arms. We used to feel guilty that middle-class women like us did not participate in the protest marches. I often spoke about it in my speeches. But we had never participated in any protest marches till then. It was on February 6, 1988, that I first participated in such a march during the *Riddles* controversy.[4] I had seen many protest marches at the Azad ground, but this time the participation was like nothing before. It was unbelievable. I walked in the march for some time and then returned home. The news about attacks on this march and the commotion continued to reverberate for a long time afterward.

Nine

One day Hira Bansode said to me, "There is a women's organization called Maitrini—women friends—in Dadar, near the Portuguese Church, and they discuss women's issues. Would you like to come with me?" I was always willing to participate in anything new and therefore agreed readily. One Saturday, after half a day's work at the office, we set off toward Dadar. All government offices worked only half a day on Saturday. Hira's husband, Mr. Bansode, joined us outside Dadar Station, and the three of us went to the meeting, held in the basement of the girls' high school in Ash Lane. Many women sat on chairs arranged in a circle. Their bobbed hair, bangleless bare hands, bare necks, and simple cotton saris made them look so different and attractive! I was simply fascinated. A discussion on women's issues was on and phrases like *women's liberation, women's decade, atrocities against women, dowry deaths* were used frequently. I knew these words, of course, but their real import was being revealed to me all over again. I started attending these meetings regularly to listen to the discussions more carefully.

Among the women who assembled here were quite a few remarkable ones like Chhaya Datar, Vidya Bal, and Usha Mehta.[1] They were involved in women's issues. They also wrote a great deal. While listening to the cases of rapes and brides burned in so-called kitchen accidents because they had not brought in "enough" dowry, I thought of the incident of the bull in our pen. I often felt that there ought to be a similar way of teaching a lesson to rapists. Later on I saw the play *Purush* by Jaywant Dalvi and liked the character of Bandya tremendously. But at Maitrini I learned that one should not take the law into one's own hands and that problems could be resolved with proper counseling. I was made aware of the biological aspects of male and female bodies. This was quite different from the titillating yellow books one got in the streets. Here I found books containing information on male and female reproductive organs with illustrations, presented in an objective, clean, and scientific manner. Just as the disciples of Lord Shiva never see the Shivalinga as a representation of Shiva's penis in Goddess Parvati's vagina, these pictures did not create any different feelings in our minds. Freud says that sex is a drive that exists in the human mind in all stages of one's life. Is it because sex is so deeply rooted in us that the first time we see a human being, we look at the person in terms of his/her gender? But our actual behavior is formed by the ways we are trained to think. And it is only humans who can think and behave accordingly. Animals cannot do so, and that is why we human beings are distinctly different.

I passed my M.A. examination with a second class. There was no reaction from my husband, Mr. Pawar. But he would tell his friends, without fail, "Now she is an M.A." My B.A. certificate, which he had put into a nice little frame, hung limply on the wall. My M.A. certificate lay on the table below, gathering dust, for a long time, still rolled up, the way the university had sent it. After a while I took it out and hung it over my B.A. certificate. Dr. Bhalchandra Mungekar formed an Urmila Pawar Felicitation Committee along with his friends, and I was publicly celebrated for being the first woman from the Konkan region to have obtained an M.A. while I was taking care of the house, children, and my job. Dr. Mungekar presented me with a set of invaluable critical books. He had had to struggle very hard against adverse circumstances to become the vice-chancellor of the University of Mumbai. His daughters had become doctors. But I had not been able to congratulate him publicly on any of these occasions. This regret is embedded deep in my heart. One must do things at the right moment, otherwise what is the point?

Before joining the Maitrini group, I knew I was a woman and looked at myself with patriarchal eyes. Gadkari's Sindhu[2] had entrenched herself deep down in my unconscious. I slogged the whole day in the office, at home, and after an arduous journey was dead tired by the time I got back home. And yet at night, though my body was a mass of aches and pains, I pressed my husband's feet. I was ready to do anything he wanted, just to make him happy. I was ready to die for a smile, a glance from him. But he accused me, "Let alone an ideal wife, you are not even a good one!" Later on he began saying that I was far from being a good mother as well! I failed to understand what exactly he wanted from me and became miserable. Gradually it became clear to me that everything that gave me an independent identity—my writing, which was getting published, my education, my participation in public programs—irritated Mr. Pawar no end. Gradually, he began to be full of resentment.

His attitude toward me was full of contradictions. On the one hand, he was proud of my writing; he admitted as much to his friends and relatives. But, on the other, he immensely resented my being recognized as a writer, my speaking in public programs, and my emerging as a figure in the public domain. Our arguments would invariably end in bitter quarrels. I would say, "Please, have a heart! I am a human being too. I too work like you. I too get tired. My work also has the same value as yours." But neither my words nor my work had any meaning for him! On the contrary, he would tell me, "Look at the village woman. The husband's wish is law for her. She does not dare to sit down or get up without his permission. Tell me, in that case, how is she able to run her home well?" Was not the answer implicit in the question itself?

When he spoke like this, the picture of our house in Bhiraunde floated before my eyes, especially the way it was during the rainy season. The day began very early for women, at four o'clock in the morning. In spite of the heavy rain, they had to fetch water from the well for everybody in the house to bathe in, drink, cook the meals, and so on. Then they cleaned the dirty pots and plates of the night before and cooked for the whole house. They breakfasted with their menfolk and went with them to work in the fields. They planted paddy till their backs broke. If the fields were far away, they had to carry lunch. After lunch they worked in the fields once again and returned home in the evening, just half an hour earlier than their men. They lit the stove under an earthen pot, which they had filled up in the morning, to keep the hot bathwater ready for their men returning from the fields. After heating the bathwater, they began preparations for the evening meals. The spices had to be pounded and grains ground. Then there was the cooking to do! Sometimes they had to even husk the rice before cooking. Even as they worked ceaselessly on these tasks, the men arrived, bathed, and sat smoking leisurely on the verandah, some of them drinking liquor. Women would again go to the well to fetch water, wash the muddied clothes of all the people in the house, hang them out to dry, light the lamps, and serve food to the men first. After everybody in the house had eaten, they ate a few morsels from the leftovers. Then they had to roll out the beds for everybody. The work was still not over. After the children went to sleep, they sat down and massaged the heads and feet of their husbands with oil. By the time they lay down in bed, their backs would be bent like a bow because of the hard work. After a few hours' rest, however, it was dawn again—time to get up and welcome the new day with a smile on one's face!

This was not an isolated picture of an unusual household. It was representative of the way things were in most of our households. All were run like this. In addition, the woman had to behave as if she were a deaf and dumb creature.

This was what Mr. Pawar had seen right from his childhood. This was his idea of how a good home ought to be run. He was perplexed as to why his wife, a product of the same mold, who had behaved perfectly well so far, was behaving quite differently now. This confused him no end. He felt that he was losing control over his wife fast and had to establish his authority with an iron hand so as to keep her within bounds! But he did not know that my horizons had expanded hugely—that I had seen the outside world, and that he did not have the power to keep me confined to the narrow space of home anymore.

My mind was in turmoil too. On the one hand, I was full of many new thoughts. I felt that a woman was also an individual, just as a man was, and was entitled to all the rights of an individual. If man has muscle power, woman has the power to give birth. These are distinctly different capacities and need to be evaluated differently, not in the same way. On the other hand, the people of my community often confronted me with, "Who are those women you are mixing with these days? Take care; they belong to a different caste. Our community does not need their thoughts and values." While they said this, their way of talking made me feel as if I had joined some criminal gang. I had realized that I now had a new vision, a new perspective on looking at women. I had lost my fear. The women's movement had given me great strength to perceive every man and woman as an equal individual. It had taught me to relate to them freely, without any prejudice whatsoever!

There was something else that I learned in the women's movement: that this was the source from which women in distress could draw support. Many women in the Maitrini group were running support centers for women. I could see many women approaching these centers with their accounts of desertion, dowry-related torture, and many forms of violence. While working with the women in the group, I was slowly learning to treat the suffering woman as an equal, a friend, and provide her with the support she needed. This was a process of assimilating something quite new. In a bus or train I began being more considerate; I began sharing my place with another woman for a little while or helping another with her heavy bags. The smile on their faces made my heart glow with happiness.

Once Mr. Pawar and I were waiting at a bus stop in Mahim, to catch a bus to Bandra, and it must have been eleven-thirty at night. Though this was the last day of the Ganapati festival, the roads were not very crowded. I saw a twelve- or thirteen-year old girl standing by the bus stop, weeping. The people at the bus stop told us that she had been crying for a couple of hours at least, but none of them had bothered to inquire why she was so upset. I pitied the young child and talked to her. She told me that she had got separated from her family when they went to the beach in the evening and she had no money to return to Curry Road. I realized that she was waiting at the wrong bus stop. So I gave her ten rupees and took her to the right bus stop. Mr. Pawar followed us all the way, constantly grumbling, "The girl is a liar. Don't be a fool. Turn back, turn back." I kept arguing, "How do you know she is a liar? Let the bus come, I'll speak to the conductor, please wait for a while." The bus duly came; I enlisted the conductor to help the girl get down at the right place and returned to our bus stop.

Mr. Pawar kept scolding me till my head started spinning, "She must have been a girl from some criminal gang! Otherwise why should she have come to the beach all the way from Curry Road? It was only because of me that you were spared. Else they would have snatched your mangalsutra, bangles, and chased you all over Curry Road." He went on and on. Oh, the things he said! There was no end to it!

I could bear it no longer. I too answered back, "Maybe what you say is true. Maybe she was a liar. But should we assume that people lie every time and do nothing? This is what makes the innocent suffer along with the guilty!"

"Then go on. Keep on being a do-gooder! Why do you come home at all?"

"Why do you ask me that? Shouldn't I have a home? A husband? Children? Can't I help people while being with my family? And why shouldn't they try to help others? At least as much as they reasonably can ... "

"Spare me these lectures, please! As if you are a scholar! Hah! I know what intelligence you possess!"

So finally it came down to my meager intelligence! We traveled the whole way back home like this, arguing, quarreling, fighting ... After we went to bed, I thought that was the end of it. But no! For many more days this incident became a handy stick for Mr. Pawar to beat me with! He used it to underscore my lack of intelligence, and his favorite theme was Urmila has no brains and no head for practical knowledge! "If somebody asks for five rupees, she will offer ten! That is how impractical she is!" According to him I had as much brains as a round stone in the river.

One day, near our office, Hira and I were talking when suddenly I saw a drunkard hitting his wife on the face with his chappals. The poor woman, a bundle of skin and bones wrapped in rags, continued to take it silently, trying to shield the emaciated child in her arms from the blows and her own nakedness from the public. Crowds of educated, middle-class people were spilling onto the street, as the offices had just closed for the day, passing the couple by, but no one had the guts to stop the man from hitting his wife. I could not bear it any longer. I stepped forward and Hira too followed me. We shouted at the man, "What are you doing? Stop it, stop it this instant! What has she done? If she has made a mistake, tell her about it, but why are you hitting her? Stop it this instant, otherwise we will hand you over to the police right away!" That finally did it: he stopped beating her.

At a slum near my house, every second day I would see drunkards swaying on their feet in an inebriated condition, their wives and children hanging onto them, being dragged to the nearby police station. Sometimes I would try to intervene from the verandah or climb down the steps to make them see reason. The people around looked at me as if I had gone out of my mind!

I liked my friends in the Maitrini group very much. In a culture steeped in the idea of women's subordination, they were trying to spread awareness about women's issues. There is a saying in Marathi, "If the rain hits you and the husband beats you, to whom do you complain?" It was an uphill task. My friends were absolutely committed to the cause of helping women in distress. That commitment used to come through so transparently, even in the way they spoke on the telephone.

Jaya Velankar's tone on the phone was assuring yet egotistical, "Ask me whatever you want and I have the answer." Even if you just said "Hello" to Chhaya Datar, she would respond with, "Look, it is not like what you said. It is quite different! So look at it this way..." Always ready with advice! Aruna Burte's "Hellow" was tinged with something like, "Do think about this problem and firm up your position," compelling her listener to be self-reflective. Madhuri Gokhale would always be worried about you. A simple "Hello" would be followed by a torrent of questions, "What's happened? Where are you speaking from? Are you all right?" Women like Usha Mehta and Vidya Bal would speak as if they were saying, "Come on, tell me whatever you want. I am here to support you, to listen to everything you say."

Hira, however, had a unique style. Even if she were the one making a call, her first sentence would be "Tell me, what is it? Come on, say it!" That would intrigue me to no end! Why does she say this? What exactly does she want? It was, of course, Dr. Babasaheb Ambedkar's thoughts that bound us so close together!

In the company of such friends, my life had taken a completely different turn. In the beginning, I used to be quite irritated by my friends' habit of addressing each other in the singular. They would never use the more respectful plural form. Even girls younger than me addressed me in the singular form, and I resented it. Here I was, I felt, a Dalit woman, on the lowest rung of the social ladder, just trying to climb one step above with the help of my education and my writing. And these women are trying to push me down again, by using the singular pronoun! Though they addressed me in the singular, I would use the plural form to address them! Then one day I met Malini Karkal, who was older than me and much more educated. Moreover, she was an administrator! And a writer as well! Yet, when I addressed her using the plural form, she scolded me,

"Hey, why are you addressing me with the formal plural form? We are all equal here, all friends! So you must use the singular form!" Gradually my tongue learned these new ways of address and got used to them.

Another thing that irritated me was their habit of using the more personal *you* rather than the impersonal *one* while discussing something. For instance, they would not say "If that person is bad and lies, what can one do?" Instead, they said, "If that person is bad and lies, what can *you* do?" This *you* made me feel as if it were a frontal personal attack on me! Gradually, however, I realized that this was the influence of English on their Marathi. So was the use of the word *sweet*! Everything was sweet! When I heard something like "She looks sweet," I felt the girl in question had her face covered with molasses!

I was, however, absolutely impressed by the scholarship of these women and their consciousness-raising programs and would tell anyone I met about both. I would insist that every woman I met came to and participated in the programs. In 1988 there was a golden jubilee celebration in honor of Dr. Babasaheb Ambedkar's visit to Kankavli. For this program I wrote a street play on the issue of Dalit women, which was performed by Sanjivani Mainkar, Shipla Yadav, Jotsna Kasle, Sunita Yadav, among others. Ordinary housewives in the Konkan performed onstage for the first time. I wanted my colleagues in the organization Stree Uwachca (Thus spake women) to see this play. I thought it would be a good idea to introduce the two groups to each other. My colleagues would learn something from ordinary women, and the housewives, in turn, would get an opportunity to see the world outside. I suggested this many times. But the elite women did not show any interest in meeting the other group. Maybe they were not ready to start with absolute beginners and their blank slates. However, I went ahead and organized the women from the street play into a group called Aakar, an organization of Ambedkarite women in the Konkan region. The organization did not progress much beyond a few programs of narration of individual life stories and participation in some conventions, the main reason being that the women were not interested.

When I saw the bare necks of the activists in the women's movement, I always asked myself, why should I wear the mangalsutra? I am a Buddhist! My religion does not tell me to wear one. It suggests only a white string, both for the husband and wife, to be tied on their wrists! Then why not do away with these ancient symbols of subservience? I resolved to get rid of the mangalsutra. But it was easier said than done. I went to the women's programs without wearing the mangalsutra, but for marriages or naming ceremonies I would invariably wear it. Sometimes my troubled conscience made me go to the office and elsewhere with a bare neck. If somebody asked my why, I would deliver a lecture on women's liberation. And sometimes, when my heart overflowed with love for my husband, I found myself wearing it again. In the beginning, my husband would throw a fit if he found me without the mangalsutra. But, later on, even he vacillated between the Buddhist and Hindu ways!

Once I was on my way to the market and heard an acquaintance of mine calling out to me from her second-floor balcony. Where are you going? She asked, communicating through gestures. I too made signs, telling her that I was going to the market. Suddenly she pointed at my bare neck and made a questioning sign. I pointed in the direction of the house to tell her that I had removed my mangalsutra and kept it at home. But she thought I was pointing toward the sky. "When?" she yelled. She thought my husband had died! For a moment her cry struck cold terror in my heart. It is interesting how external things become an integral part of a person's physical appearance and psyche!

Later, even Harishchandra started to think along the same lines. Sometimes he said, "Why do you need these surface symbols? What is so significant about the black beads? What difference does it make if a married woman doesn't wear it?" But sometimes this understanding and humane tone gave way to a temper tantrum, "Ha! Why would you wear a mangalsutra? You are just waiting for me to die!" Sometimes he would refuse to accompany me, saying in a highly pleased way, "You are a feminist! Why do you need the company of a man?" Not that I paid much attention to these tantrums. I went wherever I wanted and did whatever work I had to. This was, of course, not very easy. If I had to go out, I hurriedly tidied up everything, desperately trying to make the house look neater and cleaner so as to avoid the charge that I was a careless and irresponsible housewife. Mr. Pawar would immediately pounce on me, "Look at her! Look at the way she is trying to hide her incompetence. All this tidying up is nothing but a big facade! Nobody in her house has taught her anything about housekeeping! She knows nothing!" The words made me boil with rage. As a child I had been as carefree as a butterfly, flitting from flower to flower. Gradually I became immersed in routines: the office, children's school schedules, breakfasts, meals, milk, medicines, studies, rest, and other timings! Moreover, I had taken on many extra responsibilities: organizing programs, meetings, preparing for speeches, writing assignments, things that were way beyond what my limited strength could achieve! It was too stressful. All these things had pushed me into such tight time frames that maintaining a balance among them made me dizzy. My life had taken an inevitable and irreversible turn! But my life partner simply had no idea of what was happening to me. When he said that I did not know anything, I would try to laugh it off, making feeble attempts at humor, "All right! You are from the hilly region! You are superior people! You know how to do things well! You have even built roads in the hills!" Sometimes this would help and a smile flickered across his face, but that was rare. He was a very nice person at heart really. I realized he said such things only in the heat of the moment. However, I could not make him understand that his anger was totally misplaced. He simply refused to understand that.

Gradually, I was initiated into the Ambedkarite movement, Dalit literature, the women's movement, women's literature, but I still had'nt developed my own position regarding various issues. I lacked the depth of thinking required to organize my experiences into a coherent line of argument, like men, simply because most of my time was taken up by my job, housework, children, and education. Most of the things I said were merely parrotlike repetition. Given that there were only a few women in our community who could speak at public programs, people felt, "All right! Here is one who can deliver speeches. So we will invite her." I was a woman who could speak in public programs. That was enough for them! Or I would be invited as a replacement for another woman. And I would accept the invitation and go to deliver speeches.

Although I went to these programs, I disliked the haldi-kumkum ceremony that heralded marriage and births, giving an auspicious touch to these rite-of-passage ceremonies. Its entry in the public domain can be traced way back to the nineteenth century, to the freedom movement right from Tilak's times. Afterward it came to be commonly used to ensure women's participation in public programs. Haldi-kumkum entered the Ambedkar movement around 1975–76, through programs such as Ambedkar Jayanti (birth anniversary), Mahaparinirvan Din (Ambedkar's death anniversary) were already being held in the slums. The ceremony was inscribed in the private domain when Dalit women living in apartment houses were invited to their neighbors' for this social event. They felt if a neighbor invited them for haldi-kumkum, they were obliged to return the favor by organizing one in their houses and inviting the neighbor! Thus Dalit woman accepted the haldi-kumkum program as part of their lives. However, I never liked it, as I had read my Ambedkarite philosophy and feminism well. I considered it unnecessary and almost never participated in it or, if I had to go, I never made a big show of it.

Participating in public programs like Ambedkar Jayanti and Mahaparinirvan Din in the slums, however, made me see the poverty and suffering of our people at close quarters. A few of our relatives lived in slums, so I knew what life in the slums was like. But those slums were not like the ones I went to! Life here was impossible! Tiny, eight-feet-by-six-feet huts, crammed back to back in a very small space... cane partitions in between... low tin roofs with a couple of old rags and a few pots and pans by way of possessions... stinking open drains and gutters in front, with clouds of flies and mosquitoes hovering over them... attacking humans for trespassing on their land... mice and bandicoots chasing each other all over the place... children defecating and pigs roaming on the dung heaps nearby... people spitting everywhere... women throwing dirty water anywhere... bitter quarrels going on... and, even in this atmosphere, people with pale, emaciated faces trying to strengthen each other's resolve to live in the hope of a better life!

One day I was invited to speak in a slum in Kurla. There was no road that one could walk on to get access. The activists had created a makeshift path by spreading tiles on the open drains between rows of tightly packed huts. We walked carefully, trying hard to keep our balance, till we reached a small open space in the middle of the slum. Many children and men were sitting on jute bags spread on the ground. A table and a few chairs were assembled and a banner was put up at the back. When we got there, an activist hurriedly asked me to sit down on a chair at the far end. When I glanced at the chair at the other end, I saw a big garbage can absolutely overflowing near it. I breathed a sigh of relief. So I was sitting in a comparatively better place! I did not have to suffer the stench! But, after some time, the typical stink of public toilets assaulted my nostrils. When I looked over my shoulder, I saw five or six men standing with mugs of water in their hands behind the banner.

I did my best to sit quietly, trying to listen to the speeches for a while. But it was nauseating. Finally I got up to speak. The moment I opened my mouth, the smell reached deep inside me, and I was so revolted that I wanted to throw up. I tried hard to continue speaking, but then found it impossible to go on. Finally, I asked people to shift the table and chairs to the other side and sit with their backs to the public toilets. They said, "But there is a drain on that side!" "Let it be," I said, "even so it will be better than this toilet stink!" The poor activists did as I asked. There were many such places. In summer, especially, the huts became like ovens, with the tin roofs getting very hot overhead. People were almost cooked inside with all the heat and no air. They were human beings, but had to live like paltry hens, victims of their circumstances. Their human energy was reduced to nothing but dust!

I went to a similar slum in Wadala. By the time the program, including speeches, garlanding, and expressing gratitude was over, it was midnight. I was about to leave with an activist who was going to drop me home. I had a relative staying in the slum who said, "Tai, it is almost midnight. Why go home so late? Why don't you stay here tonight with us?" I hesitated, "I would have really liked to ... but people at home will worry about me ... how do I let them know at home? I can't even call home. We don't have a telephone." She kept insisting, and I kept prevaricating. This went on for a few minutes. Then a young girl, around sixteen, added, "If you sleep here, you would have to sleep with your feet inside a jute bag." "Why?" I asked in astonishment. A woman explained, "If the feet are left uncovered, mice and bandicoots come and nibble at the toes. Feet wet with sweat develop a fleshy smell!" I was intrigued and wished to linger, but was scared of what Mr. Pawar would say if I were late; he would get so angry if I were late. As it was he resented my going to meetings because of the late hours. Sometimes he would be particularly bad tempered and say such vicious things! Had I been a woman like those in popular fiction, I would have refused to speak to him for the rest of my life, as they were wont to do!

And yet I continued to go out even after listening to Mr. Pawar's vituperative comments because he had an exceptional quality. He loved and trusted me! He was not jealous at all. He never asked me questions like "Who's this man? What has he got to do with you?" Such questions can really destroy a woman! The activists were polite too and kept their distance. Not that they were all aware of women's issues. On the contrary, they were quite conventional. They never liked it if anybody commented on their *Manuwadi* tendencies.[3] They were only doing the job assigned to them: escorting the speaker home safely.

Once I went to Chembur for the Ambedkar birth anniversary celebrations. It was a well-organized program. I was sent an invitation letter along with a request for acceptance; a car was sent to take me to the program; tea and coffee offered as refreshment. A list of distinguished speakers, previously invited, was read out, implying that my speech had to match their scholarly discourse. We were seated like ministers in the first row, to see the cultural programs. A commentary in English was on. The speakers were politely invited to the stage afterward. All of these were signs of the changing times!

I usually began my speeches with a few quotes from Krantiba Phule,[4] besides citing Babasaheb Ambedkar's Hindu Code Bill. Here too I began on the same vein. "Krantiba Phule used to say when a woman's husband dies, she is made to commit sati, therefore if a woman dies why doesn't a man commit *sata*? He also says that a man can marry a second wife and acquire a *savat* (Marathi for "cowife") in the house. Then why can't a woman marry a second man and have a cohusband (*savata* in Marathi) in the house?" These comments, especially the play on words, were taken very well by the women in the audience, who clapped heartily. But the chairperson did not like the comments. He took out his anger on me in a different way.

I realized that humor and anecdotes carry a message rather well. I would often tell a joke while making the point that our leaders are not as aware of women's issues as they are about the internal differences among themselves; hence people get disillusioned with them. The joke went like this: once, in a mental hospital, a group of mad people were making the sound of a scooter in motion and running in a circle as if they were riding the vehicle. One madman was, however, sitting quietly, looking at them. Two doctors passed by. One of them said, "Look at that man sitting so quietly; he is my patient. I think he has improved a lot. We need to take him to another hospital for further treatment!" Enthusiastically he summoned the patient and told him, "Look, I am going to take you to another hospital for further treatment!" The patient said, "Is that so? In that case, sit on the pillion; I'll take you there," and started running like the other patients, making scooterlike sounds. I said, "This is how our leaders behave. We follow a leader because we think he is sane and then we get disillusioned! Our problems remain as they are!"

The audience clapped and appreciated the point. The chairperson was stung by what I had said earlier. He retaliated in his speech, "Like Pawarbai, I too remember a joke!" he said and went on: "Once a man was invited to speak in a program. The speech was over. The program was over. People left. Yet one man was still sitting there. I asked him, "Why, you seem to have liked the speech very much, do you want to meet the speaker?" He said, "I am just waiting for that man who invited this speaker; I want to thrash him for inviting him!" "People laughed at this as well!"

Some people in the audience wanted to see how I would react. A couple of them asked me later, "Tai, are you angry with what he said?" What could I say? People drown, the speaker stumbles, and the writer stops! What can you say to someone who does nothing?

Usually, in the Dalit movement, whenever women's conventions are organized, men are found to occupy all the chairs on the platform! Naturally, women find it very difficult to express themselves freely. Once, in such a convention, a high-caste feminist, quite highly placed, expressed her displeasure about this. She said, "I have seen many women's conventions; but this is the first time I've seen so many men on the stage!" The statement stung the men present on the stage to the quick! One speaker, a man, retaliated in his speech, "We like to be with our women always. That is our custom. I don't know what your customs are!" Women clapped loudly at this! Should not men give freedom to women at least to appreciate the point made in their favor? I realized, of course, that the import of the comment was that "men and women need to stand united in the struggle against the caste system and should not be divided on the issue, a point of which feminists are not aware!" Later on, as I listened to the speeches, bought books and pamphlets at the Chaitya Bhumi, read informative booklets, participated in discussions, I came to understand more about rationalism, humanism, scientific thinking, and the distinction between sufferings born from natural causes and those caused by man-made artificial factors such as hierarchical relations. I discovered my voice at last! I had finally reached a stage where, rather than saying, "Why did we invite her?" people said, "Good that we invited her!"

One thing was, however, very clear to me. Women's issues did not have any place on the agenda of the Dalit movement, and the women's movement was indifferent to the issues in the Dalit movement. Even today things have not changed!

There was a seminar on Dalit women's issues at a renowned institute in Mumbai. Many teachers, professors, researchers in sociology, history, and so on were present from all over Maharashtra. Many friends from the Maitrini group, like Chhaya Datar, Neera Adarkar, Lata Pratibha Madhukar, were present. I thought that their approach to Dalit women's issues was very positive. We were all sitting around a table shaped like a horseshoe.

In the context of thinking about Dalit women, naturally, Dr. Ambedkar's thoughts received a prominent focus.

A fat professor sitting at one end said, "Dr. Ambedkar did nothing for women. Hindu Code Bill was a political stunt! He never brought his wife forward like Phule, he did not educate her."

I was flabbergasted at this! "That is absolutely wrong, how can she say this?" I looked at my friends with a mute, desperate appeal in my eyes. A colleague in the movement burst out into uncontrollable laughter when she saw me looking at everyone! Maybe she found the expressions on my face very funny! But it was shocking to me that anybody could laugh, for whatever reason, when that sort of a comment was being made about Dr. Ambedkar.

It was not as if the women at the seminar were ignorant about Dr. Ambedkar's work for women, such as his insistence on the inclusion of particular clauses about women in the Hindu Code Bill or about the rights he had given to working women. Nor were they unaware of the social differences between Krantiba Phule and Ambedkar and how it had affected the formation of their wives' personalities. It was difficult to believe that they did not know how Dr. Ambedkar had coaxed his wife into getting an education. And yet they were so critical of Dr. Ambedkar! Because of Dr. Ambedkar's conversion, and Dalit literature's attack on Hinduism, they had chosen to retaliate and attack Ambedkar rather than subject Hinduism to a critical scrutiny and be self-reflective.

The same attitude could be witnessed in the women working in our organization, Stree Uwacha. This came through transparently when a discussion was held to plan the annual issue of Stree Uwacha in 1993, in the post–Babri Masjid demolition period.[5] Members were divided into two obvious camps. One group held that in the aftermath of the religious riots it was absolutely important to bring out an edition on the effects of all this on women's lives from a feminist perspective. The other group thought that being silent at this time made better sense. The positions were contradictory. Stree Uwacha would generally be edited on a rotation basis. This was a convenient excuse to push the editorship on my shoulders. My experience as a writer may also have been a plus point.

The group in favor of bringing out an edition had already started collecting poems, stories, and articles. I accepted the responsibility because religious and caste oppression was a burning issue in the Dalit movement and this was a good opportunity for me. Some very good articles appeared in the issue: Sandeep Pendse's "Sadhwi Ritambhara," Jaya Velankar's "The Drums of Ayodhya," Neera Adarkar's "The Mystery of Beharampada Revealed" did, indeed, bring some solace to minds shocked by what had happened. These articles are valid even today. Between the demolition of the Babri Masjid and the present, however, many progressive organizations like Stree Uwacha collapsed, and many others continue to collapse.

Dr. Pramila Leela Sampat, the young president of the Vikas Wanchit Dalit Mahila Sanghatana, came to Mumbai from Wardha. She organized a meeting in the office of Sharada Sathe's Stree Mukti Sanghatana, where she emphatically argued that December 25 was the true liberation day for Indian women. She said, "The *Manusmriti* has imposed many restrictions on women and built the caste system. That is why Babasaheb said that the woman is the gateway of the caste system. It was on December 25 that Babasaheb had burned *Manusmriti* to liberate Indian women from the clutches of Manuwadi culture. Our organization has been observing December 25 as the Indian women's day of liberation for the last three years. So let us celebrate this day at Mahad every year."[6]

Pramila was the only Dalit girl among the ones I knew who, in spite of being a doctor, devoted herself to organizational work full-time. She seemed to work all twenty-four hours of the day. I was much impressed with her work. I went with her to Mahad to celebrate the day.

The Bouddha Jana Panchayat people in Konkan have been celebrating December 25 as Human Liberation Day for many years. So they opposed our celebrating it as women's liberation day. We argued that human enslavement begins with women's enslavement and that is why Babasaheb had liberated women on this day. There was a debate along the lines of what comes first, the egg or the chicken. I was criticized for not supporting the Konkan Bouddha Jana Panchayat in spite of belonging to the Konkan. Later, two separate programs were organized to celebrate December 25 as both Human Liberation Day and Women's Liberation Day! In one such program I met Kunda Pramila Nilakantha. I saw for the first time how these girls had contributed to the process of transformation, beginning with using their names to establish identity. They impressed me greatly. Kunda was born in a Maratha family and brought up in the Dalit locality on Lalbaug-Curry Road. She had been working devotedly for the Dalit movement for many years. Yet she, and many like her, had no place in the Dalit movement. They do not have it even today. This reality is very disturbing.

Ten

One day a few women from the workers' building nearby came rushing to my house. They seemed very apprehensive. They knew me, since I had visited them quite often on Ambedkar's birth anniversaries, and I too knew many of them, like Sonkamble, Kardak, and Kale. Breathlessly they burst out, "Tai, Tai, you must hurry! Police have arrested our boys. They are threatening to demolish the Buddhist shrine we have built. Please come with us."

The Buddhist shrine was a tiny room built with mud by young men and women on an open space in their housing colony. I had visited the place a couple of times and advised them to get permission for the construction. Since they did not, somebody had complained to the police, who took prompt action.

Quite a few people—old men and women—gathered around the small hut. An old man with a white beard argued vehemently, "They built so many temples all around; even on footpaths and playgrounds; did anybody ask them why? Had they asked permission to build them? Then why do they stop us?"

Now this was a superfluous question. The law says, "Don't complain about the others. Explain your own conduct!" Finally strings were pulled from the top, and the young men were set free by the evening, when they resolved to work with a new vigor. Funds were collected in various ways, and it was decided to construct a proper hall with bricks and cement where various community programs could be organized. "Let them bring it down afterward," the young men said, "but we will construct our hall at any cost!" The hall was duly built and named Triratna Buddha Vihar. A statue of the Buddha was brought all the way from Thailand and installed in it. Besides programs like Ambedkar's birth and death anniversaries, seminars, meetings, panel discussions also began to be scheduled in the hall. Training programs and workshops for women in tailoring, electrical work, and so on were also conducted, along with coaching classes in karate.

I was introduced to Meenakshi and Vasantrao Moon at one of these programs. Mr. Moon was invited as a speaker and so was I. The Moons became our family friends. We used to have many discussions on the thoughts and writings of Phule and Ambedkar. Meenakshi was involved in organizing women during programs such as food distribution, prayers, and so on. Since our homes were close by, we began to visit each other quite often. The Maharashtra government had specially appointed Mr. Moon on the committee for the publication of the collected volumes of Dr. Ambedkar's writing and speeches, which was a great honor for him. He was virtually a treasure house of information about Dr. Babasaheb Ambedkar.

Every time he came to visit us, he would disclose something new about Dr. Ambedkar, and Harishchandra and I would be enthralled! Mr. Moon was extremely witty. Many people who considered humor as vulgar did not like his witty comments. Some would think he was taking a dig at them and their faces would fall. At such times Meenakshi would try to save the situation with "Umm ... err ... that was not he wanted to say ... you know ... " and that contributed to the fun all the more.

Dr. Eleanor Zelliot, the American scholar, visited India quite often with her students. She was a guest of the Moons. She was trying to learn Marathi. Once I went to meet her at their house. Eleanor and her students were sitting in Mr. Moon's mother's room, and we joined them. It was lunchtime, so naturally Meenakshi asked me to stay for lunch. Everybody was terribly hungry. The food was ready, and Meenakshi was arranging the side dishes. Eleanor asked Mr. Moon's mother, "Your name is Annapurna, isn't it? What does it mean?" Before she could reply, I put my hand to my mouth and explained the meaning with gestures: "One who gives food." And, before I could elaborate, Mr. Moon said, "No, no, she is not Annapurna! The real Annapurna is there in the kitchen! Don't ask this one for food. She will not give any. The food giver is inside. The other one! In fact, the one here keeps asking for food!"[1] This confused poor Eleanor no end! She looked at the kitchen in perplexity and asked, "If Meenakshi's name is Annapurna, what is your mother's name?" I burst out laughing!

One day, Hira and I were having lunch in her office. Suddenly she had a brainwave. "Hey, we always attend the Asmitadarsha, Dalit, Buddhist Marathi Sahitya Sammelanas.[2] It is always men who organize them, right? We women only present our writings. Why shouldn't we have our own independent platform for literature?"

I was very pleased with this idea. "Wonderful!" I said, "There is a great need to organize women in any case. So let us establish a literary platform for women where they can write, speak, and share their experiences and write with other women." We decided to float a Dalit Mahila Sahitya Sanghatana (Dalit women's literary organization). Of course, we could not have done it on our own! But we had the strength of the Phule-Ambedkar philosophy as a support and the famous pair from history—Tilak and Agarkar—as a model.

A few days later, a group of about eight of us—Hira and her husband, Meenakshi and Mr. Moon, my sister, her husband, and the two of us—went to Matheran for a trip. We shared our resolve with the others, and they all backed it strongly. We began to work in that direction.

On our return, I invited Hira to our home for lunch, along with her mother, who had come for a short visit. Hira's sister Sulochana was also present. After lunch Meenakshi arrived, and I also called Nanda Lokhande, a friend of mine who lived next door, in an adjacent block, to join us. The five of us decided to shake the world, like Napoleon Bonaparte and his five friends, with our literary activity, and, with this noble resolve, we launched our organization. That we ended up destroying the organization through lack of experience is a different story.

Even before we founded our literary forum, some young women had floated an organization called Mahila Sansad in 1984 or 1985 at Delile Road in Mumbai. Rajani Tilak, Kunda Kadam, Asha Landge, and Shashikala Dekhne were some of the women who took the initiative. But this organization also broke up because of internal squabbles. We came to know about it much later, of course. Even if we had known about it earlier, I don't suppose we would have learned a lesson from that. We took our own time to realize that an organization was greater than personal prejudices and opinions. Later on we dropped the word *literary* from the name and got it registered as Dalit Women's Organization. Some members started working on social issues.

We had to work really hard to coax women to become our members and harder still to make them retain the membership. Another equally difficult task was to convince the family members. Since Meenakshi and I were neighbors, on holidays, after quickly finishing the household chores, we would go out on a membership-collecting spree. We decided to go into the neighboring buildings and chawls to meet women and urge them to become members. We would go around mostly on empty stomachs, but who was bothered about such mundane things as food! The fire within was enough! Hira and Sulochana were supposed to cover their own neighborhoods—meeting neighbors, relatives, friends, acquaintances, telling them about the organization.

I decided to begin on a Sunday. Nanda Phulpagar, accompanied by one of her friends, and I went to meet a woman nearby. She was a little confused to find a bunch of decently dressed, educated women land upon her doorstep. She came straight out of the kitchen, a spoon still held in her hand. But she did not invite us in. She stood her ground at the threshold, her attention equally divided between the kitchen and us, and said, "Look, you can come when my husband returns from the office. Not now. Whatever work you have, you can tell him ... No, no, no ... I have no time. Come after my husband returns," she said and banged the door shut in our faces. Obviously, she was quite scared. Now what ought we to do? We looked at each other in perplexity. We had thought that once we gained entry into a house, we would find out about our own people among the neighbors and visit them. We had made up a code: A.P. (Any of Our People) and D.P. (Different People). But here one of our own women had banged the door shut on our faces! Then we thought of another trick: once the woman opened the door, we would look for images of Buddha or Ambedkar inside and just barge in.

Accordingly, we barged into another house, this time a class 4 house in a chawl,[3] after ascertaining that it belonged to the A.P. group. The lady of the house came forward, followed by a mixed audience of young and old people, both from within and without the house. Immediately we began to belt out our well-rehearsed speech.

"Bai, we have started a Dalit Women's Organization. There are so many issues concerning the women in our community, such as ignorance, superstitions, caste discrimination, employment, and others. That is why it is necessary for all of us to come forward and unite." The audience listened with a rapt attention, clinging to every word that we said, and that made us more voluble. We simply could not stop and went on to sketch before them certain rosy dreams till an old woman abruptly stemmed the flow, saying, "Bai, that is all very well! But our young men don't have jobs, what will you do for them?"

"Our organization is not meant for getting jobs for young men," we tried to explain; "It is for women's development."

"Oh, stop it," the old woman exploded. "I have seen many like you! Ha! Development indeed! Enough of this! Come on, come on, get going!" She turned her back on us and almost pushed us out.

Such harsh responses right at the outset were quite discouraging, but we were not the ones to give up. We decided to persevere. Let us have lunch first, we thought, though we had covered only two houses so far. It was two in the afternoon, long past lunchtime. The sun was particularly hot. I was feeling quite sick and extremely hungry at the same time!

But the moment I stepped inside my home, my husband thundered, "What were you doing all this while? What about lunch?"

"Oh, but ... but I had cooked ... !"

"You call that food? It's Sunday today! Do we have to eat potatoes on a Sunday? Enough of this organization business!" There was another outburst from my husband, which silenced me!

The very first day of our organizational work had thus ended in a disaster. So I decided to lie low for a while. But not for long! The bug had bitten me well and good. One day I took Jayashree Aasrondkar with me and went to Naygaon, Parel. After the experience at the B.D.D. chawls, I thought we should have "cleanliness" as the only aim of our organization. Jayashree knew a woman there, but we did not have the exact address. Parel was actually the heartland of Dr. Babasaheb Ambedkar's movement. There were so many Mahila Mandals, women's groups or societies, established. We planned to meet the Mahila Mandal members and make them our members en bloc.

When we entered the chawl, people began to ask, "What do you want?" So we told them about our plans. A stocky, middle-aged man in white clothes, sitting near the stairs, came to us, chewing *paan*. He made a gesture with his hand, asking us to hold on, spat the juice on the wall, turned to us with his eyes closed, and began to talk.

"I'll tell you," he said, "There are heaps of Mahila Mandals here, but all in bad shape. Internal quarrels, you know! Women! What else do you expect!" He guffawed loudly, showing his discolored teeth.

"Never mind," we said, "just tell us where they are. We will go and meet them."

"Oh! They have gone to a house two buildings beyond! Someone has died."

This unnerved us. "All right. We will go there," I said. We turned to go out. The man said, "Bai, don't go there; there is such a racket going on! Why do you want to go? Come sometime later."

Meenakshi lived in the officers' quarters. There were many Dalit officers living around her. But the nameplates on their doors told a different story; these were all Brahmin names like Tambe, Kamat, Sahasrabudhdhe, Barve, and so on. It was quite difficult to make out whether they were A.P. or D.P. I suggested to Meenakshi one day, "Let us go and find out!"

She readily agreed. We climbed four flights and, panting for breath, pressed the bell of a flat. Someone peeped through the eyepiece. "What do you want?" A voice inquired. The cold tone startled us a little. But soon we regained our composure and answered, "We are starting a Dalit women's organization, want to talk about it." The woman quickly lowered the chain, opened the door, let us in, and closed the door again, with a worried expression on her face. "Sit down," she said and went inside to get some water for us. We looked around. Classy furniture, color TV, phone ... quite an affluent house. But no signs of Phule and Ambedkar!

The woman returned with glasses of water. She was plump, fair, and decked out in heavy gold jewellery! "All right, what is it?" she said. So we began our well-rehearsed speech. But she was not even listening. "How did you know that we are one of you?" she asked us.

"Oh, we just guessed."

"But how could you? Nobody here has the slightest suspicion that we are like that. In fact, because of our looks, they think we are Kobras."

"Kobras?" Meenakshi was completely at a loss.

"Kokanstha Brahman!" I whispered by way of explanation.

"Oh! I thought cobras were snakes!" She whispered back, choking with suppressed laughter.

The lady, impervious to our whispers, was still chewing on her favorite theme: their high-class elite looks! We stopped her and tried to push our argument forward.

But it was of no use. Finally, bored, we got up to go. That's when she said, "You know, every individual must work for his own development and progress, mustn't he? Ultimately, it is individuals who make a community, and communities in turn make the country, right? So each one should look after himself!" The woman smiled a self-congratulatory smile as if she had come up with some great philosophy!

"But Madam, suppose Dr. Babasaheb Ambedkar also had said the same thing! Then where would we be today?" Meenakshi asked her. The woman looked a little crestfallen. I stepped forward to deliver another blow, "What you say may be right, Madam! Many people in our community look after their own interests alone; they change their surnames, hide their caste. But does it help the oppressed people in their community? Does their situation change? Don't you think this is escapism? Is it good?"

The woman grew restless. We got up to go. "This is our address," we said, giving her our card. "We meet there every Saturday at three o'clock. You can come if you are interested."

Then we asked her whether there were any A.P.s around. She gave us detailed information about everyone! They were all like her, with their surnames changed.

We thanked her and climbed down. I said to Meenakshi, "See? That woman knows so much about everybody, but thinks nobody knows about her!"

We visited a few more flats there. We came across similar women. The same attitude! We tried to locate images of the Buddha and Ambedkar to ascertain whether it was an A.P. house or D.P. Some had hung the image of Padma Pani rather than that of the Buddha on the wall as a decorative piece and some kept tiny images with their plants, so that they would not show clearly. Some had hidden them in embroidery and knitting and hung them as showpieces with decorative frames. In short, they took great care to keep these symbols of their caste hidden from the public eye, in a less prominent place.

When I returned home dead tired in the evening, I found someone had come and left an invitation, asking me to give a speech in Bhivandi. So the atmosphere in the house was very tense. There were heated arguments, but I acted as if I were deaf and dumb. That saved me. To be able to do any work, you must learn this skill first. Bhivandi was a distant place. But the program was to be several days later. That would give me sufficient time to prepare. So I decided to accept the invitation and informed the people concerned accordingly. This would be a good opportunity to talk about the organization, I thought.

In the meantime, we kept speaking to many acquaintances. Many women were quite willing to join as members. We seem to have angered a few, who said, "What are your plans? The same as our leaders? Collect money and enjoy!" Some, like Godavari Tambe and Laxman Shivdavkar, predicted in a desperate tone, drained of all hope, "We also tried doing this in our time and had to give up in sheer frustration. You will achieve nothing!" And some others told us to our face, "Your organization will get scattered like dry leaves in the wind. Wait and see!"

Pawar used to say, "Such organizations are like soda water bottles. They make a lot of noise when opened, but then they cool off. Mark my words; you will suffer the same fate!"

But, as it usually happens, there were a few well-wishers as well, besides these prophets of doom. "Good that you are doing this. It is necessary to have such organizations. Do tell us if you need any help from us. We will try to do whatever we can. You can depend on us." This encouraged us greatly.

On the way to Bhiwandi, there was a problem which I had to face as a woman. We set out in a special car. Bhai Sangare was with us. On our way, we collected Professor Ratanlal Sonagra and a couple of other activists. Sitting in the car continuously for five to six hours was quite tiring. I wanted to go to the loo. It was all right in school. You could raise your little finger and convey that you needed to visit the lavatory. But here it became a big problem. How do you convey this urgency to the others? I was the only woman among the men. I found it very awkward to tell them to stop the car because I wanted to attend to nature's call. The others stopped the car, relieving themselves, standing on the road. But I had to sit in the car. They were all people I knew well, but what was the use? And then we got down from the car only to climb straight onto the stage. The organizers were efficient and offered tea, water. But I did not drink any.

That would have meant more trouble! Then the program began. Long-winded, exaggerated introductions, unnecessary praise showered on the guests, huge reports, children's felicitations, lengthy speeches by activists and leaders went on, overstretched like a rubber band—and how I suffered! But whom could one ask?

I somehow managed to finish my speech and went to some women sitting nearby who finally took me to the right place. I remembered how Shantabai Dani also had to suffer the same way quite often. Even today the situation has hardly changed.

We had a lot of places left to cover. Our Saturday meetings were strange. Women who turned up one Saturday did not come on the next one, when there would be an entirely different set. On the third Saturday there would be still different women. Sometimes the number would be good, sometimes frightfully low. Once again we had to go on a membership hunt. Babasaheb Karande was well known to us. He was from the Charmakar community: the cobbler caste that makes shoes, sandals, chappals. We decided to include the Charmakar women in the organization. Once we went to meet Mr. Karande at his place in order to enroll the women in his family and circle as members of our organization. He was sitting leisurely in the hall. His wife was inside. When we told him that we were starting an organization to give women a voice, to help them express themselves, he was visibly moved. He lauded our work in high-sounding words.

"Please call Mrs. Karande. We want to tell her about this. Please tell her to join us." I said to him. Suddenly his face became very grave. He uttered the words, "Women's liberation!" (We had not used these words!) Then he turned to us saying, "And pray, why do you think our women need this? They are already free and liberated. If they don't get along with their husbands, they just tell them to their faces, 'I can't get along with you. Take back your *dorle* [mangalsutra].' In such cases either they leave the house or drive the husband out."

We stood stupefied as Karande delivered this speech. His wife had also come out in the meanwhile, and like us she too stared at him in utter amazement. After some time, we quietly got up and left. Our eyes were so dazed by the illuminating display of the Dalit woman's liberation that we could not even see the staircase well!

There was a sales tax officer, a colleague of mine, who lived just behind my house. His wife also worked in the same office. Usually we would not dare approach such educated Dalits in a slightly better financial position. However hard one tried convincing them, they refused to be convinced. A sheer waste of time! Yet we went and told him about our organization. He too took us to task on the issue of women's liberation. He seemed to believe that since we got together to discuss women's development and progress, we must be "feminists"! And if we were feminists, what else could we do but turn the wives against their men?

"Oh, but that is not what we intend to do at all. We are just trying to ..."

"Don't give me that! There is no need for our women to get out of the house. We give them everything they need in the house."

The man was firing away when his wife came out. Then he turned toward her, "Come on, tell them what you lack! Clothes, money, ornaments ... Go on, go on, tell them!"

The woman was completely flummoxed. What exactly were we talking about? So we turned to her and tried to explain. But the man gave us no opportunity. "How do our women suffer?" He fired away, "Are they being burned or killed? Well, in a married life, a couple of slaps here and there is nothing ... But women's liberation! What for? Because one receives a few slaps?"

The woman got the point. "You are so right," she exclaimed, "no mangalsutra, no bangles ... Silly fads!" Patting her own mangalsutra in place, she said in a shrill voice, "There are a couple of them like that in our office too. They left their homes and then came back." It was so tough to explain the objectives of our organization to the woman.

Sometimes the neo-Buddhists would explode at the word *Dalit*! "How are we Dalit now?" They asked angrily. We had to make an elaborate explanation: Dalit does not mean only socially suppressed or oppressed people! It also signals rational, secular people who have discarded the oppressive system and concepts like God, fate, and the caste system. *Dalit* is being replaced by *Phule-Ambedkarite* or simply *Ambedkarite*.

Finally, on a Saturday, some twenty to twenty-five women, some educated, some uneducated, gathered at the address we gave them. Most of them were curious to know how exactly we were going to work on women's problems.

We too did not have a concrete answer to this question. We wanted our aims and objectives to evolve out of our discussions with these women. We had ambitious plans: discover women writers, poets; bring them together;

encourage them; organize public oral narratives; print them; organize women's sahitya sammelanas. The sky was the limit for us!

First we had to find a name for the organization. Since it was a women's organization, it had to be a woman's name. Innumerable options were considered and rejected. Then names of the Buddhist Bhikshunis, nuns, such as Sujata, Aamrapali, Yashoda, Gautami, and Sanghamitra were considered, to give a historical touch. But Mahila Mandals with these names were abundant all over Mumbai. Hira came up with a suggestion, "How about Samwadini?" It means a woman who aims at communication with everyone. We all accepted this name wholeheartedly and finally our organization was named Samwadini Dalit Stree Sahitya Manch.

Now we had to decide who would be on the executive committee. I opposed this idea, saying, "It is these issues, like who will be the president and who the secretary, that ruin any organization. Do you know what Dr. Babasaheb Ambedkar has said? He has given the example of a meeting in Igatpuri where the issue of who would preside over the meeting got so heated up that finally a pillar was declared as the president before any meeting could be conducted! Many organizations have collapsed like a house of cards because of such things! So why have one at all?"

Everybody agreed with me. But we needed money if we wanted to work. Money would have to be collected from people. Thus the organization had to be registered. An executive committee needed to be set up. In the end we had to constitute a committee in another meeting. Hira became the president, Sheela Hirekar the vice president. I was the secretary, and Meenakshi the joint secretary. Our first task was collecting funds. The campaign began.

The first decision that we took was to ignore the distinctions like A.P. and D.P. and collect money from everyone irrespective of her caste. I decided to start from our office, from the highest rank. So I went to see our chief officer with the receipt book in my hand and briefly told him about our organization, its aim to work for women's development. The sahib heard the names of Phule and Ambedkar and said, "Are you sure Ambedkar belonged to the lower castes? I am asking because my son has a lesson on Ambedkar, which says that he was educated abroad! I am a little doubtful! How could he if he really belonged to the lower castes?" I was flabbergasted and quite angry with myself. Why accept money from a man who knows nothing about Dr. Ambedkar's stupendous work? I turned back and returned to my seat.

After some time the peon came to me, carrying a five-rupee note. "From the sahib," he announced. Five rupees! I wanted to throw it back in his face. But eventually I accepted it. When I gave him a receipt, he said, "The sahib gave it because you are a woman! Otherwise he normally doesn't give anybody any money!" I almost exploded with rage.

Some of our other activists also had a similar experience: of having been given money because they were women. Someone came up with a very insulting suggestion. "Instead of going in a group to meet an officer, go separately, alone, and use honeyed words! You'll be able to cull out a little more!" I remembered the incident of how Paththe Bapurao had staged a dance show of Pawalabai to help Dr. Ambedkar's work and how the latter had furiously refused to accept the tainted money. So we just listened in silence to such unsolicited advice. Some people really behaved in such offensive ways—apparently quite harmless, but very humiliating! They would avoid us in front of their wives and became quite effusive in their absence. We wanted people to look upon us as human beings.

There were many upper-class people who behaved like my boss. Some even told me, "Sorry, Madam, we are not one of you!" They would leave me speechless with indignation.

Tai, her husband, who had become a judge by this time, and my brother Shahu, who was a director in the telephone department, offered substantial donations. Generally, however, people from the Dalit communities were sick and tired of giving donations. In most of the houses we went to for fund collection we would be asked to enter with a frown that clearly said, "How much money? How many people do we pay?" Some people asked, "What happened to the money we gave you last time?" When we hastened to tell them that it was not to us they had given, they retorted, "You also are one of them!" But give they did, albeit a little grumpily. Everybody, however, asked us, "What will you do with this money?" They all seemed to feel that the programs we planned were of no use. Instead they wanted us to distribute saris or sewing machines among women or books among children or mosquito nets to save them from malaria in the slums. Such programs would indeed be useful. But our point was a more basic one. We wanted to treat the root cause rather than give a symptomatic treatment to the disease. We wanted to awaken the sense of identity and selfhood in everyone! That for us was the root cause. But educated people—who matter—also failed to perceive this. And people also told us, "You are hypocrites!"

However, we paid no attention to such remarks and continued with our work. Finally our organization, Samwadini, was opened by Eleanor Zelliot. Many Dalit writers like Babytai Kamble, Shantabai Kamble, and Padmashri Daya Pawar were present, along with Maxine Berntson, the scholar from Phaltan. This program was followed by many others including the publication of poems, public narratives, sahitya sammelana, and so on. The first Dalit Women's Sahitya Sammelana, which we had organized in Vartak Hall in Mumbai in May 1987, must have been the unique not only in Maharashtra but in the whole country.

My head would be swimming in the clouds of lofty ideas, such as having Dalit women speak and write about their lives and then be published. But once I was rudely jolted out of my dreams. A middle-aged woman came to meet me one evening at home. "I have been trying to meet you for the last two days," she said, "but you are so difficult to find."

"Why did you want to meet me?" I asked her.

"Isn't that XYZ lady in your Mahila Mandal?"

"Maybe; but why … ?"

"Why have you allowed her to be a member?" she retorted angrily.

"Look here," I said, "I don't even know who you are! Why don't you tell me everything? How can I understand what you are saying?"

The woman told me that this woman's son was married to the daughter of a family she knew. "She harasses her daughter-in-law so much! The son is transferred to another place. But she refuses to allow her daughter-in-law to go with him. Is that right?" she asked me.

"How are you related to this girl?" I asked her.

"I am her *attya!*" she said and went on to give a detailed account of the harassment her niece had to suffer at the hands of this woman. "Next month they would have the other son married off. So another daughter-in-law is coming into the house. They will harass her as well!"

"What do you expect me to do?"

"Ask her, how can you harass another woman when you too are a woman?"

"Look here, Madam, usually we do not take up such issues. But if what you say is right, and if one of our own members is behaving in this way, we will definitely try to reason with her. Now go home."

"Ha! As if she would listen to you! She is a seasoned customer!" The woman was boiling with rage. I somehow managed to convince her and sent her home.

The next day, early in the morning, when I was sipping tea, a young girl, twenty-five or twenty-six years old, stood at my door. The moment I looked at her, I understood that she was the girl the woman had talked to me about.

She came in. "Didn't my *attya* come to you yesterday?" she asked me and went on to relate the great deeds of her mother-in-law. "They have driven me out of the house now. I too do not want to go back!" she said.

"Please keep your cool," I told her. "These quarrels are like storms in a teacup! If your husband loves you, he will surely come and take you back. We have a meeting tomorrow; why don't you come? Your mother-in-law will also be present. We will listen to both of you and try to see whose mistake it is. Then we will sort it out. And you too can become a member."

This very reasonable speech of mine somehow went to the girl's head! She went home, rang up her mother-in-law, and blasted her, "Now I have got the backing of the women's liberation group and they are going to see to it that you treat me well in your house. They are going to bring a *morcha* to the wedding to spite you!" The result was predictable. Her in-laws abused me soundly. They were so scared of the morcha that they wanted to postpone the marriage. Finally, they made the decision to fight back and went to the marriage hall with sticks and other such paraphernalia! My husband was so incensed with me when he heard this that he almost thrashed me! But, after a few days, the girl came to tell me, "Now I am living with my husband. He came to take me back and we are very happy together." She, of course, said neither thank you nor sorry! That must have slipped from her memory!

I sincerely believe that a newly married couple has to be given some time together, or an opportunity to live independently with each other, so that they can understand each other well and misunderstandings can be avoided. But this view of mine drew a lot of ire from my family members. "This woman is a family breaker!" they said. There were many women who came with problems of this kind, and I would give them the address of organizations that offered counseling.

The Asmitadarsha Sahitya Sammelana was held at Dhule. Seven or eight of us were on the stage to present our views on women's problems. The audience was mostly women! After the panel discussion, I asked one of our activists, "Why did you go out when the panel discussion was on?" He said easily, "Since this was a women's panel discussion, I went out. What reason can a man have to attend that? So I went out for a stroll."

A woman activist was speaking like a spitfire on women's oppression. I was quite impressed with her fiery spirit. So when she sat down after her speech, I pushed my diary toward her for her address. But one of my friends sitting next to me poked me in the ribs with her elbow. Later I came to know that this woman had gagged her daughter-in-law and burned her alive. She had managed to suppress the whole affair because of her position in society. I was shocked beyond my wits when I heard this! My mouth fell open, and I forgot to close it for a long time!

"There really are very few cases of women getting harassed! But you feminists go hunting for them and make so much noise, making mountains out of molehills!" A friend of my husband's, called Pawar, from Naygaon, used to complain to me furiously. "Every family has some problems. They automatically get resolved with time! Why do you make so much noise over them?" What could one say to a man who himself was making so much noise?

One day Shaila Satpute and Shama Dalwai came looking for me. They said, "In Bandra, where you live, is a man called Pawar. He is from your community. He neither allows his wife to live with him nor does he divorce her. Besides he has taken all her jewellery. Is he a relative? Or do you at least know him?" I was quite intent on knowing his address. He was a Pawar. My husband too was a Pawar. Were they friends? Now the surname Pawar is a very common one—as common as the days of a week! Maybe this man too is also from Naygaon, I thought. Then Shama said, "No, he is not from Naygaon. He definitely lives in Bandra."

"How do you think I can help?"

"Well, you can get us information about the people in his house. Where has he kept her jewellery? Is he willing to live with her? What do the family members say?"

I decided to help sort out the woman's problems. When I set out to do so, however, the man's nextdoor neighbor, said, "Bai, don't you get involved in this. Tell both your friends to leave this guy alone! Nobody should be allowed to bring private problems in public."

I gave up! Going by what Shama and Shaila said, the man in question appeared to be quite a tough nut! In spite of their connections with the powers that be, he was impervious to their efforts! How was I going to make him show me where he had hidden his wife's jewellery? Such men, even if they are from your own community ...

When I could not do anything about certain things, I tried to bring these issues into my stories. In the beginning I used to be quite apprehensive about whether the person concerned or the family members would read what I had written and get furious with me. But later on I realized how silly I was. People would not be willing to open their eyes to read even if it were held right in front of their eyes. My husband would repeatedly tell the others, as he was wont to do about everything, "See, this magazine has Urmila's story." But nobody bothered. They were more scared of my stories than of his lectures.

One of my stories called "Kavach" (Shell) appeared in a collection of short stories Vilas Khole had edited with the name *Chaukat* (The frame). This collection was prescribed as a textbook for the B.A. course run by the University of Mumbai. I had studied so many authors' books while doing my B.A. and M.A., and written critically on them, saying, "according to the author," and so on, therefore, I was quite proud that students would be learning and writing about me in the same way, referring to me as the author! But no! Another rude shock awaited me. That story was termed obscene, and there was a furor!

The story was about the repulsive tendency of some men to crack obscene jokes containing ambiguous words and double meanings at the poor women who came to the market to sell bananas, mangoes, pumpkins, and other such vegetables. It dealt with the emotional reaction of a twelve or thirteen-year-old boy who listens to the crude jokes aimed at his mother. This was a reality I had experienced right from my childhood. Certain obscene words in my story were claimed to have a bad effect on the college girls. Critics like Prabhakar Nerurkar, Nikhil Wagle, and Madhav Gadkari came to the defense of my story. Finally the story reached the college students and other readers. From my place in an obscure corner, I suddenly found myself in the limelight of public attention.

I will never forget to my dying day the happy, adoring smile on Mr. Pawar's face when some journalists came to our home to interview me.

Somehow even my mother-in-law came to know of this. She reminded me that the people from Bhiraunde were reputed to be book lovers and warned me in no uncertain terms, "Don't write about just anything that comes to your mind. You must write in a tradition that will keep the flag flying high."

The Second World Marathi Conference was held in Mauritius. I was able to attend it because of people like Sharad Pawar, Madhav Gadkari, and Prabhakar Nerurkar. I was curious to know about what had happened to the people who had been taken away from India to work as sugarcane laborers. I tried to seek answers to this question during my visit there; collected some information, interviewed certain people, and then, after my return, produced a book titled *Mauritius: A Journey*. It was released by Sheelabay Bapu, the social welfare minister of Mauritius, at the Third World Marathi Conference in Delhi. My experience with people in Mauritius had convinced me that it was wrong to say caste cannot be cast off. They had done it! They knew only that they were Hindus and had forgotten their castes. But then people told me that some people from India have started digging up the history of their ancestors, giving them caste labels. Will Hindu society never be free of the obsession with caste?

During the journey to Mauritius, I came to know a writer called Asha Damle. We were both members of Maitrini, and the journey really brought us close together. I have portrayed the delicate weave of our friendship in my book *Mauritius: A Journey*. She was like a ray of light in my search for humanity in the dark.

My stories were translated into quite a few languages: Hindi, English, Gujarati, Tamil, and Urdu. I received many appreciative letters from readers in these languages. Many awards came my way for the stories, like the Sahitya Sanskriti Mandal, Asmitadarsha, Kathakar V. C. Gurjar, Ahilya Holkar Awards. I was happy that people appreciated my stories, my writing, for which I had literally burned the midnight oil! What more can one expect from life?

Eleven

One day my sister called me in my office to say that our vahini, Shahu's wife, had given birth to a boy. "Let's go to Ratnagiri for the baby's *namakaran* ceremony," she said. By 1985–86, the Sanskrit word *namakaran* instead of *barse,* the usual Marathi word for the ceremony that gave the child a name, had become a part of our vocabulary. My brother had a son after five daughters. I was very happy because I felt that now his wife would not have to go through repeated pregnancies in the hope of getting a son. The poor woman, after all, had a job. She was the inspiration for my story "Shalya." Every time she gave birth to a daughter, our family and community would react sharply! The incidents provoked me into writing this story, which was later adapted as a television play.

We, the sisters, went to the naming ceremony. The smile on Aai's wrinkled face was like the silver lining of a dark cloud. She looked very tired. Inadvertently, I thought, how much longer would she be among us? Brothers and sisters had come together after a long time. I very much wanted to be with Aai—to videotape our conversations with her, our laughing together. We would have her live image with us even after her death! I suggested as much to my brother, expecting him to jump readily at the idea, especially at the time of rejoicing over the birth of a son. But he said, "Oh no! Now I have to be very careful about money!" He was a chip off the old block! Like mother, like son!

I remembered another incident. Some time ago, we three sisters had come to meet Aaye. It was the Bhau Beej Day during Diwali. Before our conversion, we never celebrated brahminic festivals like Padva and Bhau Beej. But we did have the custom of giving gifts to newly married women when they came to visit their parents at the time of the Gauri and the Ganapati festivals. In my family, we never had the privilege of being honored this way, because Aai was nothing less than a miser. Gradually brahminic customs and festivals had stealthily entered Dalit households, especially the affluent ones, during the exuberant period of Dalit writing, though nobody would have publicly admitted it.

Now we three sisters decided to celebrate Diwali and Bhau Beej so that we could force Bhau into giving us gifts. When Bhau saw the paraphernalia we had got together—the lighted candle, the plate—he too joined in the fun. "Wow! Three sisters with the ceremonial lamp!" he said. "Prosperity will now rush to me from three different directions!" We retorted, "Ha! You live at the crossroads anyway. At the meeting point of three roads! So prosperity will come to your house anyway! But we are waiting for it to come *our* way! So get up and get ready! We are waiting for the gifts!"

Now he realized that we were quite serious. He went on, "Don't you know, Babasaheb asked us not to celebrate anything of this kind?" "Ah ha!" I said, "Don't you know that Babasaheb asked in the Hindu Code Bill to give the daughters their share of property? So come on, get up now!"

Unable to escape, he sat on the wooden seat and allowed us to perform the ceremony of moving the lamp around his face. Then he put three betel nuts on the plate instead of gifts! "What is this?" we quarreled with him. "You can't do this to us!" He put three eight-anna coins in the plate as a gift! Eight annas each! The drama ended right there! We were all play-acting really! But it hurt us to know that our brother felt that he owed us nothing after we were married. It felt like a prick of the porcupine's barb. Then Aai added her own bit to this, "You silly girls, what do you lack in your own houses? Why do you expect gifts from your brother?" These were the very sentiments of my brother! After this, one day Tai said to Aai, "Don't you feel bad that we return home with an empty bag?" So, reluctantly, Aai said that we could take some coconuts from the tree in the backyard. Of course, in the end, the coconuts remained on the trees, and our bags empty! Shahu has changed now. Maybe that's because of his wife's good nature; he is not as tight-fisted as he was before. So now at least some coconuts do find their way into our bags when we return home.

Since we were visiting Ratnagiri after a very long time, we wanted to call on Govindadada. Shantaram's wife, who came for the naming ceremony, told us that he was not keeping well. So I decided to go with her to our village. Shahu endorsed this wholeheartedly, saying, "You should really go, you know! You must see how our village has shed its old skin! It is completely transformed! Now the bus goes right up to the village. You don't have to walk any more!"

What he said was very true. The rough-hewn paths, full of stones and pebbles, were transformed into tarred roads and looked like sleek black cobras, disappearing fast through the trees. Trees adorned both sides of the road, their huge trunks painted red and white and numbered. Then there were electricity poles, bus stops, clusters of tiny, well-built houses peeping through the trees. Development from the cities had indeed flowed into the villages!

My eyes were glued to the river flowing in curves through the trees and the mountains beyond, thickly covered with forests. From the distance, I was trying to locate those tough steep climbs and the slippery paths we had walked on. I could see many familiar marks. For a moment, I thought I was hearing a murmur of the whispered conversations of women passing those roads. Looking at the river which kept winking at us, I asked Shantaram's wife, "And what about the tiny wooden bridge we used to cross during the rainy seasons? Is it still there?"

"What bridge are you talking about?" she answered. "Who bothers about whether it is there or not! Now we have the bus, why bother about that!"

"And that hill of Mirjole? And that Climb of the Lame? My memories were waking up.

"Where will the bloody hills go? They are right there ... how many women they have worn out." Shantaram's wife kept on prattling about so many things.

Suddenly I remembered the women who would walk with dry bhakris in their hands, munching on the pieces as they walked. "They must have stopped eating like that, now that they have the bus?" I asked her. I had heard something about that. A member of the State Legislative Council, Shamrao Peje, had prohibited women from eating on the road. Women found walking on the road munching on bhakri were fined five rupees. The fine went on increasing from five to ten to twenty till it reached fifty. The talathi and *sarpanch* of the village were given unwritten powers to collect the fine. Gradually even the Buddhist women stopped the practice.

This was a good thing! Not because it was bad social manners to eat on the roads. The dictate showed a deep concern for the women! Women eating on the road could choke on the dry bhakri, the fish bones might get stuck in their throats! At least the rule made them sit down and eat their food. Women would consider it a punishment to sit down and eat. Some women, of course, resisted. They would hide the bhakri under their pallavs. They would pay fines if they were caught! Shantaram's wife said, "Now nobody takes bhakri along! Women take the bus instead. They go by bus and return by bus to have their meals at home. They work as laborers on the fields of the Brahmins and the Kulwadis."

I looked out of the bus. A long red path, full of stones and red earth, as if the mountain had taken out its tongue to tease us, stayed with us for a long time and then fell back. The bus took a long turn and stopped, coughing loudly. I got down and looked at the house in front of the bus stop. "This is the house of the khot," Shantaram's wife said. Somewhere beyond this house, on the verandah of some Brahmin, Govindadada and Babi had learned the alphabet. Now there were only a few houses behind the khot's and quite a few mango orchards.

We crossed the small bridge on the stream and took the road to our house. This road was completely new to me. When I was a child, we had to walk down from the Climb of the Lame to a stream until we reached the Sati temple where the children of the toiling women stood eagerly, waiting for them to return from the market. Those children had grown up; they were doing various jobs. Now their children were going to school. This road had completely bypassed the Sati temple.

Suddenly musical notes in a high pitch came floating in the wind. Surprised, I asked, "These songs, are they being played in our wadi? So there is electricity in the wadi now?"

"Of course!" Shantaram's wife replied. "Now our wadi is not behind in anything. This evening Dhaku's daughter is getting married. You must attend the wedding." She began to reel out details about the marriage, but my ears were trying to catch the words of the song. As we moved closer to the wadi, the words became clearer. A few girls sang,

> My first namaskara is to the Bharati Buddha.
> I am leaving my Baba behind ...

I felt so happy! So the songs, which were almost shelved in the wake of the conversions, were in practice once again! I had heard songs in Marathwada and Vidarbha with Babasaheb's name woven in—and also in the Chaitya Bhumi. But here I was witnessing the first bloom of the forbidden songs in the Konkan region.

I asked Shantaram's wife deliberately, "Do they still serve the saar of ratamba leaves at weddings?" She was amused at the question! Laughing, she said, "No! Nobody is so poor now! Now they serve dal, rice, salad—everything—at the marriage feast." The mention of the word *salad* startled me a bit! But I felt so happy!

We reached the wadi, chatting away about various things. When we came near the entrance, I was surprised to find a big Buddhist vihar. Previously we used to bow down before the samadhis of our ancestors! Now the samadhis could no longer be seen. I offered a namaskara before the statue of the Buddha and went toward Dada's house. Now the words in the songs could be heard loud and clear. I decided I would talk to the girls and note the songs down in my diary later on.

The wadi had changed completely. The rooftops now sported Mangalore tiles and stone had replaced mud in the walls. My eyes began looking for our house. I could see its dilapidated condition from a distance. The tiles were broken, the walls were in a state of semicollapse, and the courtyard was rough and unpolished! Once that house had been such a great source of unadulterated joy! But the epidemic of family quarrels prevalent in the Konkan had struck our house as well. Govindadada and Shantaram, uncle and nephew, had quarreled and separated.

Dada had built a small two-storied home in his space, where he lived with his wife. His daughters were married off and lived happily with their husbands. Shantaram's wife pointed at their house and then walked off toward her own dilapidated home.

Dada was sitting in the front courtyard, with his back against the wall, a leg crossed on the other. A couple of old women, who had escorted us to the village when we were children, sat there as well. They too had grown old; their bodies were bent from the waist downwards, like bows. They laughed happily and welcomed me. We dipped into nostalgia and were lost for a while. These women had had to struggle very hard and face too many hardships! They were a little envious of the privileges enjoyed by the young women of this generation. Thoralibai came out with a jar of water and a glass when she heard my voice. She too was bent from the middle like a bow. She looked so old! She sat down and inquired after everyone. But what intrigued me most was the holy ash mark on her forehead along with the regular kumkum!

After some time she took me inside for a meal. The scene inside was strange. Behind the stove, there was a *devhara*, the god's platform, with a coconut bearing signs of regular worship. Near the roof hung many bones, goodness knows of which animals, tied in a bundle of red cloth. I had the answer to the puzzle of the ash mark on her forehead. She had become the priestess of the whole village. Long ago, she used to carry bundles of grass and sticks on her head to sell in the Ratnagiri market. Now she appeared to be selling holy ash right at home! Her profession had the backing of our family history—we were the family of priests! I looked at Dada in utter amazement. Was this the same Dada who had collected images of the gods by the basketfuls in our houses and thrown them into the stream, saying, "Ye Gods, you were never good for us; so now go to your own abodes"? He was sitting with his head on his knees.

Vahini said, "The marriage will take place in the evening. So stay for the night. You can go tomorrow." But I could not stay. I decided to leave the same evening. I did not want to see anything—the river, Chandaki's Hill. No, I did not want to say anything. I set out once again, casting a glance at the ancestors' samadhis. All I took with me were the songs the young girls were singing.

A full moon night in the huts of the poor,
And the memory of Babasaheb in my heart,
How can I live happily in my house?

I boarded the last bus from the village to Ratnagiri. The bus was quite empty. I sat beside a window and kept staring out. The devhara behind the stove in Thoralibai's house refused to budge from my sight, leaving me in turmoil! On the one hand, there was the rational, radically transforming aspect of Buddhism. On the other, superstitions' frightening hold on the human mind was back with a vengeance! It was not very long since Dr. Babasaheb Ambedkar had cleansed our minds of them, yet people got caught in the same web of superstitions, again and again. It was alarming!

A memory floated up from the recesses of my mind. We were living in Ratnagiri then. It must have been the month of May. One day, Gopal Master and some activists rushed to our house. Excited, they told Harishchandra, "Come quickly, Bhaiyyasaheb Ambedkar has arrived at the Guest House!" (Bhaiyyasaheb was Dr. Ambedkar's son and the father of Prakash Ambedkar, now a Dalit leader. He lived in Mumbai then.) Harishchandra hurried out with them. After some time he returned with Bhaiyyasaheb to our room. Prakash, Bhaiyyasaheb's son, had also come along. Our tiny room was soon overflowing with people. I cut some hapoos mangoes and offered these on a plate and then made tea for everyone. Bhaiyyasaheb looked so tired! He was completely drained. Yet he inquired about the conversions in the region, if there was trouble erupting anywhere. His language reflected his commitment and love for the people. He was a simple man, very transparent. He was deeply aware that it was because of Babasaheb that our community had progressed. He was fiercely committed to people's welfare, and the people too felt drawn to him. His work went unrecognized until the very end! He must have suffered from a guilt complex too! There was quite large number of people who backed him, as they felt it was Bhaiyyasaheb alone who could change the minds of our people in the Konkan region, especially in the south Konkan where superstitions still held a great sway and had a tremendous hold on people's consciousness. They were illiterate, still ate carrion, and refused to give up their gods and rituals of worship. They distinguished between the Bele and the Pan Mahars. Bhaiyyasaheb, people believed, could change all this.

Sadly, Bhaiyyasaheb did not live long. Both the leaders and the masses lost their confidence. They became self-centered. That is why, in spite of the Mangalore tiles on their roofs and the stone walls of their houses, they had bundles of bones hanging from the roofs, which indicated their backwardness. Throughout the journey, such thoughts kept flooding my mind.

By the time I reached home, it was dark. Aai had finished cooking. Today she had prepared a dish of fried surmay fish and curry. While we were eating, Shahu said, "So you have been to Dada's place. Did you see the village, Dada's house, Thoralibai's platform for the gods, and the hanging bones? People are simply going backward. What do you do, you writers and your so-called leaders?" I blew my top at this. He always asked me such questions. "What do you think?" I retaliated. "Have we been appointed as contractors for reform? You think you pay us a salary? What do *you* do? You too are busy earning a lot of money. You enjoy life, don't you? Aren't you a part of the same community?"

"Oh ho!" Aai exclaimed in exasperation. "What is this? You are fighting as you used to when you were children! Now eat your food quietly."

"But Aai, it is not him alone! There are so many who ask such questions! The upper castes, who live in bungalows, drive expensive cars, send their children outside India for education ... and yet ... don't they owe anything to the society? Where does their social commitment go at such times?"

Shahu listened to this outburst with a serious face and said, "All right! I will pay for your ticket to Mumbai! Done! Happy?"

I burst out laughing at this simple interpretation of commitment!

Twelve

I had noticed that very few Dalit writers from the Konkan region were present in the literary conferences like the Asmitadarsha. Truly, one could count such writers on one's fingertips. Moreover, Ramakant Jadhav, Chandrahas Gambre, Prakash Kharat, or Dr. Shashikant Lokhande would be present but had really few opportunities to interact with the others. So in 1991 I decided to organize a literary conference with the help of stalwarts like Dr. Bhalchandra Mungekar, Shantaram Nandgaonkar, Raja Jadhav, and Krishna Varde (who was a painter) to bring Dalit writers and artists from the Konkan region together. We founded an organization called Dr. Ambedkar Konkan Kala and Sahitya Movement, and the first literary conference was held in Shirodkar Hall on January 5, 1992, where more than five hundred people participated. The renowned writer Madhu Mangesh Karnik was present as the featured guest.

For the M.A. course at the University of Bombay, we were required to produce a short thesis, counting for fifty marks, on any writer or theme of our choice. This motivated me to think of doing a Ph.D. But what would I work on? I started thinking about it, and then I was struck by an idea. I had read Dr. Ambedkar's biography and about his work and also about women's participation in this movement. But where were these women? The question began to haunt me. All around me I could see only men. The case was similar vis-à-vis archival material. So I decided to find out more about the women who were a part of the movement. When I discussed this with Chhaya Datar, she said, "This is such an important project! Why do you want to do a Ph.D.? Why don't you write a book instead! Take someone's help to interview these women. Yes, you can begin by writing for our annual journal, *Stree Uwacha!*

Accordingly, I discussed the project with Meenakshi Moon, who agreed to work with me, and we began collecting information. Since Meenakshi was involved, Mr. Moon also took a keen interest in the project. He gave us access to many invaluable reference works in his library. In a short while, an amazing history of women's participation in the Dalit movement unfolded before our eyes. There was so much concrete evidence in our hands. Chhaya and Maithreyi Krishnaraj helped us get financial assistance, and we were able to publish our work in the form of a book.

Meeting people for interviews was very interesting. Some people would be so disappointed when they learned what we were working on. "What rubbish! There were no women in that struggle!" they said. Sometimes someone would confidently recommend a "very great activist" to us, and we would rush to interview her. But she would say, "What movement? Who worked in it? At least not me! I had nothing to do with it!" Again sometimes people would reject a name, saying, "This woman had nothing to do with the movement! Why go to her? You are wasting your time." There were instances when a woman's neighbors knew nothing about her work, but she came up with amazing accounts of the movement, her participation in it, and her experiences of the men and women who had worked with her.

Often while we were busy with the interviews, the children sitting around us would subject us to a keen scrutiny. "Which one do you like better?" they whispered to each other. Meenakshi scored more than me on most occasions! I liked kids who liked us both. Meenakshi had a constant refrain, "We really don't understand anything!" People loved to hear her say so! So they began with the elementary things about the movement. In such cases the focus of the interview would shift from the women we had gone to see. I used to argue with Meenakshi, "Why do you say we don't understand anything? Please don't say so!" But it was pointless telling her this.

The women in the movement left an indelible print on history through their indefatigable work. They had been harassed by their families and by people at home and outside; they had been subjected to harsh words, were berated and at times badly beaten up by their husbands. And yet their history now lay forgotten. Some women had themselves forgotten the work they had done. We awakened their memories and made them talk. Many women, like Lakshmibai Kakde and Geetabai Pawar, had tears in their eyes when we met them. They were overwhelmed to know that their work was being acknowledged.

Jaibai Chaudhary worked as a coolie in a railway station. She was educated in a missionary school and trained to become a schoolteacher. Later she opened a school, the Chokha Mela Kanyashala in Nagpur, in 1924, which has now become a college. She named it after a low-caste saint of the medieval period. Anjanibai Deshbhratar and Geetabai Gaikwad started women's hostels in Nagpur and Nasik respectively. Shantabai Sarode and Chandrika Ramteke became wrestlers in their respective fathers' gymnasia and retaliated with all their might when Dalit localities were attacked. Geetabai Pawar from Pune chose to stay with her cowife because she wanted to work in the movement. Laxmibai Kakde from Pune went through sterilization in spite of her husband's stiff opposition and cruel treatment because she wanted to work full-time in the movement.

Babytai Kamble and Shantabai Kamble endured physical abuse from their husbands because they wanted to leave the house to work in the movement. Virendrabai Teerthankar remained unmarried because she wanted to be an activist. Devki Khandare, Laxmibai Naik, and Chandrabhaga Chothmal gave up their families, shaved their heads, and became Buddhist bhikshunis.

These and many such women who made history by participating in the Ambedkar movement became a source of inspiration for us. I will never forget Chandrika Ramteke from Nagpur. When we went to interview her, she looked extremely depressed. She spoke about her work in the movement, how she was often beaten up by her husband and censured by her community, yet how she never gave up. But she spoke too listlessly. This woman, who would exercise like a wrestler regularly, building her body by doing push-ups and sit-ups, and worked as a primary teacher in a school, sounded so terribly downcast. We wondered why such a fantastic activist was now so detached and depressed. So we asked her about it. She said she was depressed because there were no good leaders left. But I suspected that there was something more to it, possibly a personal tragedy. When I pressed her, she pointed at the photograph of a young man, around twenty-five years old, and broke down. "My son! He died very recently. Now what does society and social work mean to me?" I could not bear to look at her stricken face. We consoled her as best we could. After reaching home, I wrote her a long letter, "You are a mother, but at the same time you also are an activist! An activist has no relations, no personal life. All that she has is her consciousness! That is why please forget your grief and start working once again!"

Our book on women's contribution to the Ambedkarite movement, *Aamhi hi Itihas Ghadawala* (*We Also Made History*) was released by Dr. Eleanor Zelliot in a ceremony at Mumbai in the presence of scholars like Dr. Bhalchandra Mungekar, Dr. Yashwant Manohar, Professor Pushpa Bhave, who all praised our efforts. The print media lauded us for having made history by bringing the contribution of these Dalit women to light. We honored many Dalit women activists in this program. Thus our book established an organic relationship with the women in the movement.

Life had a brutal shock, similar to the kind Chandrika Ramteke had faced, in store for me as well. When the tragedy struck, my grief and agony knew no bounds! It engulfed me completely, like boiling lava out of an exploding volcano, reducing all my emotions, enthusiasm, plans, and hopes to a heap of charred ashes! The words I wrote to Chandrika came back to me with a vengeance!

That day is like a gaping wound in my heart. I went home by bus and even got a seat. I had bought some fresh fenugreek and cleaned it during the bus ride to save time at home. Never waste time was my motto. After getting down from the bus, I went to Meenakshi's house to see if she had located any new references. I had tea with Meenakshi, picked up the references, and returned home. Mr. Pawar was back home too. I had a quick wash and went into the kitchen. My elder daughter had put the cooker on the gas stove; the younger one was studying. I made dal and hurriedly fried the fenugreek leaves with chopped onion to make a vegetable curry. Then I served Mr. Pawar his meal.

He was sitting in front of the TV with his plate in front of him when suddenly the bell rang. My elder daughter opened the door. There was a policeman standing at the door. Mr. Pawar sprang up when he saw him and went outside. I glanced out of the kitchen door but thought that it must be a friend of a nephew who was in the police. His friends often dropped in to ask after him. Then I saw Mr. Pawar asking the policeman something; the next moment he smote his forehead with his fist and, turning inside, screamed and called me. I ran forward. I saw a few more unfamiliar faces behind the policeman, staring coldly at us. "What's happened? What's happened?" I asked terror-stricken. "We are ruined ... we're ruined!" my husband shouted and ran to the staircase with those men. My heart grew cold with fear. I too tried to follow ... Then one of the strangers said, "Your son has met with an accident. He fell down from the train. Wait ... don't come. They will bring him." The ground from under my feet suddenly gave way and a deep bottomless abyss opened below.

When I regained consciousness, I could hardly breathe. Suddenly the memory of Bhai's death leapt up like a flame, scorching me with red-hot agony. That day a telegram had arrived ... at midnight. Somebody thumped loudly at the door, and Harischandra got up hurriedly to open it. A boy called Kamalakar, from my mother's place, stood outside. He called Harishchandra out and whispered something to him. I had rushed out and asked him, "What's wrong? What's happened?" But he stood dumbstruck. Then Harishchandra had said, "Let's go to your mother's place, your mother is very ill." He had started walking. Kamalakar had already moved on. Somehow I locked the door and run after them.

When I had reached my mother's house, I saw a crowd outside and heard cries of loud mourning. I had rushed into the house, thinking that my mother had passed away. But when I had entered, I saw her slumped on the floor, against the wall. She was crying, shouting, beating her breast ... it was as if all her grief was trying to burst out through her eyes, nose, mouth, and skin!

Somebody had come forward with the news, "Child, your brother passed away. There was a telegram from Mumbai." I had rushed forward and thrown my arms around my mother's neck. Her very breath had been so hot. It singed me like fire.

"How? How did it happen?" I had started to weep too. Though my tears stopped after some time, Aai's eyes continued to flow. What had she felt when her children, who were as good as her limbs, were being cut off from her one by one? Once I had asked her what exactly it meant to be a mother. I just wanted to know how she would express the feelings behind the word *mother*. My question made her wince with pain. She said, "To be a mother is to commit sati, to immolate oneself; nothing less!"

Aai had suffered that agony! Today, I was standing on the same pyre of pain.

People came, consoled us, and uttered a few words of advice. With each close relative's arrival, a new wave of pain would come surging up, swallowing me. A few tried to imagine the pain and a few relived their own tragedies.

At that time, somebody had counted the number of brothers and sisters we were. "They are three sisters; they had three brothers! Two have gone ... these sisters are alive ... Why didn't a sister die?"

"Oh yes, why didn't we die? I should have died instead. I should have ... Struck with grief, we, the sisters, had wailed. But at that moment my mother had thrown her thin hands around us, pulled us to her, and cried out with a fear for our lives, "No, no, don't ever say such things about my children."

I had looked at Aai. Through her brimming eyes, her fierce protectiveness toward us had shone like a flash of lightning in a dark sky pouring rain. To a mother, all her children are equal!

Now history was being repeated. Someone was counting my children and saying the same thing. I could see my younger daughter standing inside, her face distraught with pain. She was hardly fourteen or fifteen then. Her eyes were brimming with tears, and she too was saying the same words, "Yes, yes, why didn't I die instead of him?" And I found myself saying the same words my mother had.

I had never understood the various emotions reflected in Aai's eyes, the terrible memories deep in the recesses of her mind and her emotional reactions to them, her tearful outbursts, her mourning, her tears, and her sighs. The pain that I had been unable to understand twenty-two years ago now burned deep inside me. I found myself organically related to that agony. Aai had said, "Everybody can see the wildfire that burns on the mountains. But who can see the fire burning in the mind?" Today I could understand the meaning perfectly well. A woman had said to my mother, "The agony of your child dying is far greater than the agony of your husband's death!" And she had burst into uncontrollable sobs for her son who had died.

It was terribly difficult sitting alone, by oneself. Pain stung the brain like a scorpion. Then I started to think about new plots, imagine characters and dialogues. And suddenly I saw in front of me Gautami, who had brought the dead body of her son to the Tathagata and begged him to make him alive. The Buddha had asked her to get him some mustard seeds from a house that had not witnessed a death. In a few, well-chosen words, he made her aware of the reality of life. His kind words—and there are many such instances and that of the Buddha making compassionate speeches at such times—are together called *Udaan*, which Bhante Jagadeesh has translated from Pali into Hindi. I selected these compassionate words of the Buddha to translate into Marathi. I devoted myself to the translation to drown my grief. In the past, my writing did not allow me to sleep. Now I could not sleep and therefore started writing. I was drowning my grief in my work. And yet the painful reality kept breaking through every barricade and flooded my brain.

What exactly had happened? Nobody was willing to talk about it. I did not dare to ask. When Bhai passed away, everybody had behaved in the same way in front of Aai. But gradually she had come to know. There was some corruption in the ration cards office. The needle of suspicion had turned to Bhai. He had tried desperately to proclaim his innocence, but the system closed its ears to him. Finally, Bhai sent his wife and children to his brother and mother and hanged himself. He had given a box to his neighbor, containing two slips of paper: one was addressed to Aaye, stet Aai in which he wrote, "Only you will believe that I am innocent." The other one was for his wife, which said, "Sushila, I have been unjust to you and the children; but please forgive me if you can!"

Even now people were unwilling to talk. Oh, they gave reasons all right, but they were slight and false. One day Mandar returned from the hostel and said, "I don't want to study in this college; let me change my college." But Mr. Pawar had replied, "Why? You don't want to study. You just while away your time playing the guitar. You may be getting prizes for that, but is it going to help you in college? You must study hard. Don't give me flimsy excuses." The year before we came to Mumbai, Mandar had passed the scholarship examination, and his name was on the merit list. His photograph was printed, along with some four or five other boys, in the *Satyashodhak* newspaper in Ratnagiri. He looked cute in the photograph with his chubby cheeks, straight nose, smiling eyes, and thick curly hair combed carefully with the part on the left side. There was an artificial smile on his lips, and yet it looked so good. We had shown the photograph to so many people that it had got crumpled and dirty. Yet we had carefully preserved it at the bottom of a trunk. Mandar was very intelligent. He passed his tenth standard examination with excellent marks. Two years later he quite effortlessly found a place in the medical college after completing his school leaving examinations. We had not realized what was happening to him. The first year had been quite stressful. During the second year, he experienced stress repeatedly. Once I had said to his father, "Why don't you go and inquire at the college? See if you can get him admitted to another college. He appears to be quite serious in his complaints!" But he had not paid any attention to this. He had kept on repeating to Mandar, "Pay more attention to your studies. We are giving you everything. Whatever you wanted we have given you. Now concentrate on your studies. This is just your second year."

What had my son complained of? What was the system there like? One of my friends had said, "My husband teaches in the same college! They are all so antireservation there!" Antireservation ... opposition!

The opposition is on all levels ... explicit.... implicit ... My brother had ended his life out of frustration, and now my son had chosen the same path!

I do not remember how many days after this—I had lost all count of time—a woman from the office came to see me. She turned to my sister, who was sitting next to me, and said, "My daughter and her son studied in the same class in college." She stopped for a while and then, turning toward me, said, "But how could you say such a thing that day?" I looked at her questioningly. "Oh, I know that you won't even remember having said so, but you shouldn't have said it!"

"What? What did I say?"

"Well, I was not here that day, but this lady from our office said that you said so."

"But what? What did she say?" asked my sister in sheer exasperation.

"See, my daughter studies in the same class as her son. You said why did my son die? Why didn't her daughter pass away instead?"

We were simply speechless. This was unbelievable. My sister managed to say, "Was your daughter traveling in the same compartment as her son?"

"No, why should she? She was at home!"

"Then where does your daughter come into the picture?"

"Well, maybe your sister thought that we are in the same office. So why should she suffer? Why not me?"

"Oh, goodness me, why would I say anything of the sort? I would never dream of such a thing in my wildest dreams!" I pleaded.

Now my sister was furious. "You stay calm!" she told me, and she turned to the visitor. "Come on, lady, get up and get going. Do you realize what you are saying? Come on, out! And, mind you, go straight home. Don't you go asking such questions of other people! Go tell this to that woman in your office!"

How easily people say, "But why should this grief be mine?" It means that this grief should be someone else's, but not ours. Such sentences nauseated me right from the beginning. And this woman had thrown the acid of similar feelings in my face.

When the woman left, I was simply paralyzed.

People advised me to resume work. "That will blunt the blow," they said. So I rejoined the office. Then, one day, a colleague of mine, a woman of considerable years, came and parked herself in front of me. "Let me tell you something," she said. "Now don't be angry with me. God's justice is slow but certain! One never knows when he will decide to punish! You still have two girls to look after. You have a husband. Listen to me. Read *Dattagurucharitra* regularly."

I stared at the woman, too dazed to say anything. I felt as if she was challenging me in some way. I recovered and said, "Many of our colleagues, like Mrs. Paranjape, Mrs. Kuwalekar, read religious books, don't they? And yet they have all lost someone near and dear to them, didn't they? A son, a husband."

The woman got up and left.

It was around this time that my first short story collection, *The Sixth Finger,* was published by Jagdish More of Sambodhi Prakashan, with financial assistance from the government. Mr. More came with a copy of the book to my house and said, "We will release the book on the commemoration day of Sadanand Jadhav. I am inviting Sushil Kumar Shinde, Arun Sadhu, Prabhakar Shripad Nerurkar, and Chhaya Datar. Dr. Bhalchandra Mungekar will be invited as well. Do you want to invite anybody else?"

This was my first book. What were my feelings when I wrote it? What were my feelings now? I looked at the book in my hands from a stranger's eyes. Sanjay Pawar had drawn just a finger on the cover. But, being the extraordinary artist that he is, he gave that finger so many dimensions. But there was only one dimension for me. For me it was a finger cut off after an accident. After fever the tongue loses its sense of taste. My mind also had lost its sense.

Aai would sit in front of us. In her nine-yard sari, tucked up above the knee, the pallav on her head pulled forward from both the shoulders, leaning against the wall with her legs drawn into her stomach, her face resting on her knees. She stared ahead with unseeing eyes, her face distraught. Her grief seemed to be still dripping out of her eyes. Time conquers grief, it is said. And sometimes grief certainly conquers time.

All my life I had hated Aai for being a miser as well as for being perpetually busy. I often went against her wishes because I felt she never gave us anything we wanted. I always felt that our childhood was too austere, filled with deprivation. I realized now that was part of a treatment she had administered to herself. She never wanted her children to depend on anybody for anything. She wanted them to be self-reliant and independent. That was her way of training us. She wanted us to live life with self-respect. That was the only satisfaction and pleasure she wanted from life. That people also were aware of this quality of hers came out transparently through something I once experienced. Since all my neighbors followed the practice of buying provisions on an account they maintained with the shopkeeper, I did the same. I used to buy whatever I required and paid at the end of the month. This shopkeeper had been my mother's neighbor in Ratnagiri and knew us quite well. One day I bought something and told the shopkeeper to note it down to my credit in my account book. I turned to go, but stopped abruptly when the shopkeeper's old father suddenly called out to me and said, "Wait a minute. You must not buy things on credit. That's bad practice. Your mother lived in utter poverty but never had any payment pending, however small it was. Remember that!" I was quite angry at the old man's advice, yet, all the same, I felt so proud of my mother! I was estranged from her. But now this agony of the loss of a child brought us together once again. She had drowned her grief in weaving aaydans endlessly. I could see her hands constantly flying over the weave. For me writing was the only solace. Who knows what I was writing, whether it was of any worth. But that was the only way in which I could keep the agony at bay.

In the program for the release of the book, Sushil Kumar Shinde said, "This writer lost a son, but she has given birth to another child." How right he was! Between these two births lay our entire family life, torn asunder, bloodied by the bitter memories. I just closed it shut and turned to the outside world. Pawar, however, tried to seek solace in drinking. I tried very hard to break this addiction, but whenever I asked him to give up drinking he asked me to give up my social work. Now, of course, it was too late for either him or me to give up our respective addictions.

That same year, Aai slipped and fell down in the bathroom and dislocated her pelvic bone. My brother brought her to Mumbai and admitted her to a hospital where I went to see her. Both of us had suffered, she from the physical injury and I from the deadly blow. Who was to console whom in such a situation? When I saw the white-robed doctors moving around, I burst into tears. I sat near her dumbly. The doctors operated upon her, fixing a steel joint, but that did not help her. Her body refused to accept it. She went back to Ratnagiri. Life had dealt her so many deadly blows! She had never eaten well, never slept enough; all her life she had suffered so much pain and worked ceaselessly. Now, even toward the end, life dealt her a final blow. Aai took her revenge upon life. She refused to eat anything. Again doctors were called, but in vain! She refused to listen to anybody. Then one day the phone rang. It was Shahu with the dreaded news! We went to his place.

Aai's frail, tall, and shriveled body was laid on a soft mattress. Her hands, which used to work so ceaselessly at making baskets, were folded and placed on her stomach. It was as if they had finished giving away everything she possessed and wanted to rest. I looked at her, but my mind was devoid of all feeling. Unconsciously, I kept seeing in my mind's eye the Aai who had come to see me in Mumbai to console me, sitting in front of me with the same grief of losing a child and eating her heart out over it. Those moments were frozen in time, and they have now come to stay with me permanently.

My brother Shahu realized this. His heart bled for me. Shahu, who would drag me to school, who had tried so hard to dissuade me from getting involved with Harishchandra, who had playfully thrown a betel nut on the plate on the Bhau Beej Day, now became a pillar of support for me. He took Harishchandra and me, devastated by Mandar's death, to Ratnagiri. Many people—acquaintances, relatives, and others—came to see us. Again and again we would experience the desolation. His wife, Sheelavahini, also shared our agony. She tried very hard to comfort us.

I had wanted my son to be doctor. But since that was impossible now, I made my daughters apply for admission to science courses. They were affected by the tragedy too. Malavika, the elder one, studied science for two years after her tenth and then went back to arts. She did an M.A.B.Ed., also passing five examinations in music. The younger one, Manini, did a B.Sc., followed by diploma courses in pathology and computer science. She also learned kathak and became a professional dancer. Today both of them work as teachers and teach music and dance.

Would the picture have been different if I had not devoted so much time to education, writing, and other things? Would they have made better progress? Would our lives have acquired different meanings? Would I have been able to bring about a change? I got some answers to these questions from Malavika.

The 1991 annual issue of *Stree Uwacha* carried some interviews with feminist women. At that time, Vinaya Khadpekar, who wrote the article, interviewed Malavika. I had told her to speak without any pressure. I too wanted to know about her thoughts and reactions. At that time, Malavika was nineteen. She said,

The real change came when Aai began to educate herself. When she found it difficult to cope with her job, household work, and studies, she began to ask father to help her. After she passed her M.A., the change was still more pronounced. Education made her a feminist. She began to have more dialogue with us. When we were children, she would shout at us if we were a little late, sometimes beat us up. But now she began to discuss things with us. We tell her everything. Even if I fall in love, I don't think I will hide it. I am sure she will understand me. She is a friend now! But I have never felt this confidence about our father.

I remember our house was peaceful when we lived a traditional life. My father began to resent it when Mother got educated and involved herself in social work. He began resisting. The quarrels increased. This affected our studies, of course. But I don't think Mother is to be blamed for this. We used to feel why doesn't Mother feign defeat and not argue; that would lessen the quarrels in the house. Since Aai was a writer, her vacations would be spent in meetings and sahitya sammelanas. She never would have any leave left at the time of our examinations. That would make us angry. We wanted her to pamper us at least at the time of exams. But instead of that happening, we had to work harder. We had to work at home and study too. Now, of course, I don't feel bad about it. We have become quite self-reliant now. We have learned to accept the fact that she is a different person. Even when she is on leave, she is busy writing.

I have now realized that one has to study on one's own. The changes in my mother have had an adverse effect on my father. He keeps complaining a lot. He would have liked it much better had she behaved in a traditional way. He has the age-old, traditional expectations from Mother: she should spend a lot of time cooking, should not cook hurriedly, should give us a course in home economics, etc. He actually resents the fact that Aai is educated, that she is a famous woman. He can cook; he sometimes makes vegetables, cooks simple things in the pressure cooker. He is never ashamed to work, even in front of the guests. But I doubt whether he has accepted it willingly or whether he considers this as something that is imposed on him. That is because he never stops fighting with her. He is never ready to give up his traditional expectations of our mother and of us. We all feel that it is he who is more responsible for the tensions in the house than Aai.

My daughter had teased out all the threads of my existence as a mother and wife in her interview. If I had really kept myself confined to just my job and home, would the quarrels have been any less? When we came to Mumbai, I was doing just that. And even then Mr. Pawar invariably would go drinking with his brother-in-law in the evening. That was one major reason why we fought. Nobody would have been able to stop him from going for a drink.

Once both of us were at a function, which Mr. Pawar had been very reluctant to attend, and I had literally dragged him there. When it was time for his drinking session, he got up to go. A sensitive artist sitting there asked him, "Why, you are leaving?" "Oh, yes," Mr. Pawar answered easily, "we have to leave. This is the time when we get water in the house. So I have to go fill it up." I could not help laughing at his histrionics. After a few days, I heard this sensitive artist telling his friends, "The poor husband was going to store water at home, and this shameless woman was laughing!" How easily men appear "poor" and women "shameless"!

I did not dare show Malavika's interview to Mr. Pawar. He would have blown his top. Then he would have dug up things from the past and more fights would have ensued. "Children should be frightened of their mother. Look at this woman! She becomes younger than them and even cracks jokes and laughs with them. Stupid!" he would criticize. I, of course, never took it seriously. I never behaved like a miser like my mother was with us; I pampered my children. I thought that my daughter's interview was no less than a certificate given to me for my being a friend. But later on I realized that I was wrong. The children also kept their distance from me. There were many reasons for this. First, we gave them what we had not got in our childhoods; but their needs had increased compared to ours, and we did not realize they were different from us. And the children experienced the gap between their lives and that of their friends. They could not speak about these things to us explicitly. They felt some kind of emotional insecurity, a void inside. All three of them felt that we should have put them in English-medium schools, so that at least they would have been saved from developing a linguistic inferiority complex. They were terribly oppressed by this complex, and we never realized it. Today, with a little bit of introspection, I understand. Had English been sown in their flesh and blood, things would have been easier for them. If you do not keep up with the times, you get beaten! But by the time I realized this it was too late.

Why talk about just English? My daughters told me one day that the ayahs whom we used to employ often beat them up after we went to the office. Pinching, boxing ears, stealing money was an everyday affair. They had boyfriends too, who came to the house at the opportune time. But our children never shared this with us. The main reasons were, of course, the distrust they felt toward us and a fear of retaliation from the ayahs! We never tried to understand the ayahs either. It was all a tightrope walk! These experiences had a terrible impact on the children.

I had assured Malavika, "If you find a young man whom you like and want to marry, do tell us. Don't be afraid!" But even after this honest assurance of mine, my daughter did not open her heart to me. She could not confide her fears in me (I like a young man, but I am unable to propose to him; suppose I ask and he says no because of my caste!). Yet we had full confidence in her. We arranged her marriage with a young man, choosing him from the many proposals we received. And after all preparations were made—booking the hall, shopping, and printing invitation cards—the young man she loved declared his love for her and proposed marriage, which she accepted. She refused to marry the boy we had selected. Our house was rocked to its foundations. The relatives who had come for the marriage were speechless with shock. Everybody made the marriage a prestige issue. Everybody took a position that she would have to marry the boy we had selected and go to her in-laws' place.

Mr. Pawar was no exception. Everybody started asking me furiously, "Who is this upstart who waited till this moment to declare his love? He is not of our caste. He is from Uttar Pradesh! How can one trust him?" It was like a storm raging. And I was trying to keep calm and find a way out. I had received a mortal blow in the form of my son's death. Now I did not want to lose my daughter! Even the thought petrified me!

I could see that three people were going to be permanently unhappy if this marriage went through. My inner voice urged me, if you don't want to ruin your daughter's life, this is the time to choose well. I was aware that my decision to side with my daughter would be very unjust to the bridegroom. He was innocent. But if she married him, that would be unjust to him too! I had no other alternative before me.

The marriage ended in the wedding hall. Everybody criticized me. "What a foolish mother!" They said, "What sort of a mother is she? How could she fail to notice what her daughter was up to? But it is to be expected, isn't it? She was too busy preening at her meetings, sammelanas, and social work to notice what her daughter was doing!" My motherhood was ripped to shreds.

Mr. Pawar was furious. As it is, all his expectations from me had come to nought! Now he grew despondent and furiously angry! He began to blow his top whenever he saw me. "This woman has ruined my family. Because of her, I lost face in the community! She considers herself so intelligent! But she is plain stupid! She is selfish, useless, shameless." His anger found expression in these and many filthier words.

I was worried for another reason. The unfortunate bridegroom had been sacrificed unnecessarily. We compensated his expenses. But how could we compensate for all the agony he had suffered? And it was not just him, his mother, brothers, and relatives had suffered as well. How was I going to compensate for all that? The very thought brought me immense pain. It was only when I heard that he had married and was happy that I could at last breathe easy.

Pawar fumed. Malavika was not allowed to come home. When I said that Malavika was our daughter and she had an equal right to be in the house, he exploded. Finally, a friend of mine, Aruna Burte, who worked on women's issues, gave Malavika asylum in her house. She also went to the bridegroom and his family and talked to them, making them amenable to reason. I had no place in my house, though I had bought it with my own money; the installments were deducted every month from my salary. "Don't step into this house. I don't want to see your face!" Mr. Pawar shouted at me. Though this incensed me, where was I to go, wasn't there another daughter who was dependent on me? I continued living in the house with a smiling face. That is what a woman is trained to do in spite of such intense humiliation.

I was more worried about what Ravi, the young man from Uttar Pradesh, was going to do next. Mr. Pawar continuously prophesied, "He is going to send your daughter to the Forrass Road (a red-light area of Mumbai). And then he will make you follow the same path!"

Finally, after four or five months had passed, Ravi and Malavika got married in the Hindu way. I did not attend the marriage for the fear of being forced to do *kanyadan*. After the wedding, I made Ravi sit in front of me and asked him, "Why didn't you do this before? Why didn't you propose marriage to her? Why did you wait for so long?"

I had thought that the question would make him very stiff, that he would feel guilty. But he replied easily, "You may think I am wrong; you may not even believe me! But, please trust me, I had never even thought about marriage till then. I had come to Mumbai from Delhi to work in the film line. I was staying with a friend as a paying guest. It was absolutely crucial for me to get work. I was so preoccupied with it, I thought of nothing else! It was a struggle. Malu and I were just friends. But the day she came to give me the invitation to her marriage, I realized that she was the only girl for me! That's all! That was the moment!"

While he spoke, he never faltered. I was quite terrified of that too. Suppose tomorrow he tells Malavika as easily that she has no place in his life anymore? On the other hand, he was saying all this in such a transparent manner, without giving any flimsy reasons, that I believed him. The main point was that our caste was not an obstacle. Besides, Malavika had trusted him with her life. What right did I have to object?

Even then I asked Ravi, "And what about Uday, the young man whom she was going to marry? Why punish him? How are you going to compensate for that?"

He did not falter even at this question. He said, "Aunty, see, somebody or the other had to suffer. Had I gone to Uday to try and rationalize the matter, he would have suffered more. It would be wrong to say anything now!"

I did not have any answer to this!

One has to suffer on many counts that are not one's faults. I have had my share of such sufferings. And yet I was convinced that whatever had happened was not very decent. When I was young, I used to hide storybooks inside my textbooks so that I could read them without anyone knowing what I was doing. I remember the story of Sindbad and the old man. At that time, the burden of the old man was imaginary. But now I was aware that I had a great burden on my back that I would carry till the very end. I was under great stress and yet I had to keep a smile on my face.

It was during this period that I got an opportunity to work as a consultant for a movie with Bhanu Athaiya. Dr. Jabbar Patel was making a movie on Dr. Ambedkar and I was invited to work as a consultant on the Dalit costumes. I was reminded of my experience of having my broken leg mended in the orthopedic center at Sion Hospital.

I felt the healing of my shattered mind begin at the shooting of the movie. I derived strength from it. The movie was taking shape. In it Dr. Ambedkar was giving a form to a community that had suffered nothing but humiliation and ignominy. The dumb were finding a voice, and the blind a vision. People were standing up for their rights. They were learning to speak, struggling to walk.

One day we were shooting at Mahad. At one o'clock at night, Manini called me. Her voice sounded as if she was crying. She would not say anything except "Come back quickly." I rang up Jabbar Patel in his room and he immediately made arrangements for me to reach Mumbai. "Don't worry, everything will be all right. Go safely," he said. I was sick with tension. What more did I have to face? I had suffered so much, so I ought to have been prepared for anything now! A dead hen is not afraid of the butcher's knife! Yet I was afraid. When I reached home, Manini started complaining, "Those people are saying, if the elder daughter says no, give us your younger daughter! Marry her to Uday! And Anna, my father, is all for it!"

Now I had recovered my composure and I would have opposed anybody who dared to marry my daughter against her wishes. I asked her quietly, "What do you feel? Are you willing to marry Uday? I have nothing to say if you are willing."

"No," she said, "I am not at all willing."

"All right then. Tell your father clearly."

Mr. Pawar was standing right there. He said, "This girl now says no! Why didn't she say so earlier? Who would get her married against her wishes? Had she told me this earlier, I would not even have ventured to say anything. And had that young man seen the light earlier, this situation would not have arisen at all!" He went on speaking in this vein for a long time.

I realized that his fury had lessened to a great extent, maybe because of the conditional sentences he used. Had it been like this ... had it been like that ... He was exhausted. Now I was convinced that he would not go against Manini's wishes. And, all the while, when Pawar was fighting with me, tearing me into shreds, using the choicest of ugly words, a feeling kept surging up from the bottom of my heart. Basically, he was not all that hard-hearted. He had adopted a public posture. People had to see that he was far more concerned with morality and prestige! He wanted to show people that his values were more important than his wife and his children and that he would not compromise his principles for them!

After this incident, though, people stopped coming to our house. Among our relatives, even the educated and the young could not accept what had happened. Some relatives broke off all communications with my daughter. Manini boiled with rage at what had happened. Ravi and Malavika had subjected everybody in the house to a great deal of trouble, yet Ravi had escaped scot-free? That was her direct question. She spoke rudely to both Ravi and Malavika and told them to compensate us for all our expenses. That was her way of punishing them. She had taken the law into her own hands. But, as far as I was concerned, Ravi had arrived at the eleventh hour and managed to avert something terrible happening in the lives of all three concerned. I started trying very hard to pretend that nothing had happened and began mending the broken relationships once again.

Mr. Pawar felt very happy if someone whom he knew even slightly came to see him. He kept talking on the phone for hours on end. After he retired as postmaster, the amount of time on his hands frightened him. While talking to a visitor, he would start speaking about the recent events. If the visitor said something sympathetically, like, "This should not have happened; as it is you have had a major blow!" he would invariably begin his tirade, "This woman spoilt the daughter so much! She had no interest in the house; she never paid any attention to what was happening; she is so self-centered, selfish." He would go on and on. But, even then, his words had lost their sharp edge. He and I were aware that our home was dependent on our joint support.

Time moved on. Gradually our wounds were healing. But, at the same time, new shocks were seeking a backdoor entry. My elder brother-in-law's daughter, Sugandha, was admitted to Sion Hospital with kidney failure; both kidneys were affected. My husband and I went to see her in the hospital. On that day itself, Pawar said, "I feel quite exhausted." I thought that he was feeling tired because we had not been going out for quite a while. But then he lost his appetite; his urine turned red. We suspected jaundice. He was basically a sportsperson and enjoyed very good physical health. He had had jaundice twenty years back. So we took him to the hospital. After a sonography and a scan, we got him admitted to the hospital of Dr. Vijay Salve, a friend of Mandar's. He and his wife, Dr. Hemalata Kedare, had fallen in love, but their families had opposed their marriage. When they came to us, Pawar had taken them under his wings, became their guardian; and got them married in the Bauddha Mandir at Worli. Vijay Salve remembered this history and was grateful. He made a few more tests, consulted his senior doctors, and after some treatment discharged Harishchandra. When I asked him what was wrong, he hesitated, "Nothing much; his liver has some swelling. He will get well with homeopathic or Ayurvedic medicines. His reports are with the assistant of the senior doctors, I'll get them later."

I could see that Vijay was trying to hide something. So I said, "Please be frank with me. I am ready to hear whatever you tell me."

Vijay said, "He has cirrhosis of the liver."

I did not know what the implications meant. But I could sense that it was something serious. Then I went to see the senior doctor's assistant with my brother-in-law and my brother Shahu. A young doctor was on duty there, very busy. When Shahu asked him, he hastily handed us some reports lying around and pronounced, "The patient has got liver cancer.

It is in the last stage. There is no remedy! He has got another six months to live."

Stunned, I leaned against the table for support. Just six months! My lively husband, my life's companion, had only six more months to go? In spite of all the blows, in spite of feeling dead, my throat hurt as if there were thorns pricking it inside.

I asked Vijay, "Does he know about his condition?" He said no. So I told him, "Please don't tell him. If there is no remedy, why make him suffer more with the knowledge?"

Though there was no remedy, treatment could not be stopped. Then we took him to some other doctors. He underwent a laparoscopic operation called ambulization. We also put him on certain homeopathic and Ayurvedic medicines. Some people asked us to visit spiritual gurus. But they had no place in our lives. Then he went through a vipashyana camp, where they train people to use yoga to gain control over their emotional disturbances to achieve peace.

When I came to know that Pawar had only six more months to live, a daring thought came into my mind. Would his kidneys match Sugandha's? I proposed this to Vasudev. Only he would be able to understand it, as he was an activist. He too agreed. But then Vijay said, "The organs of a cancer patient cannot be transplanted. The cancer may have spread to other parts of the body."

The answer pushed me into a limbo of agony and relief. Suppose the kidney had matched, suppose they had made a decision to donate it to Sugandha. In that case who was going to inform Harishchandra? What would have been his reaction? Had I been in his place, what would I feel? What is more painful? The awareness that your body is on the brink of death; or the shock that one of your internal organs is to be severed? Would I have felt angry that nobody had told me about the seriousness of my condition till the last moment? Or would I have felt happy that at least I had lived my life without that pain? Or would I have been torn by the opposite forces: the urge to live and the inevitability of death, the zest for life and the utter helplessness in the face of impending death? Would everything have been hollow? Would there be a tremendous loneliness? He would certainly have felt so.

It is said that toward the end of his life, a man wants to go back to his roots, to where he had grown up. It must have been some three or four months after the people in his house had come to know about

Harishchandra's illness. The rainy season was about to start. Suddenly, one day, Harishchandra said, "I want to go to our village. I am feeling bored here. Let us go." Startled, I stared at him. Did he know that the end is near? But he appeared to be calm. We took the Konkan railway and reached the village. Harishchandra suggested going for a walk. I remembered the days after our marriage. Everything was the same. People in the fields, burning the soil, preparing it for sowing, stopped working and talked to us, as they had done at that time. Harishchandra stopped near the stones, telling stories about his mother, about her patting dung cakes, just as he had done then! But there was something else I could see now. Just as the drying water at the bottom of a pitcher leaves a thin white circle, I could see death creeping closer to the point where life had begun for Harishchandra, completing the cycle of life and death.

The very thought that Pawar was living on borrowed time was a terrible blow to his brothers and sister. His younger brothers, Vasukaka, Keshavbhai, and sister, Shalini, kept him constant company in the hospital. Aba and Dada, his elder brothers, who had come to visit him from the village, were heartbroken. When Dada broke down on seeing Harishchandra, he said, "Why do you cry? I am going to be all right, once the swelling on my liver goes away." And all of us felt the same because he looked all right. Finally the dreaded day came. Dr. Vijay Moon from Kandivali got him admitted to his own hospital and looked after him until the last moment, as if he were our own son. He refused to take any money.

Even in his last days, I got squarely blamed for Harishchandra's illness. First it was said that he was completely heartbroken by his daughter's rebellious marriage. Gradually, my education, my job, my writing, my social work, my meetings, my programs, and, last, I, because of what I was, were held responsible for his illness. But nothing affected me anymore! Nothing! Neither Harishchandra's harsh words, nor his tantrums, nor our fights! All that I was able to see was a great wave of darkness, pitch-black as coal powder, rolling toward Harishchandra, who faced it with his back turned to me. I remembered every moment of his life that I knew. Harishchandra as a child, hanging onto his mother's back, demanding molasses; as a young student, staying with his mama; then in the boarding school at Dapoli; as a young activist, clinging to every word that Babasaheb Ambedkar spoke; the shy man sitting in Khedaskar's house in Ratnagiri, the young suitor; and then as a husband and a father. So many images of Harishchandra danced around me—even that of the father who had performed the last rites for his son and was now on the same path. It hurt so terribly. And yet a piercing pain surged up time and again, overpowering everything, stabbing my heart again and again: "The death of your own flesh and blood is much more agonizing than that of your kumkum mark." The sentence uttered by a woman who had come to see my mother kept ringing in my ears.

Now I had to endure the agony of the deaths of both my son and my husband.

Another memory springs up.

During the same period that Mr. Pawar's problem was diagnosed, the All World Buddhist Women's organization, Sakkyadita, organized a conference at Lumbini. On the suggestion of Dr. Eleanor Zelliot, Karma Lekse Tosmo, her friend, sent me an invitation. But I was in no frame of mind to go. One of my friends who was going called me, suggesting we go together. I apologized and told her that I was unable to do so on account of Harishchandra's illness. "He is so ill, and I feel so depressed!" I said. Hearing this, she laughed and said, "Why should you be depressed about it?" I was simply speechless.

After the husband's death, a ritual is performed. The wife's mangalsutra is pulled out and broken at the dead husband's feet. She is made to wear green bangles, which are also broken. She is made to wear a string of flowers in her hair, which is then pulled out, and finally the kumkum on her forehead is wiped off with the toe of her husband's left foot. This ritual is a relic of the past, but it continues to be performed even after the conversion. This ritual is no less than a drama, a big show. Moreover, it is also an insult to the woman. I refused to perform it. This angered quite a few people, but they had to hide it under the garb of Dr. Babasaheb Ambedkar's philosophy. However, it surfaced in the form of comments like, "She is so stupid!" "She thinks she's so wise!" Before my husband's death, I was not particular about wearing the mangalsutra. But after his death I continued to wear it deliberately. Nobody said anything about it. I wanted people to see that the black beads are nothing but glass. Now, however, I feel that such things become a burden on human life. So why must one bear such burdens? Wouldn't it be better to discard them? But how would other people, apart from your relatives, realize that you have discarded them? If I did not wear the mangalsutra, wouldn't they think I was following the tradition of living like a widow?

After Harishchandra's death, one of my nephews, Anand, died of jaundice. He was quite young. His wife too refused to undergo the ritual of having her mangalsutra broken. Shortly after this I came across Professor Ramakant Yadav at a function. He informed me that the Buddhajan Panchayat had resolved to make this ritual an optional one. The resolution was passed on April 14, 2002.

In the final moments of Harishchandra's life, Malavika came to visit him along with her husband, Ravi. Everybody could see that she was very happy, although in those dark hours she tried to hide her happiness from the others. There was an emotional reunion. This made her feel bold enough to suggest that, since she was the elder daughter, she should perform as the son would have and light her father's funeral pyre. But my brother-in-law told her that the body was going to be cremated in the electric crematorium and it was not necessary. Ravi was at the crematorium, and many were impressed with his handsome features and pleasant personality.

Letters of condolence kept pouring in. In the meanwhile, Sugandha's health deteriorated as both her kidneys failed. Her mother was prepared to donate one of her kidneys to her; but even before anything could be done she succumbed to the illness. The condolence letters would have a reference to her death as well. Some people came to the house to offer their condolences. Unnecessarily, a couple of them also told me that it was a good thing that my parents-in-law had passed away. A couple came to see me with a proposal for Manini. They wanted Manini to be married to their son. Later, the marriage did take place, and she seemed settled in her life. My daughters give me a lot of strength to carry on.

I recall a gentleman who is a supposed to be an outspoken writer. I met him on the road one day. Even as we engaged in small talk, he suddenly asked me, "I sent you a letter when your son passed away. How did you find it?" I was struck dumb. People keep scratching at old wounds futilely. Then he went on to say, "I wrote that condolence letter in such a beautiful style! I rarely write like that. Why don't you return that letter to me? I am going to preserve that letter as a wonderful example of my writing." When my son died, I could not even bear to look at the condolence letters, let alone read them. This time, I read the condolence letters about Harishchandra and Sugandha, and some I managed to answer as well. Each time the words of that woman who had visited my mother to console her kept ringing in my ears, "the agony of a son's death is far worse that that of the husband's."

Once I met a woman whom I knew. She told me that she had come to know about Pawar's death quite late. And then, smiling nastily, she said, "Oh, you have lost weight!" I suddenly remembered the words *widow's swelling*! Oh yes, now I look much better. I have put on a little weight. One may not be directly oppressed or terrorized or face opposition. One needs a space of one's own to make decisions, to live. Why could the life partner not give it of his own free will? Only then will words like *widow's swelling* go away. Is there any expression like *widower's swelling*?

These days my correspondence has increased. The tiny showcase in my drawing room contains some awards that have been conferred on me. My sorrows have cost me the will to look at them with pleasure. Mindsets frozen in rituals and caste discrimination scare me.

Life has taught me many things, showed me much, it has also lashed out at me till I bled. I do not know how much longer I am going to live, nor do I know in what form life is going to confront me. Let it come in any form; I am ready to face it stoically. That is what my life has taught me. That is my life and that is me!

Once I was a child who used to play on the dung heap with broken toys, decorating them with rags. Then I was a young girl who accompanied the village women on their journey to Ratnagiri, through vales and hills, listening to their talk, her feet bandaged in thick leaves, running behind them in the blazing sun. I was a growing adolescent who attended school somehow out of the sheer fear of her mother, and then a married woman who tried to negotiate her married life like a trapeze artist, fighting off her tears with her pen, trying to forge a way ahead. This aaydan of my life and its weave ... what will it have to offer readers? I do not know. Maybe it will remind some of their own lives, help them cast a glance down memory lane. Again, some of them might simply want to throw it away. I expect nothing from the readers. I want them to see that each and every person's life is a social document. If they look at what I have written as part of what life is like, then that would be more than enough for me.

Notes

Preface

1. Tathagata is another name of the Buddha.

2. *Savarna* means a non-Dalit, i.e., someone who is within the *varna* or the caste system; *avarna* means someone who is outside the varna or caste sytem, i.e., a Dalit.

3. Ambedkar himself had significant predecessors who opposed upper-caste hegemony. To give a few examples, in the late nineteenth century, Jyotirao Phule of Maharashtra was a tremendously important social reformer from the low castes who fought for the education of both women and men. Iyothee Thass of Tamil Nadu was a similarly important pioneer who fought against caste oppression, funding important journals that created much social awareness. Later, in the 1920s, Periyar Ramasamy Naicker was a famous political leader of Tamil Nadu who consolidated the work of Thass and created Dravidian pride, or non-Brahmin consciousness, that eventually changed the face of southern India.

4. Schools where the language of instruction is in English, thus enabling the child to gain fluency in a language that is associated with power and prestige—and the promise of better jobs and careers.

Introduction

1. The word *Dalit* is now almost universally used by the former untouchables to describe themselves. It literally means "ground down," oppressed.

2. M. S. S. Pandian, "Writing Ordinary Lives," *Economic and Political Weekly,* September 20, 2008.

3. Sharmila Rege, *Writing Caste/Writing Gender: Narrating Dalit Women's Testimonios* (New Delhi: Zubaan, 2007). This book has references to several autobiographies by Dalit women. More such references, and some extracts, can be found in Anupama Rao, *Gender and Caste* (New Delhi: Kali for Women, 2003). Some notable Dalit autobiographies that have been translated into English from Marathi include Vasant Moon, *Growing Up Untouchable in India;* Daya Pawar, *Baluta (The Share);* Kishore Shantabai Kale, *Against All Odds;* and Narendra Jadhav, *Untouchables: My Family's Triumphant Journey Out of the Caste System in Modern India.*

4. Urmila Pawar and Meenakshi Moon, *We Also Made History: Women in the Ambedkarite Movement,* trans., with an introduction by Wandana Sonalkar (New Delhi: Zubaan, 2008).

5. Gopal Guru, "The Interface Between Ambedkar and the Dalit Cultural Movement in Maharashtra," in Ghanshyam Shah, ed., *Dalit Identity and Politics* (New Delhi: Sage, 2001).

6. The Mahars, besides being numerically the largest Dalit caste in Maharashtra, were also in the forefront of the Ambedkar movement, and even today they have made the most progress in attaining education and taking advantage of reservations, or statutory affirmative action, in educational institutions and public sector jobs. The Mahars have also been in the majority among converts to Buddhism.

7. See, for example, Eleanor Zelliot, "The Meaning of Ambedkar," in Ghanshyam Shah, ed., *Dalit Identity and Politics* (New Delhi: Sage, 2001). For more background on Dalit political movements, see Gail Omvedt, *Dalits and the Democratic Revolution: Dr. Ambedkar and the Dalit Movement in Colonial India* (New Delhi: Sage, 1994).

8. Guy Poitevin's article, "*Dalit* Autobiographical Narratives: Figures of Subaltern Consciousness, Assertion, and Identity," Centre for Cooperative Research in Social Sciences (Pune, India) is available on the Internet. I am indebted to Anupama Rao for this reference.

9. The district court of Bhandara pronounced sentences on the accused in the Khairlanji murder case on September 24, 2008. Articles on the judgement, which also give an account of the incident and its background, can be found in the *Human Rights Bulletin,* September 22, 2008 (www.isidelhi.org); the *Economic and Political Weekly,* September 27 to October 3, 2008; and the *Hindu,* September 25, 2008.

One

1. Because her husband was a school master, she was called *masterni,* the master's wife.

2. Phule wished to break the stranglehold the Brahmin priest had over the lower castes and therefore simplified the rituals that could be conducted without a priest.

3. A shrine built over the remains or ashes of someone considered to be extraordinary, like a guru.

4. The month of Phalgun falls between mid-February to mid-March of the Gregorian calendar. The festival marks the beginning of summer.

5. Playing with dirt; there is a lot of mud slinging and drinking.

6. Means "control" in Marathi.

7. A shirt, tied in the front with several tapes; traditional Maharashtrian costume.

8. A *swayamwara* is an assembly of princes who have been specially invited as suitors for the hand of a princess who selects one of them.

9. This phrase means that she gave me nothing.

Two

1. An old measure weighing around forty kilograms.

2. Ceremonial garlands of flowers tied around the bride and groom's heads in such a way that they fall from both sides of their foreheads.

Three

1. A four-yard sari (not the usual five- to six-yard one) worn by the poor that ends below the knee.

Four

1. *Panchasheel* stands for the five principles of good conduct in Buddhism: 1. no killing (because of respect for life); 2. no stealing (because of respect for other's property); 3. no sexual misconduct (because of respect for oneself); 4. no lying (because of respect for honesty); and 5. no intoxicants (because of respect for one's mind). *Trishsran* stands for Trishrana or Trishratna, meaning "three jewels": 1. Refuge (in the Buddha); 2. *Dhamma* (in the universal law); and 3. *Sangha* (a community that lives according to the principles of Buddhism.

Five

1. The crow is a bird that pollutes human beings. The root of this belief probably lies in the rituals carried out after the death (a source of pollution) of a person, when crows are offered balls of rice by the family members. If a crow touched one accidentally, a bath was required. Since the menstrual course was polluting, and since it was a taboo topic, it would be euphemistically referred to as the touching of the crow.

2. When Manjulatai started working, she helped her family move up in the world by following the practices of her Brahmin friends Manda Rege and Prabha Godbole. The family switched to using standard Marathi kinship terms, calling their mother *Aai* and not *Aaye* and giving up *bay* for *bai,* thus referring to their cousin Govindada's wife from then on as Thoralibai.

3. *Mharki* means doing jobs traditionally expected of Mahars for the upper castes: scavenging, carrying messages of various kinds, cleaning cow pens, working at the upper-caste houses as servants, at government offices as helpers. Mahars were given leftover food or grains as payment for the labor spent and had a right over dead animals. Their work was basically considered "polluting."

4. *Sunder Mi Honar,* by the famous Marathi writer P. L. Deshpande, was written in 1958; *Kaunteya* by Siravadakara (Vi Vaa, 1953), is about Karna, perhaps the most tragic protagonist in the *Mahabharata.* Abandoned by his mother Kunti (from whom the name Kaunteya comes), he is welcomed as an ally by the Kaurava princes, who are fighting a fratricidal war against the Pandavas. On the eve of the great battle, his mother, Kunti, reveals to him that he is indeed her son and that the Pandavas are his half-brothers. *Kabuliwala* is a play based on a story of the same name, by Rabindranath Tagore.

Six

1. *Kula* means lineage, often traced to a famous sage in the ancient past. One could not marry into the same kula.

2. *Ocimum tenuiflorum,* or sacred basil, is the symbol of god Vishnu's devotee who was apparently kept outside the house and is thus worshipped in the courtyard of every Hindu home. Tulsi is used in pujas and the evening is ushered in by prayers at the plant's site where a lamp is lit. In death, tulsi leaves are placed on the dead to help them make their way to the next world. Tulsi also has important medicinal uses.

3. The wife's respectful way of addressing her husband, influenced by brahminic practice.

Eight

1. B. R. Ambedkar's *Buddha and His Dhamma* was published posthumously (Mumbai: People's Education Society, 1994 [1957]); for his complete works see B. R. Ambedkar, *Writings and Speeches*, ed. Vasant Moon, 16 vols. (Mumbai: Education Department, Government of Maharashtra, 1987); Dhananjay Keer, *Dr Ambedkar: Life and Mission,*; 2d ed. (Mumbai: Popular Prakashan, 1962 [1954]).

2. *Rasa* mean emotions, as delineated by Bharata, in his *Natyashastra* (ca. AD fifth century), a treatise on classical dance and theater in Sanskrit; this particular rasa refers to disgust.

3. A *sahitya sammelana* is a literary conference.

4. Dr. Ambedkar's essay "Riddles of Rama and Krishna" took a critical view on two Hindu gods, Rama and Krishna. In 1987, the essay was being included in the fourth volume of Dr. Ambedkar's collected writings published by the government of Maharashtra, which led Madhav Gadkari, the then editor of a Marathi daily *Loksatta,* to write in his column Chaufer ("All around") that in this essay Ambedkar had maligned these two Hindu gods. Bal Thackeray, the head of the Shiv Sena, an extreme right xenophobic political party, demanded that the controversial chapter be deleted. The protest led by the left and Dalits resulted in the Congress government agreeing to retain the chapter.

Nine

1. Chhaya Datar is professor, Centre for Women's Studies, School of Social Sciences, Tata Institute of Social Studies, Mumbai; Vidya Bal is a pioneering journalist who edited the journal *Stree* for many years and is now the editor of *Milun Saryajani;* Usha Mehta is a long-time social worker, a Gandhian.

2. Ram Ganesh Gadkari was a renowned playwright in Maharashtra between 1920–1930. His play *Ekac Pyala,* which depicted the ill effects of drinking, had immense mass appeal. Sindhu is the wife of the protagonist Sudhakar, a drunkard. An Arya Pativrata, she devotes herself selflessly to the service of her drunkard husband, sacrificing her son and herself for his sake.

3. Refers to the supporters of the *Manusmriti,* the law book of Manu (complied between 200 BC and AD 200) that validated the caste system and thus supported discrimination against the untouchables and lower castes.

4. The great nineteenth-century social reformer Jotiba Phule.

5. The Babri Masjid was built by the first Mughal emperor Babar in 1527, in Ayodhya, Uttar Pradesh, and though not used for worship was of undoubted historical and architectural value. It was held to have been built on the site of an ancient

temple to the Hindu god Ram. Since the 1980s, the Hindu right agitated to have the mosque destroyed and a temple built on its premises and on December 6, 1992, its mobs, vastly greater in numbers than the local police force, tore down the mosque. Riots followed, particularly severe in Mumbai where mobs murdered Muslims. Since then court orders have prevented any construction at the site.

6. The Chavdar Lake at Mahad, in the Konkan region, was out of bounds for Dalits and on March 19–20, 1927, Dr. Ambedkar led the Dalits to drink water in defiance of the prohibition of the Brahmins. Later on December 25–26, 1927, he burned copies of the *Manusmriti*, the text most often cited to justify discrimination against Dalits.

\Ten

1. A pun on *Annapurna:* refers to the goddess thus named who never runs out of food. *Anna* means "rice" and *purna* means "full of."

2. Asmitadarsha is a prestigious literary conference, part of the Dalit literary movement of the 1970s that provided a platform for Dalit writers and had a tremendous impact on Marathi mainstream literature and on the Dalit cultures of other states within India. The conference also runs a journal of the same name.

3. Employees of the government of India are classified in a descending order from class 1 to class 4. The government provides subsidized housing according to their status. Most Dalits who work for the government would have entered on the quotas provided in the constitution, and, though a few would have moved upward, most would be in this category and thus found in the same kind of housing.

Glossary

abir	fragrant black powder applied on a worshipper's forehead by a priest; also thrown on people during the Holi festival.
amlas	Indian gooseberry, *Amlica embillicus*, light green sour fruit, richest source of vitamin C, of great medicinal use
amsul	dried ratamba, a kind of plum, also called kokum, used as a souring agent in cooking
arhar dal	a lentil dish cooked with yellow split peas or pigeon peas
Baman	a derogatory form of the term *Brahmin*
banosa	a small stove on the side of the main one
barse	naming ceremony of a child
betel nuts	areca nuts that are cut into slivers and used to flavor a paan
Bhadrecha Shimga	a day after the festival of Holi, which some people celebrate as the main day
bhakri	flat bread made from a kind of millet, coarser than wheat
bhajans	religious songs, some dating back to the middle ages, composed by itinerant saints
bhatji	an ordinary Brahmin priest

bhausaheb	a respectful term of address to men in authority
bibbe	a black nut, of medicinal use
bidi	Indian cigarettes where the raw tobacco is wrapped around a piece of leaf
burfi	desserts of flour, sugar, coconut, almond, carrot, or squash cooked in milk and ghee, then cut up into diamond or square shapes
bundi larus	a desert made of chickpea batter, dropped through a sieve into hot oil, then dipped in syrup and molded into balls
Burud	a Dalit caste—weavers of bamboo baskets by profession
chakarmani	people from the Konkan who worked in Mumbai
Chambhar	a Dalit caste of leather workers
chana	roasted whole chickpeas
chawl	a tenement
chiranjeev	"may he live for a long, long time," placed before a groom's name in invitation cards
choli piece	material to make up a blouse to wear with a sari
crore	ten million
dadpe pohe	pressed rice flakes soaked in coconut water, drained, and flavored with salt and chillies
dakshina	fee given to a Brahmin for performing rituals
darshan	the experience of being in the "presence" of god or an extraordinary person
Dasera	the nine-day festival of the mother goddess Durga, culminating with Vijaya Dashami on the tenth day, to commemorate her killing of the demon Mahisasura; to commemorate also the defeat of the demon Ravana by the god Rama, both events celebrate the victory of good over evil
dashmi	bhakri made from flour mixed with milk
dhabu paisa	a large old coin with a hole in the middle; no longer in use
dhapate	spicy flat bread made from coarse flours like millet and whole wheat, roasted on a griddle
Dhor	a Dalit caste—curers of the skins of dead animals
dhoti	men's clothing, a piece of cloth tied at the waist and draped around the legs
Dhulwad	The day after Holi/Shimga when men get drunk
garhane	prayers of supplication/pleading for aid or a particular boon
ghana	a measure for pouring grains in the grinding stone
Gandharva	celestial singers
gharge	deep-fried bread made with flour and molasses
ghov	husband in Konkani

gilli-danda/ *viti-danda*	a game of two teams, a little like baseball or cricket, played with a bat in the shape of a longer stick and a short piece of wood that acts like the ball
going to Kashi	giving up on the world forever and retiring to a life of piety at Kashi
gulal	powder of different colors, originally from plants, used in the festival of Holi
haldi-kumkum/ *kunku*	a mixture of turmeric and vermillion smeared on women participants for any auspicious event like a wedding or a puja or a naming ceremony
haliv seeds	brown seeds of a plant, to be added to larus, that increase a new mother's lactation
handa	brass/copper pitcher with a wide mouth
havildar	noncommissioned officer, equivalent of sergeant, in the Indian army
jatra	village fair
jalebi	a desert made of a mixture of farina, wheat, and rice flour, piped in a cluster of rings onto hot oil, later soaked in hot syrup and drained
jatra of Sada- *nandaswami*	prayers and recitations to commemorate a local guru
kabaddi/ *hututu*	two teams of twelve players each; a player from one team enters the other team's "territory"and, shouting *kabaddi*, tries to touch any of the players, who is then "out"; the team that gets the most players out wins
kameez/kurta	a loose-flowing long shirt
kankol	Ayurvedic medicine for a sore throat
karanjya	a dessert made with wheat flour and sweet filling
khadi shakhar	crystallized sugar sucked to soothe the throat
khakre	pappadoms, flat and round like chapatis, that can be stored
khele	a form of folk theater
kheer	a desert of thickened milk, sweetened with sugar or molasses and flavored with bay leaf and cardamom, heavily garnished with almonds and raisins
khot	an important administrative officeholder of the village
Komti	nomads
Kulwadi	a farming caste
kumkum	a vermillion powder that includes turmeric, worn as a dot on the forehead of Hindu women, signifying that she is married, a suwasini
kanyadan	gift of a virgin, the bride, from her father to the groom
Kunbi	farmer caste
Kashi	another name for Varanasi, also known as the kingdom of Kashi

khokho	two teams of twelve each, one team of the "runners," who try to escape being touched by the team of "chasers"; once touched or tagged, the runner is out
lagorya	a pile of stones is placed, and players of two teams have turns in trying to lop them off with other stones; the hitter then runs before another stone is made to fall
langdi	a player hops and chases the other players, who try to evade her; whoever is caught then must take her role and give chase in the same way
majghar	a room in the middle of a house used by women
mamlatdar	government official responsible for tax collection, land surveys, solving land disputes
Mang	Dalit caste, below the Mahars in status; makers of ropes
mangalsutra	a string of black beads, sometimes with some gold, worn by a married Hindu woman of Maharashtra and south India
Modi	an old script used to write Marathi before Devanagari replaced it in the nineteenth century
mool purush	founding father, a key male ancestor; from the Sanskrit *mool,* for "primary root," and *purush,* for "man"
morcha	a large group of protestors
mridunga	a drum originally made of clay now of hollowed jackfruit wood
oti	a ritual in which a married woman is given a coconut, with kumkum to put in her pallav, signifying prosperity
ovi	oral poems and songs by women
owale	impure; polluted
paan	an edible leaf filled with aromatic spices and betel nuts that aids in digestion; sometimes containing tobacco; consumed for centuries, intricately associated with social life
padayatra	walking long distances on foot for a cause
Padmashri	a fourth-level honor awarded by the president of India for service to art, science, industry, or public life; the other levels in ascending order are Padma Bhushan, Padma Vibushan, and Bharat Ratna
panch	five male members who act like elders in the caste council and make decisions on matters that concern the community
panchapatra	five pots for rituals, used by Brahmin priests
pantoji	a name for a Brahmin teacher; *ji* is an honorific suffix
patwadi	made of chickpea flour and spices, roasted, and then cut into small pieces as a savory snack
phugadya	a game played by women in pairs; the two cross their arms and grasp each other's hands, then tap out a rhythmic thumping sound with their feet and go round very fast in circles

pithale	a fried savory snack made with chickpea batter and spices
pranayam	basic yogic breathing exercises that enhance mental and physical well-being
prasad	offerings to a god/goddess that is then served to people
puja	worship of a god/goddess with flowers, offerings, chants, and lamps, with or without a priest
ramphal	*annona reticulate,* a large round fruit, six inches in length, native to the West Indies, with white sweetish flesh, called custard apple, bull's heart, chirimoya
sangdi	a spicy dry lentil dish
sarpanch	the elected head of a village's administration by the local community, the smallest unit of representative government
satwik	associated with ritual purity; especially vegetarian food cooked by Brahmins; being Brahminic
saubhagya-kankshini	"may she always be a fortunate woman," placed before a bride's name in an invitation
shendi	tuft of hair at the back of their heads kept by Brahmins and others aspiring for higher status as a marker of status and superiority over others
shirkhanda	a dessert made with thickened milk, yogurt, flavored with spices or mixed with fruit
sowale	pure
sutradhara	the narrator in classical or folk theater who links the many aspects of the play before the audience
suwasini	married women who are traditionally considered to have the highest status among women, as the state of marriage is considered auspicious
tashe	a drum that is played with two sticks
tabuts	decorated towers, created with bamboo and cloth, that are carried round by the shias at Mohurram, commemorating the tragic deaths of the Prophet's grandsons in the Karbela desert
talathi	officer in charge of administration in a village
tamasha	traditional folk theater
Tambat	a Dalit caste—the makers of brass pots and pans
vaidya	a village doctor; also, a practitioner of Ayurveda
thikraya	small flat stones are thrown from a distance to hit stones arranged inside a circle; the team with more hits wins
Vijaya Dashami	the tenth day of Dasera when the goddess Durga kills the demon Mahisasura, and the slaying of the demon Ravana by the god Rama, both symbolizing the victory (*vijaya*) of good over evil

wadi   neighborhood; a small settlement

Yaksha   a celestial being with magical powers

zhimma   a woman's game, played in pairs or groups, clapping palms, one against anothers', creating intricate rhythms and movements

zhumka   dangling earrings, the bottom part formed like a canopy with beads

Readers' Reactions to Aaydan

When *Aaydan* was about to be published in 2003 by Granthali, Dinkar Gangal, the publisher, suggested that it should be placed in the context of Marathi literary history. *Aaydan*'s publication was planned to coincide with the silver jubilee of *Baluta,* the first Dalit autobiography by Padmashri Daya Pawar, marking this anniversary and offering an opportunity to readers to consider what developments had taken place in the lives of Dalit women for a quarter of a century. The publication of my book was quite hurriedly organized, so much so that it seemed as if I sat glued to a chair in the Granthali office and wrote the *Atmabhan* (Sense of selfhood), the preface, as fast as I could, and finally *Aaydan* did get published toward the end of December.

Mr. Gangal was firmly convinced that there are only a few readers of Marathi books, most of whom are on the wrong side of fifty. Such readers, according to him, find a book with more than 250 pages boring. "Why don't you choose a small font size?" I asked him, thinking that would accommodate more material. But Gangal coolly answered that then he would have to consider the problem of the readers' glasses as well. Apart from the joke, what he was saying was quite true. As a result, my stories about the thieves from my village, which were published in the Diwali issue of *Akshar* in 2002, had to be left out of *Aaydan*.

Many more things were left out, especially the account of the help that I received from my brother Shahu and his wife Sheela and all three of my sisters-in-law, which made my life easier. Many more people who have had a major role to play in my development were similarly left out. And I have not talked about how my children grew up. The famous writer P. S. Nerurkar, who often threatened me in his typical Konkani style ("If you don't bring a story, don't enter my house!") and encouraged my writing, and his wife, Umavahini, also did not get any place in *Aaydan*.

Readers were appreciative. The book was reprinted four times between 2004–2006. I received some two hundred letters from readers. There were some thirty-five reviews. Many notes were published. *Aaydan* got an honourable mention in Sharad Pawar's speech in the Seventy-Seventh Sahitya Sammelana, held in 2006, and Madhavrao Gadkari, the eminent journalist, also took a special note of it in the Konkan Marathi Parishad held in Thane. Many writers, like R. G. Jadhav (the erstwhile president of the Maharashtra Sahitya Sammelana), Anant Dikshit, editor of the daily *Sakal,* intellectuals like Rawsaheb Kasbe, and Ramdas Phutane, a well-known poet and president of the Maharashtra Sahitya Sammelana, were present at the awards ceremony organized for *Aaydan*, and many people praised it.

I found readers' letters to be very memorable. G. P. Pradhan, an eminent writer, appreciated *Aaydan* greatly. He wrote, "Because of the so-called high-caste people like us, you have had to suffer unnecessarily humiliation and insults. You had to suffer poverty and adverse circumstances. I hold you in great regard." Similarly, Baba Amte also took note of *Aaydan*. Vidya Bal wrote "Now Urmila has overtaken me." Many more told me how moved they were after reading the book. Many realized that I had had a deprived childhood, and they became my family members, invited me to their homes, and cosseted me. This brought far greater a joy than the award.

Many readers told me that they liked my style and also my perspective of looking at a woman as an individual without any prejudices. I was somewhat overwhelmed to read reactions like "We read the book at one go"; "I lost a sense of the outside world when I read your book"; "I read your book without having slept"; "You have scaled a new pinnacle of success"; "You introduced us to a new world"; "You gave a sense of selfhood"; "You touched my heart"! So on and so forth. I was a little embarrassed as well. That is, I blushed with happiness, satisfaction. There was, of course, criticism as well: of my direct, outspoken style, use of dialect, and especially of racy words in it. Many felt I should have written about my children. I also was aware of this. But I did not dare to write about those wounds; I was afraid of reopening them.

Aaydan received four major awards: Maharashtra Foundation, USA; Priya-darshini Academy; Padmashri Vikhe Patil; and the Matoshree Bheemabai Ambedkar

Award. It was also prescribed as a textbook in the syllabus for M.A. II of Mumbai University. Some parts of *Aaydan* were also included in the predegree syllabus at the same university. *Aaydan* became a topic of M.Phil. and Ph. D. research. I was quite overwhelmed and felt honored.

A woman missionary had offered to take my father to England, and my grandfather turned it down because he did not want to send his son beyond the seven seas. Had he been allowed to go to England, maybe we, his children, would have been born there, and our lives would have taken a different turn. I often regretted that this did not happen. Now *Aaydan* will be able to reach foreign readers because it has been translated into English. This gives me great happiness.